IT HAPPENS AMONG PEOPLE

WYSE Series in Social Anthropology

Editors:
James Laidlaw, William Wyse Professor of Social Anthropology, University of Cambridge, and Fellow of King's College, Cambridge
Maryon McDonald, Fellow in Social Anthropology, Robinson College, University of Cambridge
Joel Robbins, Sigrid Rausing Professor of Social Anthropology, University of Cambridge, and Fellow of Trinity College, Cambridge

Social Anthropology is a vibrant discipline of relevance to many areas—economics, politics, religion, science, business, humanities, health, and public policy. This series, published in association with the Cambridge Department of Social Anthropology but open to all scholars, focuses on key interventions in Social Anthropology, based on innovative theory and research of relevance to contemporary social issues and debates.

It Happens among People

Resonances and Extensions of the Work of Fredrik Barth

Edited by

Keping Wu and Robert P. Weller

berghahn
NEW YORK • OXFORD
www.berghahnbooks.com

First published in 2020 by
Berghahn Books
www.berghahnbooks.com

Library of Congress Cataloging-in-Publication Data

A C.I.P. cataloging record is available from the Library of Congress
Library of Congress Cataloging in Publication Control Number: 2019037952

British Library Cataloguing in Publication Data

A catalogue record for this book is available from the British Library

ISBN 978-1-78920-428-5 hardback
ISBN 978-1-78920-537-4 paperback
ISBN 978-1-78920-429-2 ebook

Contents

Figures

Introduction

Robert P. Weller and Keping Wu

The passing of Fredrik Barth marked the end of an era in anthropology. Nevertheless, his contributions also promise new beginnings. As his students and colleagues, we felt nothing could honor our debts to him more than an intellectual effort that brings attention to his relevance to anthropology today, rather than simply celebrating his legacy. This volume attempts to do that by offering chapters that expand on his work, sometimes argue with it, but always honor its humanist approach. In the process, the book may also serve as a summary of some of his main themes, and it may illustrate how much we owe him intellectually, but our main goal is neither intellectual biography nor commemoration. It is instead to pass on Barth's humanistic tradition of knowledge, so it can live and evolve.[1]

Such a process of continuous intellectual evolution characterized Barth's own career as well. In the late 1970s, when Robert attended his graduate seminar at Johns Hopkins, Barth was already highly celebrated. This was above all because of his introductory essay in *Ethnic Groups and Boundaries* (1969), which had appeared a decade earlier. Though Barth repeatedly said that he was not an expert on ethnicity, this essay fundamentally shifted the way people conceptualize ethnicity—from "cultural stuff" to the boundaries actors set out to maintain. However, instead of dwelling on his fame or reiterating his earlier ideas, it was clear that Barth at that time was wrestling with new issues, especially with the problem of how to understand a person as both a potentially creative individual and as a product of broader social processes. In retrospect, the period marked a fruitful point in his career as he extended his thinking about how social forms can be generated from a primary focus on individual transactions to a new concern with how ideas can come to be shared and passed down through what he called traditions of knowledge.

Barth's next monograph thus moved not only to a brand-new field site, but also to a new interest in rituals and symbolic systems. *Ritual and Knowledge among the Baktaman of New Guinea* (1975) marked the beginning of what was to become his brand of the anthropology of knowledge. In the concluding essay of his edited volume *Scale and Social Organization* (1978), Barth wrote, "What is required is a truly dynamic and empirically valid model of the entire process of cultural transmission and behavioral enactment, capable of showing how encounters both reflect and generate culture" (Barth 1978: 272). This concern with the relationship between individual behaviors and the shared culture they both make and are part of was one of the central theoretical concerns of Barth throughout his career.

Almost two decades later, when Keping attended his graduate classes at Boston University, Barth had already published his final major monograph, *Balinese Worlds* (1993), in which he most clearly established his position on those issues. By the time Keping was working with him, Barth's teaching focused more on the central importance of methodology than anything else. He taught the seminar on anthropological methods each year, and on alternate years he would teach a seminar on ethnicity or anthropology of knowledge. Even in those classes, however, methods—how one collects the data and what constitutes the material for analysis—were always the starting point of his discussion. In a way, theory and methodology were the same things for him. His methodological "naturalism" and insistence on the "worm's eye view" about "real people doing real things" left a deep mark on all the students who were in his classroom in those years. His anthropology was humanistic in the broadest sense, since it requires us to consider how we behave as true humans, in the fullest and most complex sense of the term. One of the lessons all of us learned from him is that human social life is neither simply the product of individual calculations or of cultural categories; instead "it happens among people" at particular places and times.[2]

Even if we distinguish an "early Barth" from a "later Barth," there is a continued concern with working through the implications of human agency that matured over the course of a long career. From his thesis-turned-book *Political Leadership among Swat Pathans* (1959a) to *Balinese Worlds* (1993), Barth's theoretical attention was always focused on how individuals thought and planned their ways through political systems and social organizations that seemed to have set rigid roles for them. His orientation is significantly different from the kind of anthropology that treats the person as the product of his or her social structure and/or culture. Nor is agency ever the product of an isolated and autonomous individual. Instead, Barth's is an actor-centered perspective that emphasizes actions based on existing knowledge and interactions situated in the local context. Though Barth was not interested in starting a new school of theory—he has never even given his theory a name—by emphasizing a *transactionalist* and *generative* model, he steadfastly improved and perfected his understanding of agency.

Barth's concern with individuals, agency, and generative models foresees developments that would follow later in anthropology. This introduction and the chapters that follow trace at least four themes that Barth's works bring to contemporary theory. First, Barth's work on traditions of knowledge and people working through their networks and interactions with others resonates with the "ontological turns" in contemporary anthropology by challenging the conventional ways culture or society is conceptualized. It insists that we begin with real people in their environments, and not from abstracted concepts of society or culture. Second, a burgeoning anthropology of ethics and values can benefit from Barth's discussion on values that guide transactions and the dialectic relations between moral codes and moral actions. Third, though much of Barth's work has been on societies with a weak state presence, his interest in political leadership, power, and authority sheds light on classical and contemporary questions in political anthropology. He has sometimes been criticized for failing to deal adequately with the state, but many of the chapters that follow show how fruitfully his work can be applied to such problems as well. Fourth, Barth has always given variation central importance in his writings, and this resonates with much of later anthropology's debates on multiculturalism and pluralism. In many senses, Barth was to develop an anthropology that we can build on today.

Traditions of Knowledge and Other Ontological Turns

One of the ways in which Barth's work continues to inspire us today is the dissident relationship he always had to the Durkheimian mainstream in anthropology and sociology. Emile Durkheim had been the great champion of "society" as the proper unit of analysis. For him, this society was always greater than the sum of its individual parts and exerted a powerful influence over what anyone could do or think. As Durkheim wrote in *The Division of Labor in Society*, "The totality of beliefs and sentiments common to average citizens of the same society forms a determinate system which has its own life; one may call it the *collective* or *common conscience*" (Durkheim 2013: 173). In this sentence we can see both the omnipotent "society" and the overbearing "culture" that characterized a great deal of twentieth-century anthropology.

Barth's intellectual lineage, which one might trace back from Edmund Leach to Bronislaw Malinowski, ran counter to the most extreme versions of that Durkheimian tradition (Kuper 2014). It left far more room for conflict (e.g., Gluckman 1955) and change (e.g., Leach 1973) than the stronger Durkheimian models of culture and society. Nevertheless, Barth's predecessors never fully succeeded in leaving behind a fundamentally Durkheimian anthropology or the functionalist assumptions that accompanied it. Thus, when Barth began his career in the 1950s, "culture" and "society" were perhaps at their height as taken-for-granted ways of understanding people's lived worlds. Almost from the beginning we can see him struggling, more radically than most of his teachers and colleagues, for some kind of alternative that would allow room for human agency.

Much of the first two decades of his work was dedicated to finding a space for creative individual thought and action that let people be more than automata controlled by a larger culture or society. Examples discussed in the chapters that follow include the choice of some nomadic Basseri to become sedentary (Barth 1961, discussed by Thomas Barfield in chapter 5) and of course his famous introduction to *Ethnic Groups and Boundaries* (Barth 1969, discussed in chapters 9 and 10, among others). In these and other early works, Barth pioneered his concepts of transaction and process. He highlighted the individual as a strategic thinker and thus built "society" up from its many transactions, rather than seeing decisions simply as the reflex of social position and cultural inclination. This focus on the individual as a counterweight to an overpowering concept of society, however, left Barth open to being dismissed as a methodological individualist.

Had his career ended in 1969, it might make sense to discuss whether this critique was an adequate response to his approach. His continued work over the decades that followed, however, makes clear that his transactionalism cannot be reduced to a sort of early rational choice theory (discussed further in the following section). When Robert studied with him in the late 1970s, it was already quite clear that much of Barth's theoretical labor was going into the problem of how to think through the dynamic interactions between individuals and groups in some way that would not be reductive. The results appear especially in his works on New Guinea and Bali, the last of his major ethnographic studies (Barth 1987, 1990, 1993). Here we see a focus less on the individual decision-maker and more on traditions of knowledge.

This was the topic of his 2000 Sidney W. Mintz Lecture, where he began by explaining how his understanding of traditions of knowledge differed from and offered advantages over the concept of culture as used by someone like Clifford Geertz:

> Knowledge provides people with materials for reflection and premises for action, whereas "culture" too readily comes to embrace also those reflections and those actions. Furthermore, actions become knowledge to others only after the fact. Thus the concept of "knowledge" situates its items in a particular and unequivocal way relative to events, actions, and social relationships.
>
> Knowledge is distributed in a population, while culture makes us think in terms of diffuse sharing. Our scrutiny is directed to the distributions of knowledge—its presence or absence in particular persons—and the processes affecting these distributions can become the objects of study. (Barth 2002: 1)

This view led toward an understanding of people as fundamentally diverse rather than culturally alike, because traditions of knowledge do not flow evenly over the ethnographic landscape. It also pushed us to think of knowledge as something that moves along varied networks, that changes in the process of transmission, and that has its roots in action. Barth takes pains to show, in all his late work, that he is trying to provide an alternative to the Durkheimian inheritance of static concepts like culture and social structure.

We thus see Barth's work in part as a push to break through the limits of an earlier anthropology. While he did this very much in his own way, it should be no surprise that his work often resonates with (and indeed generally predates) other traditions of knowledge in anthropology that were also trying to break new conceptual ground. Unni Wikan, in chapter 1, for example, includes some discussion of Barth's reactions to postmodernism. He undoubtedly recognized a kindred spirit in some postmodern writing, for instance when she quotes him as saying that "in that sense the whole gang of Bergen folks in the 1960s was part of such a postmodern hubbub without any of us knowing it; we played with some ways of thinking that now can be given that sobriquet." In his influential article "The Guru and the Conjurer" (discussed at some length by Michael Herzfeld in chapter 2 and Charles Lindholm in chapter 7), to cite another example, he points out similarities to Renato Rosaldo's postmodernism, while also arguing that it is not enough simply to rest on the assertion that life is polyvocalic (Barth 1990: 651).

Equally striking are the reverberations with what has recently been called the "ontological turn" in anthropology, especially with those theorists most concerned with moving away from the Durkheimian legacy and reconceptualizing society and culture. Barth's conception of traditions of knowledge, with their networks and transactions, is not identical to Bruno Latour's discussion of assemblages and actor-networks, but one can see that both scholars are setting themselves up in opposition to conventional notions of culture and society, and both are looking to related alternatives that center on interacting networks of people and their worlds. As Gunnar Haaland points out in chapter 6, even "large-scale society . . . takes place between people" in Barth's understanding (Barth 1978: 256).

Had Barth been more prone to grand pronouncements, it would not be difficult to imagine him saying something quite like Latour's "The very notion of culture is an artifact. . . . Cultures—different or universal—do not exist" (Latour 1993: 104). There is no doubt that Barth was aware of this work: when Keping took his course on the anthropology of knowledge, one of the assigned readings was Latour and Woolgar's *Laboratory Life* (1986). One of our hopes with this volume is that it might encourage a deeper dialogue about what an alternative anthropology will come to look like, perhaps as suggested by some of the chapters that follow. Barth's ideas continue to provide us with an important trove of conceptual possibility.

Generating an Anthropology of Values

Graduate students under pressure to study for their comprehensive examinations often reduce the key thinkers of anthropology to a simple shorthand: Franz Boas the historical particularist, Malinowski the psychological functionalist,

Geertz the theorist of interpretation. For Barth, as we mentioned above, the so-briquet is usually "methodological individualist," meaning someone who stresses above all the "rational" and strategic decisions of autonomous individuals.

All of these intellectual shortcuts draw on real features of the work of these thinkers, but of course none of them do justice to the complexity of their ideas. The problem seems especially egregious for Barth, who we think never imagined himself in those terms, and whose progression as a thinker shows him working systematically against such a view of what people are. This side of Barth's opus is best understood as an early attempt in anthropology to think seriously about the problem of agency. As Chee-Beng Tan discusses in chapter 10, on the history of Barth's thought, Barth's strongest early influences in anthropology were probably Raymond Firth and certainly Edmund Leach. Both men helped lead the move away from the very muscular functionalism of A. R. Radcliffe-Brown in order to conceptualize problems of change and conflict. Barth's early work was more radical than theirs in a sense: if we were not going to allow some abstracted "social structure" to explain everything, then individual agency would have to be taken more seriously. He thus never began with methodological individualism as a philosophical position or a theory of human nature. Instead, he was searching for alternatives to the conceptions of an all-powerful social structure, which dominated the anthropology of the 1940s and 1950s. Even his dalliance with game theory is framed primarily as a critique of "a Durkheimian conception of mechanical solidarity" (Barth 1959b: 5). Real people for Barth were always the core of the analysis and could never be reduced to mere puppets of a social structure. Coming from such a position, it is natural that he would be attracted to a theoretical position that left space for people to strategize, to choose, and to think. As Tan points out in chapter 10, the same was true for Pierre Bourdieu, writing at roughly the same time and responding to many of the same intellectual problems, even though their solutions are not entirely the same.

Barth's work in the 1970s and beyond helped clarify the ways in which he differed from methodological individualism. For him, the answer to an overly powerful Durkheimian concept of society was not the autonomous individual, but instead the processes through which shared or differing values could be generated and regenerated in humans' interactions with each other and their environment. By the time of his last major ethnographic work, *Balinese Worlds* (1993), this had matured into an extended discussion of multiple and partly competing "traditions of knowledge," which are passed down over time, but which also change in the process. There is still ample room for agency, but this is emphatically not a world of autonomous rational choosers.

Barth's approach here can be expanded in a number of fruitful directions that lead us, more or less, to some of the issues currently being discussed as a new anthropology of ethics. Much of that recent literature has also been phrased as an attack on Durkheim and then struggles with how to find room for agency. As Didier Fassin phrases the problem in a useful quick review:

Do human beings act morally because they obey socially defined rules and norms as the result of a routine of inculcated behaviors, or an embodied fear of sanction, or perhaps both? Conversely, do they act morally because they decide to do so as a consequence of a rational evaluation, or transformative endeavor, or inseparably both? (Fassin 2014: 429)

Durkheim is generally associated with the first view, that there are socially defined rules and norms; most of the current anthropologists of the topic are searching for alternatives.

Ethics are one sort of values, and it is thus not difficult to see that Barth and the anthropologists of ethics share a sense of problem, because Barth had a great deal to say about values. In chapter 6, Gunnar Haaland gives one example of how Barth's thinking about the generation of values can be extended, in this case concerning issues of trust. In keeping with the call for an "ordinary ethics" (e.g., Das 2007) in some of the recent anthropology of ethics, Haaland draws especially on Barth's insistence that we focus on behavior and on the unspoken acts as much as the spoken ones. This leads him to identify two quite different traditions of knowledge, which offer very different bases for an ethic of trust. The first is highly local, experience-near, and concerned above all with solidarity rooted in the mother-child complex. The second, and historically more recent in the Darfur region, is much wider-scale and rooted instead in a universalizing idea of Allah. As he shows, these differences have translated tragically into competing political movements in the decades since Barth was there. Part of the power of this analysis is the recognition that scale can make an enormous difference in the social consequences of traditions of knowledge, which Barth explored in his edited book *Scale and Social Organization* (1978). We thus see two very different ways of generating an ethic of trust out of lived experience, one relying on intimate experience at small scales, and the other on nation-spanning forms of literacy and formal institutions to shape and define orthodoxy.

In chapter 8, Joel Robbins also tackles the problem of the generation of values. Like Tan, he focuses our attention on some of the evolution in Barth's thinking about the problem. Like Haaland, Barfield, and Lindholm, Robbins bases his contribution on fieldwork carried out not far from one of Barth's many sites, but somewhat more recently. Most of those other chapters use the changes since Barth's fieldwork to pose questions about how far we can generalize Barth's work across places and times. Robbins, however, is more concerned with the broad theoretical issue of how we can understand values. He points to a conundrum already apparent in Barth's work on New Guinea: If values are generated by transaction, then how can the Baktaman generate their value of secrecy? Secrecy, after all, is a refusal to transact.

Robbins's answer is that secrecy has to be performed and enacted in order to be secret and to show the value of secrecy. In that sense, his argument is not far from the parts of Herzfeld's chapter that address secrecy among master artisans in Crete (see chapter 2). His goals, however, are different. Robbins is concerned to show the utility of a distinction between what he calls the production of values and the realization of values—between creating value and enacting it. By showing how both aspects of value are necessary, he is trying to move beyond Barth's emphasis on the production side, which led to the puzzle of Baktaman secrecy. Barth's uneasiness with the "realization" approach to values may have stemmed from his distrust of anything that might reinforce the idea of a disembodied and all-powerful idea of culture, but Robbins is suggesting that a more balanced approach can help us solve some difficult problems.

Much of the current thinking about an anthropology of ethics proposes a turn from "Kantian reason to Aristotelian activity," as Michael Lambek phrased it (2010: 13). That is, these anthropologists are now less concerned with explicit moral codes than with the ways that ethics is embedded in daily life. Barth has not been an especially direct influence on this movement, and yet the chapters by Haaland and Robbins show how much he anticipated some of these developments and how much his thinking about values (of trust or secrecy, for example) still remains a potential source of inspiration today.

Power, Authority, and the State

How is political power generated? How do forms of authority differ from one another? Barth was concerned with political power and various forms of authority throughout his career. He paid particular attention to local political organization based on kinship networks. In his *Political Leadership among Swat Pathans* (1959a), he compared political power between the saints and landowners, each relying on different but intertwined constructions of legitimacy. Though sometimes criticized for lack of attention to the issue of class differences (e.g., Asad 1972), Barth's discussion of political organization builds on native categories and resonates with much of today's anthropology.

The apex of Barth's theory on authority comes with the article "The Guru and the Conjurer" (Barth 1990). The guru and the conjurer represent two paths of knowledge transmission and two different forms of authority. The guru (in the Balinese case) transmits knowledge overtly through verbal and textual means, whereas the conjurer (in the case of the Baktaman) reproduces knowledge by maintaining secrecy. While one generates authority by demonstrating knowledge, the other gains authority by demonstrating how much the others do not know. Though Barth is often regarded as a Weberian, Barth's types of authorities are different from Max Weber's ideal types because they are "native categories" and therefore context-specific. The same goes for Barth's concept of power, which is different from Michel Foucault's power that is everywhere the same. In chapter 7, Lindholm uses this Barthian logic and sketches out two indigenous forms of authority in Swat: the khan and the Sufi saint, which are "based on opposing premises, modes of inculcation, and styles of performance." The khan gains influence over his co-equals through his "natural" expression of his manly virtues. The saint, on the other hand, gains authority through empty-ing himself in submission to a spiritual master. Lindholm argues that Sufis can sometimes gain power over khans, but only at the cost of their own sanctity.

Most of the peoples and groups Barth worked with lived in a stateless soci-ety or a society in which the state had a weak presence (with important excep-tions like Sohar and Bali). Whether Barth's transactional model was useful in studying societies where the state has a strong presence was sometimes raised as a question. Some of the chapters in this volume address this issue. For in-stance, in chapter 5, Barfield revisits Barth's work on the Basseri, *Nomads of South Persia* (Barth 1961). Though the Basseri fell increasingly under the in-fluence of the Iranian government and market economy in comparison to the time of Barth's fieldwork, Barfield concludes, "After more than fifty-five years, *Nomads of South Persia* still stands the test of time in spite of the many mono-graphs about Iranian pastoralism that came in its wake." This is not because the state is unimportant in what happened, but because Barth's approach gives us an avenue to understand the state's role.

We suggest that there is potential in his transactional model to deal with societies with strong state presences. On the one hand, one-sided transactions are still transactions. In chapter 9, on the paradigm shifts in Chinese ethnology, Ke Fan illustrates the role of the state in solidifying categories and in influenc-ing the ways academics study *minzu* ("ethnic" or "national") groups. Though it seems that there is little room for the ethnologists to talk back to the state, there is some room for agency when new theories such as Barth's ideas about ethnic groups and boundaries were introduced to Chinese academics. On the other hand, in some cases the state can dominate or even monopolize the terms of transaction. In Keping Wu's chapter about a mountainous area on China's periphery (see chapter 4), the state has been an increasingly powerful actor, affecting the transactions among other actors as well. In this actor-centered view, the state participates in the local transactions and engages in the bound-ary-making processes. Wu shows how such transactions have led to increased boundary-making, almost entirely as an unintended consequence. This only becomes sensible when we see how people are interacting locally with the state, its infrastructure projects, and each other. Herzfeld's chapter also deals with a strong state, especially where the Thai government shows its strong hand in cultural heritage narratives and management (see chapter 2). However, even in this case, state ideology is never a fully successful project. Barth's transactional model, with its room for individual agency, illuminates the intricate processes in which state interacts with society.

The Problems of Variation, Group Formation, and Pluralism

How do we live with those who are truly different from us? This is how people often phrase the problems of pluralism, which once again dominate news headlines around the world. The post-Enlightenment solution of privatizing our differences while displaying only our "universal" characteristics in the public sphere (seen most recently in headlines about wearing headscarves in France, performing circumcisions in Iceland, or speaking Spanish in American public spaces) is no longer providing much comfort. This is because another modern invention continues to expose that façade: the nation-state, with its conflation of culture, ethnic origins, and political structures.

Barth wrote directly about such things primarily in his position as a public intellectual, rather than in his academic writing. Nonetheless, we could see his entire career as a process of continued wrestling with underlying theoretical and moral issues of pluralism. As one of the pioneers in trying to return some sense of agency to anthropology, he naturally became very concerned with the process of group formation, which always includes the possibility for intolerance. The existence and boundaries of groups had been taken for granted in much earlier anthropology, but Barth's move toward an emphasis on generative models made the process suddenly problematic and interesting. For that reason, his work brought an improvement in how we can think about the related policy issues.

This had two important consequences for anthropology. The first, of course, was his work on ethnic boundaries as something produced through generative contact with others, rather than being natural and simply inherited. The key idea generalizes to any kind of group—it is often more fruitful to see the group as something created by interactions at its edges, he suggests, rather than the expression of some shared essence. Few works in the social sciences have had as much impact as Barth's 1969 *Ethnic Groups and Boundaries* volume (which has over thirteen thousand citations as of this writing), and few have such clear lessons for policy makers. Failure to appreciate the dynamics of group formation that Barth clarified helps explain numerous policy problems. In this volume, evidence of those includes chapter 6, where Haaland's final few pages discuss some of the relation of political violence in the Sudan to conflicts over essentializing understandings of Islam (that is, seeing group formation as coming from a religious core rather than from boundary construction) and ultimately of the nature of group trust. In chapter 4, Wu, in a very different context, also shows how the government's essentializing ethnic categories have brought completely unintended consequences to seemingly unrelated economic development policies. Thus, constructing roads, resettling people in new villages, and even building basketball courts have hardened ethnic boundaries and increased group tensions, compared to the "plastic pluralism" she saw there in the past.

The second consequence stems more clearly from Barth's later work, where he often focused on the problem of variation. After all, if groups are constructed, the construction materials are the myriad differences that make each person unique, out of which we can manufacture both similarities and differences. His work in Bali focused especially on the enormous variation that had already attracted significant anthropological attention, although he offered a new kind of explanation. The exquisite ritual variety that spread across tiny neighboring groups in New Guinea (including the people Robbins discusses in chapter 8), however, seemed more surprising. This was especially true because these groups shared almost entirely identical material lives and languages.

If we begin from Barth's theoretical standpoint, however, the variation no longer seems so astonishing. For him, there is nothing automatic about sharing culture or practice. Sharing only comes about because knowledge (in a broad sense that includes practice) can be reproduced over space and time. Yet the very acts of reproduction, whether through socialization or schools or ritual performances, create the possibility of change. Barth thus started at almost the opposite place from Geertz in the analysis of Balinese variation. Instead of assuming that cultural similarity is a given and the high degrees of internal variation are thus puzzling, as Geertz did in his classic work on Bali (e.g., Geertz 1959), Barth began with the understanding that change and variation are natural and that our hardest job would be to explain the continuities instead of assuming them. From this point of view, we can see the continuity in Barth's sense of problem throughout his career, with the earlier work focusing more on how groups can be created out of people's varying understandings, and the later (e.g., Barth 1987, 1993) seeking to illuminate the variation itself and to show more flexible forms of organizing shared life than just ethnic identity— especially in his concept of traditions of knowledge.

In chapter 2, Herzfeld shows one way in which these lines of thought can be extended. In a broadly comparative study that moves between the Mediterranean and Southeast Asia, he draws inspiration from both strands of Barth's thought. On the one hand, he works out of Barth's influential article on two very different modes of institutionalizing knowledge and their social consequences—the guru and the conjuror (Barth 1990). These show how we can begin to make sense of broad lines of non-ethnic variation that extend across social and national boundaries; for Herzfeld, this approach offers an alternative to what he calls methodological nationalism (following Wimmer and Glick Schiller 2002). On the other hand, Herzfeld extends Barth's thinking in *Ethnic Groups and Boundaries* (1969) to focus explicitly on how these processes help us to see how we can take a new approach to some idea of culture areas freed from the conceptual bonds of the nation-state.

In chapter 3, Robert P. Weller extends Barth's work on variation in a different direction. His cases take place within a single small region of China but still show wide variability, which he explains primarily as stemming from different ways of thinking about time and about how knowledge can flow across it. He identifies three main lines of variation (which he calls continuous, folded, and emergent time), each of which frames different possibilities for how groups form and relate to each other. Conflicts and interactions among these frames are leading to changes from new senses of place to identity claims with implications for the relations between Taiwan and the Chinese mainland.

Toward a Broader View of Barth

The essays collected here touch on a great deal of Barth's intellectual legacy as it continues to shape our field: specific studies that shaped thinking on topics ranging from nomadic and sedentary agricultural economies (chapters 5 and 6) to ritual secrecy (chapter 8); essays that continue to be touchstones for new thinking, from *Ethnic Groups and Boundaries* (chapters 2, 9, and 10) to more recent work like "The Guru and the Conjurer" (chapters 2 and 7) or *Cosmologies in the Making* (chapters 3 and 8); and broad theoretical problems that continue to challenge us (all the chapters, as we have been discussing). Nevertheless, Barth's lasting influence extends even farther. In this final section, we want to make quick mention of three areas that do not always receive extensive discussion in the chapters that follow or in the academic literature, but that we feel are just as important a part of his legacy. These include his understanding of an appropriate anthropological method, his commitment to public anthropology, and his lasting contributions as teacher.

Only our bookend essays by Unni Wikan and Ulf Hannerz begin to do justice to these issues.[3] In chapter 1, Wikan emphasizes how much Barth felt that theory and method in anthropology were inextricable. For him, as she says, theory could only grow from field experience. It is not so much that he disapproved of armchair theorizing. Rather, he simply considered it impossible, at least for him. He was interested, above all, in how people interacted with each other as people. He thus frowned on reliance on key informants, whose overuse encouraged a kind of disembodied and abstracted anthropology.

Barth was always full of fieldwork advice, although he never wrote the text on methodology that he had long contemplated. Robert remembers Barth telling him that the first job is to learn everyone's name—not their official name, but whatever everyone actually calls them. And at the same, one should learn all the place names, again not the ones on the map, but the ones people actually use. Otherwise, he explained, you cannot understand half of what people are saying to each other. It seemed like common sense, but only after he said it. In a way, it was absolutely typical of Barth, showing his interest in how people lived and dealt with each other, and not just with an anthropologist. It was, above all, a humanistic anthropology.

By the time Keping took his methodology course in the early 2000s, Barth was still not given to grand abstraction, but rather to stories showing how specific ideas grew out of unique experiences in the field. The method was to accept people as people (as Wikan says), rather than types. He thus had little patience for methods designed to reduce the complexity of daily life, whether those were statistical summaries or pile sorts. In some ways, perhaps *Balinese Worlds* can stand in for the methodology book he never wrote or at least give us some idea of where he would have headed. Even for a very difficult topic like Balinese sorcery, for example, he emphasized the importance of starting from open-ended engagement with people he had good relationships with and only then trying to build some model of what was going on (Barth 1993, 249). Theory and method, for Barth, are one.

Bringing anthropology beyond the academy is the second broad area of Barth's work that is underrecognized in discussions of his contributions to anthropology, as both Wikan and Hannerz make clear. In part, this took the form of extensive consulting on applied projects, where Barth's enormous field experience must have provided a significant advantage in trying to make sense of local data quickly, as such projects almost always demand. Some of his consulting work took place in areas where we already know his academic work well (like the New Guinea gold mine mentioned in chapter 8, with Barth's role discussed at more length in chapter 1). Much, however, took place in areas that led to very few or no academic publications. He consulted extensively in Southwest China, for instance, toward the end of his career but published on it only in Norwegian. Wikan describes his long-term work on child health in Bhutan, which may have been his most lasting and important such contribution. Barth was equally committed to bringing anthropology to a broader public. He did this more in Norwegian than in English (as Wikan says, he was always a Norwegian first). This included numerous television appearances and several books in Norwegian, including a policy-directed book on Afghanistan and the Taliban (as Hannerz discusses), as well as a memoir.

Third, Hannerz reminds us of Barth the editor. His first edited book concerned entrepreneurship in Northern Norway (Barth 1963)—a classic topic for someone interested in human agency. Hannerz points out that editing a book is itself the act of an entrepreneur, and we can see this very clearly in Barth's three edited books, where he is using the books to help build a Scandinavian anthropology and an anthropology of Scandinavia. Perhaps more importantly, Barth is also hoping to construct new ways of thinking about problems—entrepreneurship itself in the first, and then ethnicity and scale in the two that followed. We can see Barth as entrepreneur as well in the way he constructed an anthropology program at Bergen.

Finally, although not all of the contributors to this book knew Barth personally, he was teacher or colleague (or both) for many of us. It is no surprise that Wikan begins her reminiscence about Barth with a description of him in the classroom. None of the other chapters discuss Barth in this sense, but all of us who knew him found him quietly inspirational, both in and beyond the classroom. When Robert first knew him, he was already so established and successful that all the graduate students (and all of them flocked to his class, of course) expected him to be resting on his laurels. Nothing could be further from the truth, however. He was actively thinking about how to maintain an emphasis on people's agency through transactions while still recognizing the force of what is shared. In retrospect, we had the privilege of hearing him think out loud as he was moving toward the new ideas that would shape his late work, culminating in *Balinese Worlds*. His frequent stints as visiting professor meant that his influence as teacher extended far beyond the sizable impact he had on Norwegian anthropology.

His humility was as remarkable as his knowledge and his ability to communicate. He would not hesitate to ask students for advice on the next project he was thinking about (although he certainly felt no compunction to follow that advice). Even the fact that he consistently pushed his theoretical positions forward throughout his entire career showed a kind of intellectual humility—he was never satisfied with his earlier positions, no matter how influential they became. It is not just the attitude of a proper southern Norwegian (as Wikan describes it); it is the attitude of a genuine scholar, one who was never satisfied but continued to question throughout his life.

For many of us collected here, Barth was a model of how to do fieldwork, how to craft theory, how to teach, and how to be a human being. That is why this volume does not attempt simply to celebrate his life and accomplishments, but to extend them and to try to push even further at the frontiers of anthropology. Such an effort, we feel, honors his memory better than just memorialization.

We have organized the chapters that follow into three broad sections (and alphabetically within each group). We begin with Wikan's chapter, which approaches Barth in a personal way that no one else could. It builds on her intimate knowledge of him in many contexts, from teacher to intellectual collaborator to husband. The next three (Herzfeld, Weller, and Wu) deal with parts of the world on which Barth never published (at least not in English). Each chapter takes inspiration from parts of Barth's oeuvre but does not hesitate to push the ideas in new directions. The next set of chapters (Barfield, Haaland, Lindholm, and Robbins) is based on more recent studies of areas in which Barth's work was a benchmark. This lets those authors address some important issues that come up in the work of almost any influential pioneer: how much can the results generalize to other similar groups or to later times? Each of these essays makes clear that Barth's legacy in the field has sometimes led people to be too quick to read his work as broad general claims, rather than as the empirically grounded studies that he intended. These are followed by two chapters that address Barth's work in a more general way, including Fan's essay on how Barth's approach is causing a rethinking of how ethnicity should be conceptualized in China, and Tan's review of Barth's work, especially as it evolved over time. The book concludes with an afterword by Ulf Hannerz, who draws on Barth's oeuvre and on personal experience to show him as a "rooted cosmopolitan" and cultural broker.

Robert P. Weller is Professor of Anthropology at Boston University. Most of his work concentrates on Chinese societies in a comparative context. His early work began with the problem of religious meaning and authority. His most recent book is *How Things Count as the Same: Memory, Mimesis, and Meta-*

phor, coauthored with Adam Seligman (Oxford University Press, 2019). He is currently working on urbanization and religious change.

Keping Wu is Associate Professor at the Department of China Studies in Xi'an Jiaotong–Liverpool University. She held previous teaching and research positions at Sun Yat-sen University, National University of Singapore, and the Chinese University of Hong Kong. Her research interests are ethnic and religious diversity, urbanization and gender. Her recent publication includes a coauthored book (with Robert Weller and C. Julia Huang), *Religious Charity: Social Life of Goodness in Chinese Societies* (Cambridge University Press, 2018).

Notes

1. The chapters here are the result of meetings that took place at the School of Sociology and Anthropology at Sun Yat-sen University in June 2017. We are enormously grateful for their sponsorship. The tireless help from Drs. Luo Pan, Duan Ying, and Zhang Wenyi and the wonderful graduate-student helpers there were crucial for the success of this conference. Special thanks go to Professors Liu Zhiyang and Zhang Yingqiang for their generous support and for creating an excellent academic environment for doing anthropology in China. We are also grateful to those participants whose work is not directly represented in this volume, but who certainly contributed to its development: Abdel Ghaffar M. Ahmed, Ying Duan, Jiansheng Huang, Yuanlong Li, Ke Man, Haimei Shen, Gen Tian, Tenzin Jinba, Liping Wang, Andreas Wimmer, Da Wu, Wenjiong Yang, and Yongming Zhou. Thanks also to the Fritt Ord Foundation for their financial support.
2. "It Happens among People," from which we take the title of this book, is also the Norwegian title of Barth's currently unpublished memoir, discussed in chapter 1.
3. See also Eriksen's very useful biography (Eriksen 2015).

References

Asad, Talal. 1972. "Market Model, Class Structure and Consent: A Reconsideration of Swat Political Organisation." *Man* 7(1): 74–94.

Barth, Fredrik. 1959a. *Political Leadership among Swat Pathans*. Monographs on Social Anthropology 19. London: Athlone Press.

———. 1959b. "Segmentary Opposition and the Theory of Games: A Study of Pathan Organization." *Journal of the Royal Anthropological Institute of Great Britain and Ireland* 89(1): 5–21.

———. 1961. *Nomads of South Persia: The Basseri Tribe of the Khamseh Confederacy*. Boston: Little, Brown.

Barth, Fredrik, ed. 1963. *The Role of the Entrepreneur in Social Change in Northern Norway*. Bergen: Norwegian Universities Press.

———, ed. 1969. *Ethnic Groups and Boundaries: The Social Organization of Culture Difference*. Boston: Little, Brown.

———. 1975. *Ritual and Knowledge among the Baktaman of New Guinea*. New Haven: Yale University Press.

———, ed. 1978. *Scale and Social Organization*. Oslo: Universitetsforlaget.

——. 1987. *Cosmologies in the Making: A Generative Approach to Cultural Variation in Inner New Guinea*. Cambridge: Cambridge University Press.

——. 1990. "The Guru and the Conjurer: Transactions in Knowledge and the Shaping of Culture in Southeast Asia and Melanesia." *Man* 25(4): 640–53.

——. 1993. *Balinese Worlds*. Chicago: University of Chicago Press.

——. 2002. "An Anthropology of Knowledge." *Current Anthropology* 43(1): 1–18.

Das, Veena. 2007. *Life and Words: Violence and the Descent into the Ordinary*. Berkeley: University of California Press.

Durkheim, Emile. 2013. *The Division of Labor in Society*. Translated by George Simpson. Digireads.com Publishing.

Eriksen, Thomas Hylland. 2015. *Fredrik Barth: An Intellectual Biography*. London: Pluto Press.

Fassin, Didier. 2014. "The Ethical Turn in Anthropology: Promises and Uncertainties." *HAU: Journal of Ethnographic Theory* 4(1): 429–35.

Geertz, Clifford. 1959. "Form and Variation in Balinese Village Structure." *American Anthropologist* 61(6): 991–1012.

Gluckman, Max. 1955. *Custom and Conflict in Africa*. Glencoe, IL: Free Press.

Kuper, Adam. 2014. *Anthropology and Anthropologists: The British School in the Twentieth Century*. 4th ed. London: Routledge.

Lambek, Michael. 2010. Introduction to *Ordinary Ethics: Anthropology, Language, and Action*, edited by Michael Lambek, 1–36. New York: Fordham University Press.

Latour, Bruno. 1993. *We Have Never Been Modern*. Translated by Catherine Porter. Cambridge, MA: Harvard University Press.

Latour, Bruno, and Steve Woolgar. 1986. *Laboratory Life: The Construction of Scientific Facts*. 2nd ed. Princeton, NJ: Princeton University Press.

Leach, E. R. 1973. *Political Systems of Highland Burma: A Study of Kachin Social Structure*. Oxford: Bloomsbury Academic.

Wimmer, Andreas, and Nina Glick Schiller. 2002. "Methodological Nationalism and Beyond: Nation-State Building, Migration and the Social Sciences." *Global Networks* 2: 301–34.

1

Humility First
Fredrik Barth in His Own Words—and Mine

Unni Wikan

Fredrik Barth passed away on Sunday 24 January 2016. His death came unexpectedly but peacefully. He lived to be eighty-seven years old. We were together for forty-four years.

He was born in Leipzig, Germany, of Norwegian parents, who shortly after moved to Washington, DC, where his father, a geologist, had a research appointment. They returned to Norway when their son was seven years old so he would have an ordinary Norwegian school experience, which he did, until 1940, when the Germans invaded Norway and ordinary schooling came to a halt. Fredrik has described how during the next five years he received little formal education and passed his exams through sheer luck. He trained as a sculptor in his youth and envisioned that as a possible career. But then his father, Tom Barth, was invited to the University of Chicago as visiting professor in 1946, and Fredrik got the chance of his life. He got an MA in anthropology from Chicago and later a PhD from the Cambridge University in England, where he studied with Edmund Leach, who, beside his father, provided the most important intellectual influence on him.

Like his father, Fredrik was a Norwegian at heart, and though he held positions at elite universities in the United States and elsewhere, there was no doubt in his mind of where he wanted to *live*. So when the chance came up to develop social anthropology at the University of Bergen, he jumped at it, though his father advised against it. Too many good scholars, warned his father, had gone there and lost out. It was at the University of Oslo that things happened and where you had to be if you were to count. But Fredrik did not get an offer in Oslo; on the contrary, it seemed evident that he would not be getting it either. There is something in Norway called the Jante Law: "Don't you ever think you are something!" Fredrik Barth was clearly an upcoming man, and it was not to everyone's liking. Fortunately, in Bergen there were people at the university who realized that here was someone who could make a difference, and he was invited to join. The long story of it all is entertaining and educating reading and appears in his memoirs, to be published.[1] The short story I shall provide here starts in 1967, just two years after he established the Department of Social Anthropology at the University of Bergen. It was then that I came to Bergen, and my first memory of Fredrik Barth is the following.

A Teacher's Teacher

We were seated at the back of a large auditorium hall, a fellow student and I. We had both just arrived in Bergen to study social anthropology, but Professor Barth would not be teaching that semester or the next or the next. He was preparing to go off to Papua New Guinea, where he would remain for a long, long time. We hadn't even seen him as a shadow, and we didn't have a clue of what he looked like or what fieldwork really meant. But we knew we were in for an experience. In those days, "everyone" came to Barth's lectures: colleagues, professors in adjacent disciplines, students, and ordinary folks. It was an event. You could sense it by the atmosphere. We had heard talk of his charisma, though I am not sure we even knew what that meant. The one thing we understood was what older students had told us: "*Onkel Barth tegner og forteller*—Uncle Barth draws and tells." That was how *they* summed up their praise for his lectures. And we were soon to understand why.

He entered the podium, a tall, slim man with gray curly hair and a moustache. He had a very dignified appearance. But his lecturing style was entirely down-to-earth. He drew us in with his words. He made it all seem so simple. No big talk, no jargon. He had a child's playfulness and delight in telling stories, reaching out to the audience as if that was all that mattered. It was apparent even as I saw him that first time from the back of the auditorium. It was apparent till the end of his days.

Fredrik Barth has been described as an ethnographer's ethnographer and a theorist's theorist. In a beautiful article to his memory, that is how Richard Jenkins (2016: 412) summed up his legacy. Barth was also a "teacher's teacher." I think that few who heard him lecture or give a talk were likely to forget it. He prepared for each and every talk by writing down a few notes that would give an outline of what he was to say. Whether the audience was undergraduates, the general public, or postdoctoral students, the procedure was the same. Then he threw his heart into it. The paper with his notes might just be lying there, for he knew his stuff and had prepared himself. He always felt that something was at stake and never took success for granted. It used to surprise me. But that was how he was.

In his memoirs he tells how his experience of talking to public audiences in Northern Norway through the Folk Academy helped shape his style of lecturing. Without a steady job, after his first fieldwork in Kurdistan, he took on engagements to travel to remote regions. North Norwegians are known to suffer no big talk. He experienced how he could not just reach but *keep* audiences through a certain narrative style. It was a lesson that was to stay with him always.

But I also think that he was by nature a *communicator*. His letters from Chicago to friends in Norway during his student days are a parade of funny, often self-mocking observations, with caricature drawings filling the margins. His articles to a Norwegian main newspaper sent home from Kurdistan and Swat with his own inimitable ink or pencil drawings are both instructive and hilarious.[2] Fredrik was a man with a great sense of humor.[3] No wonder children too loved him.

(For our son Kim he produced a new story every night for years. "The Wolf in Peshawar" was an all-time high. I used to think that I must tape-record these stories—they often had an ethnographic bent—but I never did.)

On Shyness and Fieldwork

Fredrik Barth was a shy man and well aware of it. He sometimes pondered the intricacy of fate by telling this tale of himself and his two best friends: "The kindest one became a criminologist, the clumsiest one became a diplomat, and the shyest one [*den mest folkeskye*] became an anthropologist!"

In an interview in October 2015 he further reflected on shyness. To the question "Why do you think that social anthropology has become so popular here in Norway?" he thought for a moment, then said, "Perhaps because Norwegians are so shy. Anthropology gives them a method to come a little closer to people. I think they are longing for that" (Fatland 2015: 27).

Now there are *some* anthropologists who work primarily from (or on) texts, and there are diverse ways of doing *social* anthropology. It has room for people of different dispositions. But for Fredrik Barth there was only one way, and it obliged him to be always *with people*, closely observing acts and interaction. *People* were central in his anthropology. There was no shortcut to actually observing what happened among people.

The shy young man developed an orientation within the discipline that required him to overcome himself. But then, this was not a first-time experience. In his memoirs he tells of how in childhood he had been a sissy who was afraid of "everything"—darkness, water, everything . . . He eventually forced himself to overcome his fears by facing them head-on. It is heartening to think of the benefits of this for future anthropology.

Fredrik Barth has been described as an adventurer—indeed as Norway's foremost living adventurer as of 2015 (Fatland 2015: 24). He *was* adventurous. If he was ever afraid, he never showed it. Nor did he complain about hard living conditions. He took things in stride.

But don't think he didn't suffer. Fieldwork was sometimes excruciating for him. He always regarded it as hard work. He experienced it as exhausting time and again. That was in its nature. That was how it was. Anyone following in Barth's footsteps should be prepared for this.

It Happens Among People

So why did he do it again and again? It was not just from an insatiable sense of curiosity but also for sheer professional reasons. He needed practical, empirical issues to deal with to move forward analytically. His theories were developed in the encounter between his mind and life on the ground. He needed new input to move on. One might say, he needed concrete puzzles, practical issues, real-life problems. It was by *observing* life on the ground, between people, in empirical contexts under varying circumstance that he produced the materials that provided the basis for nearly all his own analytical thinking.

Naturally he was inspired by, and stood on the shoulders of, a host of scholars, anthropologists, and others. But I think he was also to a considerable extent a self-made man in that he made his own field studies "carry the burden" of his analyses; it was from them that his thinking developed, and it was through his field materials that the *evidence* for the plausibility of his analyses was produced.

He was a "methods man." In his view, theory and method went hand in hand. He thought that method was not given enough attention in anthropology. From the 1990s he worked on and off on a book on method that was never finished due to too many other tasks. But readers of Norwegian could savor a firsthand narrative account of *his* method through his book *Vi mennesker: Fra en antropologs reiser*, first published in 2005.[4] The title really does not lend itself into English: "We Humans" is a poor rendition of *Vi mennesker*. The subtitle, "From an Anthropologist's Journeys," works better. He planned to rewrite the book himself in English rather than having it translated, knowing full well that translation *is* rewriting. But again, time was too short. It will be for me to see to it that this important and beautifully written book finds an international audience, and I am steadily encouraged to do so. There is nothing resembling it in anything he wrote in English.

An Ethnographer's Ethnographer

The ethnographer's ethnographer did fieldwork in a host of different places. Starting with Kurdistan in Iraq in 1951, he went on to Swat in the Northwest Frontier Province in Pakistan; then to Basseri nomads in South Persia (later Iran); Darfur in the Sudan came next; then Baluchistan in Pakistan; next followed Papua New Guinea. Together we did fieldwork in Oman, Bali, and

Bhutan. He also did some fieldwork in Sichuan in China in connection with a consultancy job.[5]

Brief fieldwork early on in his career in Norway should also be reckoned: among itinerant gypsies, among small-scale farmers in a mountain community, and on a fishing boat off the coast of Norway. All resulted in scientific articles and were important for his development as an anthropologist. His first monograph, however, would be *Principles of Social Organization in Southern Kurdistan*, published in 1953 when he was twenty-four years old.

It was submitted for the Norwegian doctor philosophiae degree—and turned down: a scathing experience for him, though he was to regard it retrospectively as his good luck.[6] But for that, he would not have gone to Cambridge and Leach. What *that* experience meant to him cannot be overestimated. He held Edmund Leach in the highest possible regard and had a deep affection for him. Out of Cambridge came also Fredrik's PhD thesis and book *Political Leadership among Swat Pathans*, which was to be critical also for what he could later do on ethnicity.

Because Fredrik wanted me to meet some of "his" people with whom he had done fieldwork before we met, I had the opportunity to observe him with Pashtuns in Swat, Basseri in South Persia, and Baktaman in New Guinea—in addition to the Omanis, Balinese, and Bhutanese among whom we worked together. It was a privilege.

People loved him, and he them. He had a way with people that was attentive, respectful, and humble. In Swat, on his return nearly twenty years after his first fieldwork there, "everyone" welcomed him, and some shed tears when we left. With the Basseri likewise, it was as if the lost son was coming back. The Baktaman had planted a pine tree to remember him—Fredrik loved pine trees. It had grown to be a considerable tree when he returned in 1983. Fredrik's special quality was to make as little as he could of himself, thus giving the other person the feeling that it was he who counted. On my showing some photos of him doing fieldwork, Robert Weller and Keping Wu remarked how he fitted in so well that it could be hard to see who was *he* in the picture! And it was true: his body language took on the form of those he was with, not because he *made* his body do it, but because it fell into that pattern. In some early photos of him from Kurdistan, Swat, and Persia, at first glance even I could hardly make out who was he and who "the other." His black hair helped. But even as an elderly man in Bhutan sitting on the ground with villagers, he loses visibility. And he sat cross-legged till the end of his days. That part of his fieldworker self had become *him*, *his* self.

The Challenge of Novelty

On why he continued to go so many places and pursue so many different themes in fieldwork, he said:

I see my task as an academic not in discovering things in libraries but in discovering things in the field. That is where we can find new understanding and new data. It has also been important to me to confront totally new places; this somehow keeps me young and enables me to think in new and original ways. It surprises me that many of my colleagues have chosen anthropology and yet have not followed this course of action. I suspect they feel that fieldwork is exhausting—which it is, certainly, and that might tempt one to give up. But I think if you stop collecting new data, you stop being a scientist. (Korbøl 1985: 34)

Asked whether he was concerned with specific questions, he answered:

Here too I probably have my own way of working. Sometimes I do continue to pursue the same theme from one fieldwork to the next. But I prefer to cast my net very wide. I have made a conscious decision not to become an expert—on a region, on comparative politics, on economics, on whatever it may be. Again I believe that the challenge of novelty, in methods and problems and themes, keeps you intellectually alive. (Korbøl 1985: 34–35)

He also came to realize that pursuing different thematics actually led him to develop new theories and perspectives. It became apparent to him especially after he undertook his study on ritual and knowledge in New Guinea:

Earlier I had understood the changes in my perspective as primarily thematic, with a focus on ecology, on politics, and on economy as a kind of shifting of scientific fields of cultivation. Now I understood much more clearly that a thematic shift had also each time enforced [*fremtvunget*] theoretical and perspectival shifts—that corresponded with my father's intellectual wandering through crystal structures and mapping of rock types and geochemistry: in other words, that my new thematic focus was about to drive through an even deeper "sea change," yes.[7]

Swim or Sink: The Making of an Anthropologist

My first meeting with Fredrik Barth was toward the end of 1967, shortly before he went to Papua New Guinea. I was a first-semester anthropology student in Bergen. I had been reading the book *The Social Organization of the Marri Baluch*,[8] which was not on the curriculum, and there were some things I could not figure out. So I went to Barth's close colleague Blom and asked him. "Why don't you go and ask Fredrik?" he said. I said I could not. But he urged me, and a meeting was set up.

I remember entering a large office with a big beautiful kilim in brilliant colors covering the wall opposite the sofa where I was motioned to sit. Barth sat in a chair to the left. The furniture was red. I was afraid to waste his time and had my questions clear. He listened attentively and responded thoughtfully, as if my questions mattered. Perhaps in due course they did.

More than a year later, I received a letter from him that was to change the course of my life. He had just returned from fieldwork in Papua New Guinea, whereas I was in Cairo studying Arabic. I had completed *grunnfag* (basic anthropology) at the department in Bergen in the summer of 1968 and then gone to Egypt to do a year's Arabic in preparation for later fieldwork in the region. I had lived in Egypt in 1964–65 and was keen on studying the Bedouin. But I would have to go back to Bergen first. Three semesters of anthropology were required before we could do fieldwork. I had only two.

Barth's letter came out of the blue and advised me to try to do some fieldwork while I was still in Egypt. He wrote that he thought I was qualified enough to manage to do it and that it would save me major expenses. Most importantly, I should grasp the opportunity while I was there to try to get *something* done. He had prospects of building up a Middle East studies program with the aid of the Norwegian Social Research Foundation, and there might be a place for me.

Imagine yourself in my stead: I had just one year of anthropology. True, I had done my exam with exceptional result, and he would have heard about it on his return from Papua New Guinea. But he did not know me other than secondhand, and he might have vastly overestimated me. That was my concern. I was overwhelmed and proud to receive his letter, but not happy. How could I possibly live up to his ideas of (and for) me?

Moreover, I did not have a clue, really, as to how one conducted fieldwork other than what I had intuited through seminars and the books of others. Still, in those days, it was not common to tell much of how one *did it*. I was a fieldwork illiterate, and Barth must have known it.

Yet he trusted me to do it. And it made all the difference. It was sink or swim. I relate the experience for what it says of Barth. He was generous to a fault but also demanding of his students. Anthropology was no holiday; you had to do your best, be your best, and if you did, he was behind you. I had to manage by myself the business of trying to get a research permit—something he knew from his own experience in the Middle East could be well nigh impossible, but I stood a better chance if I was there.[9] I realize how his own experience of doing research in Kurdistan, Swat, and Iran had made him all too aware that you have to make the best of your opportunity on the spot. Don't expect to get a second chance. Use all your abilities there and then, and endure. I did. And when I was about to give up, the knowledge that Barth believed in me kept me going.[10]

I have thirteen letters from him from the time I was in Egypt. I did fieldwork in a slum in Cairo. I returned to Bergen after four and a half months in the field, spent one semester in Bergen, then back to Cairo for four more months. After that, I was on the verge of giving up; I was utterly exhausted and self-deprecating. I went home to my parents to recuperate, not knowing if I could continue as an anthropologist. I didn't feel I had what it took.

Fredrik started writing to me to save this nearly lost soul for anthropology. In those days, there were not so many of us who had done fieldwork in hard places. He was *building* a department. He needed good recruits.

I returned to Bergen to write my magister's thesis. A year later, in May 1972, Fredrik Barth and I began our life together. It was to last for nearly forty-four years. Anthropology was at the core of it. We lived the discipline. We breathed the discipline. When our son Kim was born in 1976, he too became a part of it. He was a born traveler, like his parents. And besides, there was no choice. One does not choose one's parents, as they say.

Team of Two: Fieldwork in Arabia

In 1974, Fredrik and I moved to Oslo. He had always wanted to live there. It was home. He had a deep sense of belonging there. The stark and dramatic contrasts of the west coast were not solace for his soul. He loved the forests, woods, and valleys of the southeast. It had always been his plan to move to Oslo once the professor at the Ethnographic Museum at the University of Oslo retired. He expected to be the strongest applicant for the position. He was. So in February 1974, we left Bergen.

In Oslo, on settling into our home, the first thing we did was to hang the kilim from Fredrik's office in Bergen up on the main wall. It provides an anchor piece to this day. To me it stands also as emblematic of Fredrik's qualities as a fieldworker. It was a gift bequeathed to him by the family he stayed with among the Basseri. It had been a part of the wife's trousseau; she had woven it for her marriage. She wanted Fredrik to have it to remember them by.

In August 1974, Fredrik brought me with him to visit the Basseri. It was like a homecoming, and it made me see with my own eyes what they had meant to him and he to them. Indeed for Fredrik, his happiest experience as a fieldworker was with the Basseri.

That was not the case of Oman, where we did our first fieldwork together. Oman was horrific physically, though we did not know it when we went there. Why did we go? Let me give the word to Fredrik, though the translation from Norwegian will be mine:

> Both Unni and I wanted to do fieldwork. Most importantly, we felt that the task of doing urgent anthropology still remained—what would be better than beginning with it ourselves, at once? Urgent tasks do not just concern hunters and gatherers from different outposts of the earth, but to the greatest extent also archaic and complex societies that in our generation are about to disappear even more quickly.
>
> Our original plan was to work both in southern Arabia and eastern Afghanistan, where we both had special qualifications for studying undocumented areas. I wanted to look at ethnic relations in non-Western large-scale societies, those that had not been created by colonialism but functioned on their own, traditional premises. Unni would use her excellent language competence of Arabic, and I my Pashto, and we should each participate in the other's fieldwork—that was the plan.
>
> And we started naturally with her part, for it was for her that it was most urgent [I needed a PhD]; so we wanted to get to southern Arabia in some way or other.

Our dream was really South Yemen, a series of old oasis towns in the valley of Hadramawt—but North Yemen was possible, and so was Oman. We applied for visas to all three places. In South Yemen it was impossible, the communist party there was too extreme and did not want anthropologists. But we got a quite positive reaction from both North Yemen and Oman. So we thus traveled to London, where both countries had embassies and had talks with the ambassadors—and the decision was taken because the Omani ambassador said yes, we were welcome, but he wasn't sure if Oman would be "a suitable country for anthropologists—you see, there has never been one!" That decided the matter and we headed straight for Oman.[11]

We settled in the town of Sohar, midway between Muscat and Dubai, reputed home of Sinbad the Sailor. It had everything we wanted in terms of a plural society with a multiplex population. And the people were a pleasure to be with. But the climate was not. For months, the temperature never went below body temperature even at night. And we had no fans; the humidity was up to 100 percent. After four months we could bear it no longer:

> What next we did was to flee from the coast and into the Empty Quarter, on the inside of the mountains, where it was even hotter . . . up to 52°C, but where the air was dry. Thereby it became actually more livable. So we extended our stay beyond what was humanly possible by staying there, in inner Oman, for six weeks more, and got some very special material, both there and on the coast in Sohar.[12]

We returned for fieldwork in Sohar the next year, but in winter. The government generously provided us with lodgings and a car with a driver. I was eight months pregnant. We left two weeks before our child's expected birth.

What was it like for me to do fieldwork with a master fieldworker? And what was it like for him to have somebody *se ham i kortene*—watch him close-up? Fredrik loved telling the story of how shocked he was to discover how I did fieldwork. He told it especially to students as a lesson on method. It went like this: "I am humble and respectful and accommodating; she speaks her mind and engages in discussion. And yet they like her better than me!"

It was fun. We had fun together doing fieldwork, however hard it was. And I think we were the perfect pair; for though clearly people liked Fredrik at least as much as me, we each had our roles and positions. We were two different people. We made sense. People *are* different. And we were a couple as different as most couples. He was always very kind and gentle and accommodating, it is true. And people appreciated it. He was polite, he was humble. He was also obviously someone of stature. He gained respect. He did not really have to win it. He seemed to get it, easily.

My advantage on our first fieldwork, before we had got used to one another, was a good command of Arabic and a sense that I knew "how to do it." I had survived the slums in Cairo. I had gained good materials.[13] I had learned to cope in a difficult environment. And I did *not know* that there was any other way of doing fieldwork well other than how I had done it. I had no comparison. So when I spoke my mind on occasion and challenged this or that, it was because I behaved like a good Cairene woman. Moreover, I had age on my side. A young female has leeway to make a fool of herself in a way that a man of Fredrik's stature could not. He had learned how to behave among honor-driven Kurds and Pashtuns, where by virtue of *his* age at the time, he had to act carefully. Now he was a senior man, he was forty-five years old; still it was natural to him to be attentive, gentle, low-key.

And people loved him for it. Till he died, whenever I went back to Oman, they said, "But where is Fredrik?" And when he died, though they never used to phone me, now they did. I had to go back to grieve with them. We shared the sorrow.

Barth on *Sohar*: Transformed Conceptions of Ethnicity and Scale

Fredrik and I each wrote a book on Sohar. His *Sohar: Culture and Society in an Omani Town* was published in 1983; my *Behind the Veil in Oman: Women in Oman* came in 1982.[14] We pooled our field materials, then as always. But we kept our writings separate. I was happy to read in Richard Jenkins's commemorative article that his favorite two books by Barth were *Political Leadership among Swat Pathans* and *Sohar* (Jenkins 2016). I think the latter has been entirely underrated in anthropology.[15] But what did Fredrik himself think of the book?

> My understanding is that my book on Sohar was not theoretically and analytically the most important I have done, but it has unique data and an important analysis. What the Omani fieldwork did for me was to get me to understand how open local cultures can be in archaic states. It is not enough just to think of [Sohar] as a plural urban society—for it was an ancient town with twenty thousand people—every one of the groups that lived together in this town had its own extension in completely different directions. Some of them lived, and had always lived, in a world that consisted of all of the Arab Gulf; and the Bedouin lived in a world that consisted of the Arabian desert; and some had only a small world that consisted of a thirty kilometer sector of the beach and the coast, for they were fishermen—and so on and so forth. And beside Arabs, there were Persians there, and Baluchis from the regions north and east on the other side of the Gulf, and a little linguistic group that is not found anywhere else in the world, and Gujarati tradesmen from India. . . . So the picture was not just large scale and local, and a plural mosaic . . . but it was that the whole world fell apart with these belongings and memberships in different directions. That transformed both my conceptions of ethnicity as culture, and of scale as variable, and of how complex social systems can be constituted.
>
> . . . Asked to compare his view of Sohar with that of Swat, he said, *Swat* deals with large systems, but with a tighter and more small-scale model, so the analysis becomes focused in an entirely different manner.[16]

To the question of whether he thought that by opening up the systems analytically one gets less emphasis on the stuff inside, he answered, "That's true, and
then one wonders about all the other stuff that may have been there also, but
that I didn't see any reason to embrace and include. When something is open,
then you cannot give the reader the feeling that the description is complete!"

Ethnic Groups and Boundaries: An Unexpected Success

In the spring of 1968, when I was a student in Bergen, the chair of the department asked me if I would proofread an article by Barth that was to appear in an
edited collection. Barth himself was in New Guinea. I admired the clarity and
elegance of the text; it seemed to flow more easily than some other writings I
had read by Barth such as *Models of Social Organization.* There were a few mis-
takes, and I corrected them; then I handed the text back to Blom, who thanked
me. I never read the text again, but many others did. It was to become one of
the most cited articles in the social sciences, the introduction to his edited
book, *Ethnic Groups and Boundaries.*

Barth had not expected *Ethnic Groups and Boundaries* to take off so much.
Asked why he went to a parochial press, the Norwegian University Press, with
it, Fredrik said that it was because it was the easiest thing to do. But in those
days, he added, a book could have a life irrespective of its publisher. He felt
that he was lucky with the book's timing; the larger intellectual community was
ready for it, as there were others too engaged in issues on ethnicity.

He did *not* regard the much-cited introduction as his best work in any way,
and he always underscored that the insights stemmed from a joint venture and
that Gunnar Haaland's (1969) contribution had been particularly significant for
developing the theory.

Fredrik liked to stand things on their head. He was playful with theory and
liked to try out new perspectives to see where they might bring him. He was the
opposite of doctrinaire. As he said, "Instead of being scared when somebody
throws rocks at the fundaments . . . let us try to see what is constructive in the
new." In an interview, he applied this to postmodernism:

I find aspects in postmodernism that are easy to grasp because they are similar
to ways of thinking that I have grappled with. Through the whole strategy and
rationality debate I recognized—though without being able to get it quite explicit
in theory formulations—the deeply arbitrary in how people construct their point
of departure, their values, and thereby the reality they live in. To deal rationally
with things means only that people reason in terms of the understanding they
have—at that historical moment. Therefore, all rationality is in flux and culture
relative: each time it leads to constructions that reflect the specific experience
that just that person has got in life. So here is both circularity and paradox: prin-
cipal rationality in human experiences builds necessarily on a set of accidental
(or more precisely: stochastic) experiences that persons come to have by trying

to be rational in the world, in just that culturally created and experience created world that they happen to find themselves in. This gives rise to a dynamics that postmodernism dramatizes, and that obviously is in tune with [*er samstemt med*] the way I tried to build my models in the 1960s. The clearest case where I grasped for that insight was in the argument about ethnicity—that yes, ethnicity is about the social organization of culture difference, but although people themselves construct it as if it was the differences of culture it was all about, that is not so: it is their specific selection and construction of *some* cultural differences that it is all about. Anthropological thought had mixed the two and assumed that here you have "cultures," as totalities, that stand against one another in ethnic opposition, when on the contrary it is only *groups* that can stand in opposition to one another; and when their choice of symbols for group identity draws on culture, they do it in a way that is not representative of the totality of cultural stuff that is there. This was a kind of postmodern thought. It was a thought, I mean, that was akin to a postmodern way of thinking. So in that sense the whole gang of Bergen folks in the 1960s was part of such a postmodern hubbub without any of us knowing it; we played with some ways of thinking that now can be given that sobriquet.

. . . Postmodernism came much later and on entirely different premises than what we had grappled with—and partially in ways I can feel *great* impatience with, yes.[17]

On the Value of Revisits

After our first fieldwork together in Oman in 1974, we had taken the long way back to Norway by flying to Islamabad in Pakistan and making it by local buses up to Swat, where, after a stay, we headed west on the road through Afghanistan, Iran, and Turkey until we reached Istanbul and flew home. It was the trip of all trips in our shared memory. We were to re-create it in part the next year when we started out from Shiraz in Iran and traveled east overland through Meshed, Herat, Kandahar, Kabul, and Jelalabad back to Swat. In Swat the Wali asked Fredrik if he would write his biography, an offer Fredrik was happy to accept, but it had to be fitted in between various commitments. In the fall of that year, 1975, we traveled all over India, even up to Assam, Fredrik as an honored guest of the Social Survey of India giving lectures, I as the wife; I was visually pregnant and was constantly viewed as the lucky mother-to-be rather than me. After India, we flew to Oman for a last stint of fieldwork before our child was due. Kim was born in March 1976. Two years later we returned to Afghanistan, this time by air. We were on our way to Swat, where Fredrik would do the interviews for the Wali's biography, but with our shared love of Afghanistan we could not think of *not* going via the Khyber Pass. We were the last, the only tourists at the Kabul hotel. The American ambassador had been killed there shortly before—but we reckoned we had no reason to fear, and we did not. The place was calm, calm before the storm. We proceeded over the Khyber Pass, down into Peshawar, hired a taxi to take us up to Mingora in Swat; it was April and spectacularly beautiful with the poppies in full bloom—future source of income for the Taliban. Kim and I stayed for a couple of weeks, then left Fredrik to his job and went home.

Fredrik gives me credit for enabling him to understand that one could actually revisit former field sites. He wrote:

> Until that time [the first return to Swat in 1974] I had thought about fieldwork, really, as something you do once ... and then you write a book, and then the world is so large that you never come back; while Unni had from the very beginning continued to return to Cairo. For my own part, I was uncomfortable about returning, I imagined that it would be both sad and embarrassing to return to a place where it had been as if I belonged, but where I now no longer remembered all, knew all, had a place ... and some of the places I had forgotten what I knew of the language, and so on. So I was hesitant about it. But on the other hand, it was an attractive thought that I should show Unni the places where I had worked! I had gone with her to Cairo and seen that, and she should come with me. . . .
>
> So this also became the opportunity for a job I could do—the biography on the Wali in 1978. And it was also exciting to come back.[18]

Fredrik met again his beloved servant and assistant, Kashmali, from the time of his fieldwork among the Swat Pathans. He writes:

> And Kashmali was there, and when Unni and I left, he sat behind when the bus took off ... then Kashmali sat by the wayside and wept openly. . . . It was the last time I saw him, then in 1978. . . .
>
> It was a new pattern for me, this thing about revisits. And when the question came up whether I was willing to revisit the Baktaman in connection with an advisory job regarding the development of the gold mine that had been developed in that area ... if not by the Baktaman ... then I said yes, because I had learnt something and knew that it was possible to return. But furthermore, the Baktaman book [*Ritual and Knowledge*] had been published in 1975, while I was doing Sohar and Oman, but it did lay the ground for a wish for more fieldwork and a wider perspective. So here was a way to return to the region. We went there in 1981–82, and had four to five months.[19]

His Best Work: *Cosmologies in the Making*

Fredrik was thrilled to go back; I was reluctant and deeply so: a rain forest held no appeal to me, having had more than my share of bad weather growing up way above the Arctic Circle. We also had few trees. A thick forest would be claustrophobic to me. But I decided to give it a chance, as Fredrik would not go unless Kim and I came along.

In retrospect I am very glad I did. Out of this journey came what Fredrik himself was to regard as his best work: *Cosmologies in the Making*.

As for the Ok Tedi gold mine job, he was less satisfied:

The study of the Ok Tedi mine and its effects was methodologically very diffi-cult—insoluble, I would say. I did not feel that I mastered it. Very striking, really: When you travel the first time to the Baktaman, where everything is strange, you have to ask what things mean. You have to learn it from bottom up, and you learn it on local premises, for there are no other premises to learn it from. If, on the other hand, you travel to the Ok Tedi mine, . . . how was I to build an understand-ing of all this from [the people's own] perspective and find out what it meant for them? It is in a way technologically—methodologically—insoluble for us with anthropological techniques! So with my hand on my heart I had to accept that no! I had no methodology for analyzing what this form of life meant for them.[20]

But he learned other things. The stay in New Guinea enabled him to travel around and collect other empirical materials from a diversity of communities:

I had *Cosmologies* in my head when we left; and working out that analysis went easily, for the analytical breakthrough had come to me while I collected the data. I wandered around and visited a few local communities that I had never seen be-fore. And it was fantastic—the story about this white man who had lived among the Baktaman for many years (!) and become initiated and knew all the secrets, it had spread over large areas. I was famous in dozens of isolated tribes, and was received as a wise man and a colleague. Temples that would have been closed to me when I was with the Baktaman were now open for me, and secret information flowed my way! I got a great grasp of the world of knowledge that was cultivated in the cult. . . .

   While the materials for the Baktaman monograph had been very difficult to work through, with *Cosmologies* it was very different. I saw the structure in *Cos-mologies* almost as soon as I came home from New Guinea.

He wrote the book in no time at all. It took years to be published due to delays at the press. But the book itself was an easy-go and one that, unlike his usual self, he enjoyed writing:

I think myself that *Cosmologies* is the best work that I have done. *Swat* was good, and especially in light of my qualifications at that time; but *Cosmologies* does some things that my readers still have only partially managed to grasp. If it does what I believe, then it is the first time that Western anthropologists have been able to explicate the intellectual process of creation in a writing-less knowledge tradition and been able to follow the steps of thought that this entails. I believe that work will be standing, long.

Bali and an Anthropology of Knowledge

When *Cosmologies* appeared in 1987, we had already been at work in Bali for some time. Bali was *not* Fredrik's choice. He would have wanted to continue in New Guinea, and I said, "You can have it; I am going to Bali!" I was really so tired of always being to such physically unpleasant places: a mega-city slum, an

Arabian sauna, a jungle where you were eternally soaked. I wanted a pleasant place. Fredrik said, "What are you going to do in Bali? *Everyone* has been to Bali!" I said I didn't care. So we went. Fredrik wrote:

> I have always told students that you can find gold everywhere. So from that point of view, the choice of where you go is not so important. But I was used to seeing before me a kind of thematics in my choice of fieldwork places. . . . I had the feeling still that we had to choose a place that would be suitable for a thematics that I wanted to take up. And what gave itself for me, on Bali, the thematics that the place seemed to invite, was how different traditions of knowledge are produced, maintained, and changed through the splendid ritual imagery of the place. . . . For this Bali was a fantastic place.

Truly, Bali was a rich experience. After a first fieldwork of six months, we had to take turns, going and coming over several years except for a few ritual occasions when we all went back together. Kim was in school, and Norway is extremely strict about permitting children to be taken out of school. But we pooled our field materials, then as always. We had a rich store. But we were not Bali *specialists*. And Fredrik more than me was aware of the cost.

He has written of how the specialists will grind you for going on their turf. His interest was in an anthropology of knowledge. That was what he had been developing after his return to New Guinea. Bali with its composite cultural traditions—Hindu-Balinese, Muslim, Bali Aga or Asli, and more—provided fertile ground for his explorations. We settled in the city of Singaraja on the north coast—practically all anthropologists had worked down south or in central Bali; from there he ventured out over a wide region to villages of various kinds, and we also stayed for a time in a Muslim village. He titled his book-to-come *Balinese Worlds*. Nothing more, nothing less. No subtitle. He was comfortable with that. But it was not exactly a selling title for a book on an island described as "an anthropologist's favorite of favorite places" about which books upon books had been produced, and some by highly renowned scholars in our discipline.

Fredrik's attitude was to think he could afford it. He really did not need to please readers. Promotion was an unknown word for him. And Balinese worlds—traditions of knowledge—was what the book was about. He had ample data. It added up to about three years in the field with his notes and mine combined. Now the quality of those data is what matters, and Bali specialists could with good reason fault us for not knowing Balinese and skimming surfaces where they went in depth. What Fredrik had that was special, though, was *comparative* insight from fieldwork in ever so many other places. He was well positioned to grapple with what people were *not* doing. And he could see Balinese Islam from standpoints in the Middle East. Cosmologies in Bali—though part of a written tradition—were also not exempt from naturalistic and supernatural influences akin to what Baktaman struggled with; and the Baktaman tradition of secrecy of knowledge—the idea that the value of knowledge depended on its being kept secret—certainly had some resemblance to a critically important tradition of black magic in Bali. I am not saying that this is how he thought. But he would definitely have had perspectives on Bali that stemmed from his wide experience of studying human relations.

He reflects on the value of working in a way that combined intensive periods in the field with times away, periods of reflection:

> That was one of the reasons why the fieldwork could grow and my questions and perspectives adapt themselves to the realities on the ground in a perhaps optimal way. But the other important thing about these revisits was what we already knew from Unni's experience: that people love you if you come back. So it was almost as if we learned more by being gone for six months and then coming back than what we would have by remaining there for those six months! People perceived our revisits as clear signs that we were linked with them and belonged in their world; and they also talked more openheartedly and freely with us because we had been away and should be brought up to date. So in terms of field technique it was an unexpectedly great advantage, really. But analytically, I don't know how fundamentally different it was from what I do in the field anyway, for I have always very consciously made sure that I work on my understanding analytically at the same time that I work empirically in the field. And I have steadily taught this to students too.

Barth's Special Field Method

Let us pause here for a moment. For here lies a key to how Fredrik worked in the field. It was brought out cogently in a discussion once with Edvard Hviding, where Hviding remarked, "This is an important point for it is easy to think that anthropology consists in going on fieldwork, finding out some things, and then coming back and do—what is it they call it—'writing up'; and that the under-standing is generated through writing—but that must be completely wrong!" Fredrik remarked:

> Yes, I think it is very unfortunate if that is the case. By all means, it is creative to write, new insights come to you through writing; and incompletenesses in your own thinking are revealed. But when I succeed more quickly in fieldwork than many, then it is because I more consciously than many others undertake this con-tinuous analytical working through [*bearbeidelsen*] . . . there is a steady analytical activity while I am doing fieldwork—even by my writing short essays to myself in the field. And I try to identify types of data, types of places, variants, whatever it be—not just as lacunae in what I have of data, but selectively, so that I might be able to falsify my hypotheses, and then I get it done at once and so I get further at work there in the field, while I am doing that.

He added that it was very hard to do this while being simultaneously socially at-tentive and attuned to people's continual concerns. No wonder he found field-work exhausting, however rich and rewarding it could also be.

I think a part of his special giftedness was that he was able to work at several levels at once. He did not just have his eye to the ground; he could also take flight and observe things from high above. There is a passage in Thomas Hylland Eriksen's rich and interesting intellectual biography on Barth where he notes that "he is a social scientist of the kind that thrives best by crawling on all fours equipped with a magnifying glass. Helicopter trips above the planet, with or without a pair of binoculars, may have fascinated him, but in the last instance they become too remote from experience" (Eriksen 2015: 204). I think the imagery is misleading. Fredrik could be down on all fours if that was required, but never without keeping sight of things higher above. That was the crux of his method: he did not just observe. A magnifying glass would have distracted him. He used all his senses at once. He also relied on intuition and was explicit about that.

And yes, he did love helicopter rides. Helicopters do not hover very high above the ground. That's their great advantage, as I learned in New Guinea. Barth's method was to make use of several methods of observation at once.

Multiple Compelling Concerns

Fredrik had planned and wanted to make revisits after the publication of his Bali book. However, as he wrote:

> The world is so big, the experience of new places so enriching and challenging. And with time, I have also learned enough about Bali to experience a darker side that wears on me—yes, that wore on me already after a couple of revisits. Bali seems claustrophobic to me; it is a civilization, a large-scale society, but the complexity of culture, and people's fine-registering experience of pressure from their surroundings means that when you come in there with knowledge about what is going on under the surface, then the place closes itself around you, and you lose freedom, you are caught by an immensity of complications and concerns that is pressing [*påtrengende*] and doesn't give you space . . . so it resembles claustrophobia. You know that every movement, . . . absolutely everything you do will be seen, will be interpreted, will be noticed; . . . everything that surrounds you has meaning and is part of a very invading and intense social life! It is an enormous experience. But it is too much.

Asked if it was difficult to write the book, he answered, "Not very. Only this: that I had such large masses of data that had to be handled." And then he talked of the Baliologists and the challenge facing anyone who is not an expert on language, religion, tradition in a civilization. It was a challenge he had met before in the Middle East. His take on it was to try to produce good enough data and analysis that the experts might say, "Perhaps this guy has something to contribute after all!" He was happy not to be an expert. It had been his deliberate choice.

Bhutan: Not a Shangri La, but a Fieldworker's Dream

In 1987, Fredrik got a dream fulfilled: to go to Bhutan. He had talked about it for a time and written some letters to the authorities asking about the possibility for fieldwork. I did not share his ambition. I felt I had more than enough on my hands. I was still "wrapping up" fieldwork in Bali and in addition going yearly on revisits to the poor in Cairo. Bhutan was not on my horizon when in Bali I received a telegram from Fredrik saying, "Meet me in Calcutta. Stop. We are going to Bhutan."

I remember rushing to the telegraph station in Singaraja in North Bali to try to connect with him to ask what on earth was on. But the lines were down. So I had to go by bimo (minibus) the long way to Denpasar, where I could make an international call. Fredrik was thrilled.

He had received a telephone call out of the blue from a Norwegian water engineer working for UNICEF in Bhutan. He was just about to arrange a workshop on water and sanitation and had come to think that having an anthropologist on board would be good. So he invited Fredrik and me. We had a fantastic two weeks. But it could have ended there had not Karl-Eric Knutsson, a Swedish colleague and friend of Fredrik, former chair of the Department of Social Anthropology in Stockholm, become head of UNICEF South Asia in 1989. He secured us permits to do baseline studies for a project on mother and child health. From 1989 to 1995, after an initial four months of fieldwork together, we went in turns over several visits. Kim was in school, and there were limits to how much we could be away together.

In an interview in 1989, just as we were starting up in Bhutan, Fredrik was asked to respond to the observation: "Your recent projects have been undertaken in collaboration with your wife, Unni Wikan, who is also an anthropologist. It must surely make a difference to travel as a married couple?" He answered:

> It has been a great pleasure to work with Unni. As a couple, we can also work in a different way and achieve much more. It is extremely useful to combine the fruits of full participation in both men's and women's affairs. In the Bhutan project, that will be particularly helpful. But it is important not to trespass on one another's territory. Our method is to use each other's results with total freedom, and we work side by side and study the same people. But we have always chosen to write our things and publish separately. I think this is good advice to pass on to other anthropological couples. (Korbøl 1989: 35)

Our work in Bhutan had a practical purpose: to help improve mother and child health. It was a piece of medical and of applied anthropology. But as Fredrik had always said, it is easier to apply basic anthropology than applied anthropology. In other words, baseline studies were needed. And we were very fortunate: we were given free rein by the authorities to go wherever we wanted in this culturally fabulously rich and complex society of some five hundred thousand people speaking at least twelve different languages and adhering to different branches of Buddhism and Hinduism. English was a first language in school, so that eased our situation linguistically, but we depended on interpreters for a large part.

Now Fredrik always felt that he had an advantage in the field over anthropologists dependent on discourse and verbal articulation. With his focus on *acts* and *interaction*, he could always find gold even "without" or before knowing "the language." He could start from day one to observe. And he did. I think this is part of the clue to how he could be so productive. Add that he was a naturalist with a naturalist's delight in landscapes, flora, fauna, animals, insects, what not . . . He had much knowledge about zoology, botany, biology, geology. It aided his ecological observations. But most of all he never tired of watching people and social interaction in real-life situations and *wondering* what it was all about. Bhutan provided him with ample opportunity for that. But he also worked very closely with several learned Bhutanese who were experts on their own culture and the written Buddhist traditions.

At one point Fredrik came up with the idea of arranging a workshop bringing together traditional and modern health workers, that is, the vastly influential Central Monk Body (Bhutan's official organization of Buddhist clergy) with members of biomedicine. He has given me credit for developing the idea together with him, and I may have helped nurture it, but the idea was truly his. It was evident that cooperation was needed, and indeed there was basic distrust between the parties, and the people were the losers. It was a sensitive idea, and it was taken to the king for approval. In 1989, the first workshop on "Religion and Health" was held. It brought together lamas and monks with modern health personnel and was a success. Fredrik and I were key persons; it meant we could take the blame if things went wrong. With time, similar workshops were arranged over the whole country at the district level, opening up a space for much-needed dialogue and cooperation between various sectors of health care. For our status in Bhutan with the Central Monk Body, it was a breakthrough, establishing us as persons of respect.

For someone of Fredrik's disposition and interest in an anthropology of knowledge, Bhutan was a godsend. He knew it and sometimes joked that Bhutan was his "Sunday off." He said he knew that with all the problems in the world and all the issues of globalization, he should have put in more time on such serious issues. But he did not want to be that kind of man.[21] He did not want to be that kind of scientist—he needed to be able to *enjoy* some of what he did, and Bhutan was enjoyment for him—even as the fieldwork conditions were horrible and the rats (which could not be killed due to karma) overflowed and the food was awful because most people were dirt-poor, and starting days with rancid butter tea was not helpful. But that was secondary. What he found— what *we* found—compensated for it all.

Together, we wrote a report for UNICEF—a baseline study—that was published as a book by the Centre for Bhutan Studies in 2011. It was titled *The Situation of Children in Bhutan: An Anthropological Perspective*. In the foreword the Centre notes that the insights produced by our research were still highly important and relevant for an understanding of Bhutan. I might add that very little anthropological work has been done in the country at all.

Fredrik had about twelve months of fieldwork in Bhutan; I had twenty-two because I was also engaged by UNICEF to do a study of the "situation of the girl child," and with the cultural, economic, and religious diversity in the country, this in itself became a major undertaking. I also took on work by the World Food Programme (WFP), which brought me to schools and monasteries in the remotest parts, and for other agencies on hydroelectric power/resettlement programs. Fredrik for his part became involved as a consultant on resettlement programs in China. He had previously worked on hydroelectric power development in the Hindu Kush in Northern Pakistan in 1988, and doing practically oriented work that could help improve people's lives and condition was something he valued. He saw a large part for anthropology in that. But our fieldwork in Bhutan added up to so much more than expected thanks to the fact that we were given absolutely free rein by the authorities to research what we wanted and under the conditions we deemed necessary. It is a rare prerogative of anthropologists, and we had it! But it does not make writing easier. On the contrary, so many people at so many levels had put their trust in us. We were not just spokesmen of the poor and downtrodden or the marginalized, as we had been in some of our other fieldwork. We had also been "studying up," something much more difficult, I think, and ethically more problematic than many are ready to consider. We had obligations and commitments in many directions that were ethically and morally demanding. That is how it *should* be. Anthropology *is* humanly trying. But neither of us had been before in exactly this kind of situation, and a publishing experience of mine did impress upon us how delicate the situation was.[22]

The complexity of our Bhutan materials was enormous and really too much. In recognition of this, Fredrik did something he had never done before: he invited two eminent young monk scholars to come to Norway to stay with him for one month and work together. They went on to become scholars in their own right. Not long before Fredrik died he received a parcel sent via Norway's embassy in New Delhi to him. It contained a beautiful Bhutanese hand-carved mask and a letter from one of the students, now a graduate from Oxford, thanking him for having made his studies possible. Perhaps with the help of scholars like him and others in Bhutan, we shall be able to put to good use the materials we have produced.

Fredrik was highly respected in Bhutan, and a beautiful article on him was published in the national newspaper *Kuensel* on his death, written by Dasho Karma Ura.[23]

Public Anthropologist

Fredrik's view of anthropology was that it should serve the public. That is one reason he emphasized from the very beginning that Norwegian anthropologists must also work in Norway, not just on exotic peoples and places. He himself put in much time giving public lectures and writing for the public. He made a television series in 1980 that became enormously popular; the book that was produced from it sold in several editions (Barth 1980). His last book was *Afghanistan and the Taliban*, published in 2008. It was made obligatory reading for all Norwegian military personnel serving in Afghanistan. Fredrik had a political agenda with it. He wanted both the Norwegian authorities *and* the public to understand that the Western powers' policy in Afghanistan was bound to fail. He used his insights among the Pashtuns of Swat to educate and warn—not with much result on politicians. But they too had their hands tied due to Norway's membership in NATO.

I found in his papers a letter from a former foreign minister whom Fredrik had upbraided in an interview, thanking him for his perspectives and expressing his regrets that he could not do more.

Fredrik was explicit that he did not think anthropologists had taken the task of public anthropology seriously enough. He felt that anthropology should be *in* the world, not just *of* the world.[24]

Back to Humility

Fredrik believed that he had a way of working in the field that was different from many anthropologists. And I think it is true. As I observed him, he listened much more than he spoke. He did not go around asking a lot of questions. He listened to what people had to say among themselves or to him. And when he did not have a common language with them, he paid much attention to nonverbal cues. He was not out for "information" in the asked-for sense of the word. He relied more on things happening and coming to the fore. He depended much on his own powers of observation, interpretation, and intuition. He liked playing "second fiddle" in that respect. He did not want to be in the foreground.

Secondly, he was not interested in people as informants. He was interested in them as people, persons. He has written beautifully on this in regard to the person most important to him in Swat, his servant and friend Kashmali. Barth was never on the lookout for "big men" or "chief informants." As he wrote, if he met a "big man," his interest in him would be as a person—what can this person make me understand?—rather than in the fact of him being important. It was a universalist approach, in a way; Fredrik was interested in persons as humans in social context. That was his forte. That is a part of his legacy.

But it had its drawbacks. Anthropology lost out on insights he could have produced. In Bali there was an incident where, with the Bali Aga or Asli (original Balinese), he had the occasion to find out about their concept of god. He was able to meet the chief "priest," who turned out to be a priestess, and on hearing of his interest in the concept she suggested he ask god himself. So she went into trance, and then god appeared. Fredrik and his assistant were so perplexed and awed, they asked for blessings and left. As Fredrik said, how can you ask god about god?

In His Own Words

Now to his own words:

> I think it is something with the way I do fieldwork that . . . I have . . . this is really impossible to say about oneself . . . I think I have practiced humility in the field in a more basic way than most anthropologists. If I meet a big man in the field, then he is not primarily my informant, but especially interesting fellow being. And though he possesses a lot of knowledge that I seek and ask to get a part of, I am not primarily interested in tapping him, in an interrogating relationship, but I am very interested in his vision of the world.
>
> But of utmost importance: I don't sort people in the field in terms of how "big" they are, how much they know—for I am very taken by [*betatt av*] ordinary people that I come close to too. So to go back in time: Kashmali was the most important person in Swat for me. He was not any "big man." He was neither a chief nor a saint, he was not even especially gifted. And his vision was not something that was so dazzling, but he was a human being who stood in a sincere relationship to me, and where I could develop a degree of intimacy and richness of relationship which meant that he gave me enormously much insight in himself and his life, and thereby in some parts of his society—and it is that which gives the deepest basis for an anthropological understanding. So besides the fact that I developed a great kindness for him and for many others, it means that it is not the experts that have the most precious material for an anthropologist; it is the relations you can establish that have the human nearness and richness that give the most secure [*tryggeste*] and most valuable basis for anthropology. Whoever those people happen to be.

Interpretation, Not Explanation

In the last public interview he gave, Fredrik was asked, "Why did you yourself choose social anthropology?" He answered:

> First and foremost because I believe that the condition of the human being is influenced to a large extent by the cultural. I am fascinated by how different everything can be. I have wanted to know what it tastes like to live like others. Curiosity drove me. I wanted to formulate and understand why it is like that, but not to explain.

"Not explain, what do you mean?" The interviewer, herself an experienced anthropologist, looked incredulously at him. "Doesn't that go against the very nature of social anthropology and what you yourself have tried to achieve? You have been known as someone who wants precisely to explain how different cultures have come into being." Fredrik answered:

> To a large extent there is no explanation of why the human variation is like it is, I think. The diversity is too great. I am more interested in how people live than to explain why it has become like this or that. It becomes too simple, too impoverished, when one tries to explain. (Fatland 2015: 27)

In an earlier interview in 1989, he was asked, "In your work, where does your loyalty lie?" He answered:

> That's a hard question to answer. I might say in the discipline itself, but then I think of colleagues, and do not feel it can be with them—I disagree with their priorities too often. My loyalty is probably grounded on a basic belief in knowledge and understanding, that this is important. On the other hand, something I would wish always to hold on to is humility in relation to the understanding and insights of other people. We live in a world where so much is being lost and destroyed—not because it is valueless, but because it is powerless, lacking political power, economic power, military power. As a result, the fruits of outstanding human effort and thought through millennia are lost. An anthropologist can help to slow down this destruction to a certain extent, strengthen what is being threatened and make the world conscious of things that have value, in all forms of culture and life. I see this as a colossal task. (Korbøl 1985: 34)

Acknowledgments

I deeply appreciate the inestimable efforts of Keping Wu and Robert Weller to arrange this collection and let me be a part of it. I shall always remain immensely grateful to them for this and for all the work they have expended on making this book materialize. Without them, nothing would have been.

I am also very grateful to all who contributed to this book.

I also want to extend heartfelt thanks to Sun Yat Sen University and Boston University for their generous support.

Unni Wikan is Professor Emerita in the Department of Social Anthropology at the University of Oslo, Norway. She has done fieldwork in Egypt, Oman, Bali, Bhutan, and Scandinavia on various themes and issues. She is the author of ten books; the most recent is *Resonance: Beyond the Words* (University of Chicago Press, 2012). Her forthcoming book is *Arabian Grace: Pursuit of the Good Life in Oman through Five Decades.*

Notes

1. The memoirs to which I shall be referring are a manuscript in Norwegian originally based on interviews done by the anthropologist Edvard Hviding with Barth in 1996–97. For various reasons, the planned book did not materialize. Barth then used the transcripts as a basis to write his own memoir, while keeping the dialogic form. All translations from the Norwegian text are mine and less fluent than his would have been; he was entirely bilingual and would surely have rewritten the text for publication in English.
2. Seven essays on Kurdistan and Pakistan were published in *VG*, Norway's leading liberal newspaper at the time. They were accompanied by his inimitable drawings, some in cartoon-like style. He was at heart an artist and always liked to draw.
3. This is also brought out in Michael Herzfeld's memorial article on Barth, which begins with these words: "It was always hard to take offense at Fredrik Barth's teasing, which was deeply grounded in his anthropological convictions; he was a living reminder that anthropology without a sense of humor is not likely to be very good anthropology"; see Herzfeld 2016: 95.
4. Ulf Hannerz in his contribution to this book also speaks appraisingly of *Vi mennesker*.
5. The work concerned hydropower development on the Yalong river, a tributary to the Yangtse, in southwestern China, entailing the resettlement of 50,000 people. He writes of the experience from an anthropological angle in *Vi mennesker* (2005: 61–80).
6. The reason for the thesis being turned down was this: the committee of three distinguished professors set up to evaluate it did not really know what to do. The field of anthropology was still non-existent in Norway. So they asked the opinion of Professor Evans-Pritchard at Oxford University. He replied that at Oxford, two years of fieldwork were required for a doctorate. That decided the matter. But to make up for the rejection, the candidate was offered a scholarship that enabled him to pursue studies in England.
7. Interview with Edvard Hviding, quoted in Barth's memoirs.
8. Barth had written the book based on the fieldwork materials of Robert Pehrson, who had died in the field, supplemented by a short fieldwork of his own.
9. I never did gain a formal permit, but after months of turning up weekly in the Ministry of Interior—a formidable building in Tahrir Square—the authorities must have realized that I would be hard to get rid of. Perhaps they also appreciated my sincere desire to study the poor. So they offered me a scholarship, for which I had not applied and that had actually been granted to another student. I turned it down. But it was a tacit permit. I went my way, and they looked the other.
10. This is not the full story. At one point I was truly about to give up. I had given up. I walked with heavy steps to Professor Laila Shukry el Hamamsy, an eminent anthropologist and Director of the Social Research Center at the American University in Cairo. She had supported me, and she knew Fredrik. Now I had to tell her it was all over: I was a failure. I could not endure fieldwork in the Cairo slums.

    She took one look at me (I was thin as a telephone pole) and lectured me—on my teachers! I remember that she did not mention any name, but it was not necessary. Those teachers, how *could* they imagine that *anyone* could do what I had done! Just recently a student, himself an Egyptian of lower middle class, had given up on fieldwork in the slums. What I had done was impressive, but my *teachers* should know better than . . . !

    Three years later I had the satisfaction of bringing Fredrik with me to my turf: an urban slum that was not situated in the picturesque old Cairo and had nothing to show for it but the people. Fredrik was enchanted by them and abhorred by the conditions. He said he could never have done fieldwork there, and I think this is true. He could bear any discomfort without complaint, but he was a nature man, and there was not much nature in *my place*—nothing to lift the mind. We both agreed that it was my luck in life that I had ended up just there, by his encouragement; he visited me several times and loved the people. But without Professor Laila Shukry El-Hamamsy, would I have endured? She certainly said the right things at the right moment in time: go get yourself your own lodgings so you can at least have a bed of your own! I did. She paid for it through a stipend. She and Fredrik were good friends and deeply respectful of one another. But her perspective on "my teachers" taught me a lesson: there is no ideal of fieldwork that you need to follow: be pragmatic and do as best you can.

11. Citation from Barth's memoirs.
12. Ibid.
13. My first book on the poor in Cairo was published in Norwegian in 1976, and later translated into English and Japanese. I wrote two more in Norwegian (the last in 2004) and one in English (1995). An Arabic translation of *Tomorrow, God Willing: Self-Made Destinies in Cairo* (University of Chicago Press, 1995) was published in Cairo in 2013. I continued fieldwork there until 2014 and wrote several op-ed articles on political developments, earning me much criticism from Middle East specialists as my analysis indicated that the Arab Spring would make matters worse in Egypt. It did, and not just there.
14. Unlike Fredrik, I had the good sense to get my Oman book republished in paperback, which secured it a long life. His Oman book, unfortunately, went quickly out of print after a small run of just 1,500 copies. I wish I had taken it on myself to try to have it reissued. It was not a task he was fit for, or perhaps even cared much about.
15. That Fredrik´s book on Sohar should be almost completely overlooked by scholars with a particular interest in ethnicity, and in *his work*, has always puzzled me. It continues to do so even more as the fiftieth anniversary of the publication of *Ethnic Groups and Boundaries* was marked in various ways this year, with Fredrik´s introduction to the book gaining ample praise, but with hardly a mention of how he himself questioned his own analysis and developed it further through his work in Sohar. Richard Jenkins is one of few anthropologists who has seen and appreciated that. I think it all shows how politicized scholarly work on ethnicity has become. Fredrik was aware of this politicization, mentioning it explicitly in papers and interviews, and took little interest in the field over the last twenty to twenty-five years of his life. He remained surprised that the book (and his own introduction in particular) should have become such a "hit." It pleased him, but I am not sure that it meant very much. He was on to other things, as always.
16. Interview by Hviding, quoted in Barth's memoirs.
17. Ibid.
18. Ibid.
19. Ibid.
20. Ibid.
21. Interview with Hviding, cited in Barth's memoirs.
22. I published an article in the *American Anthropologist* in 1996 that made me unwelcome in Bhutan for some years. I think this experience alerted Fredrik as well to the sensitivity of publishing about the country. The situation was wholly resolved in 2000 when we both went back and were very gracefully received. But it was a reminder of the difficulty and the ethical dilemmas of anthropological publishing. I think it may have affected Fredrik as well. An article of his, written as a paper for a talk at Yale University in 1995 and labeled "Not for Citation," was fortunately discovered by a Bhutanese anthropologist and recently published, with my permission, in Bhutan. But it is perhaps telling that he had kept it. I am hoping to find other such pieces with time.
23. A taped interview with Fredrik on the Ura Festival—from which the cover photo of this book is taken—was conducted by Dasho Karma Ura in 1993 for the Center of Bhutanese Studies. The photo was probably also taken by him.
24. He supported me wholeheartedly in my own engagement as a public anthropologist, and I would not have endured it without him. However much it wore on us, he remained steadfast. The only thing I ever wrote that I did not share with him was an article for an

edited book by Didier Fassin: *If Truth Be Told* (2016). I did not want to remind Fredrik of the hard times. But the story is a testimony to his generosity of spirit and his belief in independent thinking; anthropology *mattered*, and he was proud to see that I could make it matter.

References

Barth, Fredrik. 1952. "Subsistence and Institutional System in a Norwegian Mountain Valley." *Rural Sociology* 17(1): 28–38.

———. 1953. *Principles of Social Organization in Southern Kurdistan*. Universitetets Etnografiske Museum, Bulletin 7. Oslo: Universitetets Etnografiske Museum.

———. 1955. "The Social Organization of a Pariah Group in Norway." *Norveg* 5: 125–144

———. 1959. *Political Leadership among Swat Pathans*. Monographs on Social Anthropology, 19. London: Athlone Press.

———. 1961. *Nomads of South Persia: The Basseri Tribe of the Khamseh Confederacy*. Universitetets Etnografiske Museum, Bulletin 8. Oslo: Universitetets Etnografiske Museum.

———. 1963. Introduction to *The Role of the Entrepreneur in Social Change in Northern Norway*, edited by Fredrik Barth, 5–18. Årbok for Universitetet i Bergen, Humanistisk serie. Bergen: Universitetsforlaget.

———. 1966. Preface to *The Social Organization of the Marri Baluch*, by Robert N. Pehrson, vii–xii. Compiled and analyzed from his notes by Fredrik Barth. Viking Fund Publications in Anthropology, 43. London: Athlone Press.

———. 1969. Introduction to *Ethnic Groups and Boundaries: The Social Organization of Culture Difference*, edited by Fredrik Barth, 9–38. Bergen/Boston: Universitetsforlaget/Little, Brown & Co.

———. 1975. *Ritual and Knowledge among the Baktaman of New Guinea*. Oslo: Universitetsforlaget.

———. 1980. *Andres liv—og vårt eget*. Oslo: Gyldendal.

———. 1983. *Sohar: Culture and Society in an Omani Town*. Baltimore: Johns Hopkins University Press.

———. 1985. With Miangul Jahanzeb. *The Last Wali of Swat: An Autobiography as Told to Fredrik Barth*. Oslo: Universitetsforlaget..

———. 1987. *Cosmologies in the Making: A Generative Approach to Cultural Variation in Inner New Guinea*. Cambridge: Cambridge University Press.

———. 1993. *Balinese Worlds*. Chicago: University of Chicago Press.

———. 2005. *Vi mennesker: Fra en antropologs reiser*. Oslo: Gyldendal.

———. 2008. *Afghanistan og Taliban*. Oslo: Pax.

———. 2018. "Power and Compliance in Bhutanese Rural Society." *Journal of Bhutan Studies* 38: 46–64

———. Forthcoming. *Det skjer mellom mennesker. Memoarer*. Ferdigstilt av Unni Wikan. [*It Happens Between People: A Memoir*. Completed by Unni Wikan].

Barth, Fredrik, and Unni Wikan. 2011. *The Situation of Children in Bhutan: An Anthropological Perspective*. Thimphu: Centre for Bhutan Studies.

Eriksen, Thomas Hylland. 2015. *Fredrik Barth: An Intellectual Biography*. London: Pluto Press.

Fatland, Erika. 2015. "Den gamle mannen og verden: Intervju med Fredrik Barth." *Morgenbladet* 41 (16–22 October): 24–29.

Haaland, Gunnar. 1969. "Economic Determinants in Ethnic Processes." In *Ethnic Groups and Boundaries: The Social Organization of Culture Difference*, edited by Fredrik Barth, 58–73. Boston: Little, Brown.

Herzfeld, Michael. 2016. "Barth's Boundaries: Anthropology in the World." *Norsk antropologisk tidsskrift* 27(2): 94–107.

Jenkins, Richard. 2016. "Fredrik Barth: An Ethnographer's Ethnographer and a Theorist's Theorist." *Nations and Nationalism* 22(3): 411–14.

Korbøl, Aud. 1989. "Barth to Bhutan: Other Worlds, Other Forms of Fellowship." *Norwegian Literature* 2: 34–39.

Pehrson, Robert N. 1966. *The Social Organization of the Marri Baluch*. Compiled and analyzed from his notes by Fredrik Barth. Viking Fund Publications in Anthropology, 43. London: Athlone Press.

Wikan, Unni. 1980. *Life among the Poor in Cairo*. Translated by Ann Henning. London and New York: Tavistock/Methuen.

———. 1982. *Behind the Veil in Arabia: Women in Oman*. Baltimore: Johns Hopkins University Press.

———. 1990. *Managing Turbulent Hearts: A Balinese Formula for Living*. Chicago: University of Chicago Press.

———. 1996. "The Nun´s Story: Reflections on an Age-Old, Postmodern Dilemma." *American Anthropologist* 98(2): 279–289.

———. 2016. "Perils and Prospects of Going Public: Between Academia and Real Life." In *If Truth Be Told: The Politics of Public Ethnography*, edited by Didier Fassin, 228–260. Durham: Duke University Press.

2

Transacting Knowledge and Value
Fredrik Barth and the Tactics of
Mutual Incomprehension

Michael Herzfeld

Imagine two places: one, a Cretan mountain village, known for the swash-buckling antics of its doughty shepherds, and located far from the classical and pre-classical ruins that have for long been mainstays of both the tourism industry and national cultural ideology; the other a small urban community in Thailand desperately fighting for its survival as the authorities close in on it and attempt to expel the last remaining residents from what they have deemed to be a "historic site."[1] These are both communities that, in an apparent paradox, have been raucously proud of their respective national identities and yet, at the same time, are deeply at odds with their respective countries' official author-ities. In both cases, each side professes not to understand the other's motives and to dismiss the other's claims as unfathomably immoral—as betrayals of the true national character that each local community claims to represent. In other words, in both cases, each side professes total incomprehension of the other, but they do so in more or less identical and highly nationalistic terms.

The tactics of incomprehension are elements in a war that is ongoing be-tween European-inspired models of the nation-state and the claims of local communities to moral autonomy. Admittedly these two cases are fairly ex-treme, but they illustrate an important point that was implicit but strongly represented in the work of Fredrik Barth: if we wish to understand what is distinctive about regional culture at any level, we should attend to its repre-sentation by the local communities rather than the conflationary and ideolog-ical portrait drawn in more or less identical format, ironically in the name of national uniqueness, by national governments. It is the local resistances that exhibit cultural difference in the face of the revealingly paradoxical cookie-cutter style of official talk about national uniqueness. The local communities may claim not to understand, and certainly do not always heed, the claims of their respective states; but they do so in locally distinctive ways, whereas state authorities everywhere appeal to a more or less similar state model.

Let me illustrate with a simple example. In the Cretan village Zoniana,[2] road signs pointing both toward the village center and toward other villages in the area are so riddled with bullet holes that they have become a staple item of cartoons about local violence in the media. Inside the village there is virtually no public signage. One old shopfront sign announces the presence of a dance troupe that has in fact given up performing, while another indicates a historical museum that its creator, a non-local person who married into the community, rather forlornly hopes will appeal to passing tourists and other outsiders. Here, a semiotics of silence resists communication with the state.

In the second place, the tiny Bangkok community of Pom Mahakan (Herzfeld 2016), we find the opposite situation. Profuse signage in both Thai and English parody official forms. In front of what is technically the inside of the circumvallation of the capital established by Rama I in 1782 when he declared Bangkok the new capital of Siam, as Thailand was then called, the authorities have erected a sign of the kind they use for heritage sites, describing the history of the fortress (*pom*), mentioning the royal construction of the wall, but without even indirectly alluding to the past or present existence of a community of living souls. Inside the community, however, there are numerous signs describing individual houses as sites of various kinds of activity—fish maw soup production, gold smelting, water purification, laundry—some of which no longer occurs in the community but is part of its collective memory. In addition, a small and stereotypically "Thai" house contains a collection of documentation concerning the community's past existence and present struggle; it is fronted by an official-looking sign in elegant gold-on-red lettering, announcing that it is the "pavilion of the community's local knowledge"—an ambiguous nod to official rhetoric but suggesting an alternative vision of history. All this signage, in fact, is potentially, but not too directly (given the Thai aversion to direct confrontation of any sort), parodic. It was long an effective weapon in the struggle against the official policy of demolition but has now been demolished along with the houses and shrines of the living population. One of the most ironic scenes I can recall is watching teams of wreckers removing the remains of houses they had demolished, while one of the community's signs points toward the "heritage museum" and photographic display about the community. Here, the resistance to authority is a form of apparent engagement that is so parodic that the authorities cannot really accuse the residents of insubordination; after all, they are politely offering the highest form of flattery, imitation of the state's own way of representing culture.[3]

In drawing up this contrast, I am suggesting that there is a radical difference between two communities both of which, for very different reasons, find themselves in opposition to the authority of the state. Zoniana, the Cretan village, is notorious for its endemic animal theft (Herzfeld 1985) and became a household word in quite the wrong way when, in 2007, some of its inhabitants engaged in a violent confrontation with an armed police patrol and killed one of the police officers. Pom Mahakan, officially now deemed to be a community of squatters, is arguing back against the official historiography of the Thai state on the grounds that they, too, are part of the national polity.

These two scenarios represent two very different understandings of how knowledge is to be handled. As Fredrik Barth (1990) would have expected, the difference is not purely local but arguably distinguishes whole regions—Mediterranean Europe and mainland Southeast Asia—from each other. The people of Zoniana are necessarily secretive about immediate acts of an illegal nature, although openly proud of their long history of defiance.[4] They are adroit performers of their secretiveness; all secrecy is contingent on someone knowing that one *has* a secret, and these villagers are experts at conveying that message while daring anyone to ask any further questions.

To these two sites I wish to add two more, one again from Crete and the other from the old section of Bangkok. The Cretan site is a coastal town, Rethemnos, where I studied artisans and their apprentices (Herzfeld 2004) and where both a shared sense of cultural identity and a town-village opposition hold sway concurrently in the popular imagination. And in Thailand, having briefly now considered the implications of the signage posted inside and outside Pom Mahakan, I will also turn to a nearby second community, one of artisanal goldsmiths and jewelers called Ban Maw,[5] where what I had already learned in Pom Mahakan has helped me to decipher a pattern of mutual solidarity and suspicion that contrasts dramatically with what I have reported from Crete. Neither Rethemnos nor Ban Maw is at war with official authority in the way that Zoniana and Pom Mahakan have been. Rather, we can say that Zoniana and Pom Mahakan, as extreme cases, help us to discern patterns that characterize a larger cultural region. I specifically write of regions rather than of nation-states in order to avoid the "methodological nationalism" in the same way that Barth's (1969) treatment of ethnicity transcends the rigidity of "nationality" as a concept.[6]

At issue here is the extent to which, and the reasons for which, we sense that research in adjacent sites gives us a deepened understanding of each, whereas research in very different cultural contexts serves more to bring out contrastively what might be the dominant features of each. The risk for the anthropologist is that of reproducing the local residents' self-stereotypes. But as is true for stereotypes generally, the self-stereotypes they express do contain elements of ideal-typical models that motivate, albeit neither completely nor always with clarity, the ways in which they act toward one another and toward outsiders. People perform idealized selfhood for strategic and tactical ends.

The result of such comparisons is something akin to the emergence of a sense of local or regional culture identity—what anthropologists have often re-scripted as "culture areas." The culture area concept is fraught with difficulty and, especially in the Mediterranean, requires acknowledgment of the role of anthropology itself, as well as of local official and unofficial social forces, in more or less consciously creating some of the apparent homogeneity (see Ben-Yehoyada 2014; Herzfeld 2014). But when local actors or the politicians who directly affect their lives acknowledge and even generate cultural features that emphasize their collective similarity, we must acknowledge that these stereotypes index and reproduce, however imperfectly, some sense of shared social experience. I phrase this in deliberately inchoate terms because we are talking about a necessarily inchoate phenomenon.

In his classic work on ethnic identity formation, Fredrik Barth (1969) demonstrated the processual and transactional nature of the boundaries that delineate ethnic allegiances, showing that these are neither as fixed as nation-states would like them to be nor as imaginary as some scholars had previously assumed. He thereby focuses our attention on the creative aspect of cultural identity and on the conceptual labor involved in generating and maintaining the associated collective self-recognition. What he said about ethnic groups would seem, *a fortiori*, to be valid for the culture areas recognized—created?—by anthropologists.

Barth was not the first, of course, to note that Southeast Asia displayed some common characteristics. Heine-Geldern's (1942) reconstruction of its historical development gave a chronologically deep basis to Tambiah's (1976) elaboration of the spread and evolution of the mandala model of the polity. Others (notably Day 2002) have noted a measure of coexistence between political impulses, egalitarian and authoritarian respectively, that would be inconceivable in many self-styled Western democracies. But Barth's argument, I suggest, pushes the idea of cultural commonality further, along the lines of what we would expect the author-editor of *Ethnic Groups and Boundaries* to do when reflecting the insights of that seminal book back onto the process whereby that relatively inchoate phenomenon of cultural commonality emerges. The "cultural stuff" is gradually recognized and to some extent mutually assimilated over a long period of time; the consciousness of commonality, by contrast, represents a late development that only transnational awareness has made possible. It was the emergence of modern nation-states that gave form to this particular sense of common cultural heritage. But the much-needed critique of methodological nationalism does not require us to fall into the opposite trap of denying the nation-state any role in the formation of cultural consciousness; it simply warns us not to let the concept of the nation-state determine our perception of where cultural commonalities lie or lead us to impose boundary-like divisions on what in reality is always a fluid and unpredictable process. Regional patterns do not spring from the bureaucratic obsessions of national authorities and often do not resemble the artificial arrangements that those authorities call "national culture."

In one of his most daring papers, Barth (1990) demanded that anthropologists raise their heads above the level of local ethnography and contemplate the significance of such regional commonalities. To achieve this goal, he elevated two contrasted models of knowledge possession, exemplified by social personae, to the status of ideal types for their respective culture areas: the didactic guru for Southeast Asia, the secretive conjurer for Melanesia. Arguing that anthropologists should escape the narrow confines of specific field sites in order to paint comparison with a broader brush, he argued that even if we disagreed with the kind of diffusionist historicism that would trace civilizational features to origins at particular regional centers, we should not ignore the effect of cultural contact in generating distinctive (and distinct) cultural zones around those centers. In short, he invokes a kind of "big history," as we would call it today, to remind us that the sense of regional identity is never purely the product of anthropologists' imagination—even if the boundaries they place around it can be arbitrary and artificial.

It was certainly not anthropologists who generated the phrase *una faccia, una razza* (one face, one race), which we instead apparently owe to Mussolini—a phrase that many Greeks have enthusiastically embraced as *mia fatsa, mia ratsa*, even as most Italians would rather forget the phrase, together with its embarrassingly racist pedigree. Political forces, reinforced by trade and warfare, have long shaped the consciousness of commonality to which the phrase was supposed to lend genetic authority. We may productively read Barth's essay in counterpoint to some of Julian Pitt-Rivers's work,[7] including those papers in which the latter scholar argued passionately for the recognition of a distinctive Mediterranean culture area, with its commonalities anchored by a shared cosmology with shared consequences for social relations. While I have always approached the concept of culture areas with a good deal of skepticism, the "weak version" thus proposed by both authors does provide us with at least a provisional basis for critical comparison. "Big history," over a *longue durée*, had already done much of the work of reification long before anthropologists came on the scene.

My goal is thus to complicate Barth's conclusions to the point where, while the original heuristic of the culture area concept will have led us to a useful comparison much as he proposes, it can then be strengthened against the all-too-easy danger that it will end up reducing culture areas to nation-like entities. I want to sketch a way of probing the origins of such regional patterns in cosmology as much as in location—this being an approach that I believe remains faithful to the respective visions of both Barth and Pitt-Rivers[8] but owes more to the former in addressing very specifically, and in a comparative frame, the significance of esoteric knowledge for the social relations of those who possess it.

Such comparisons are urgent because both areas are now undergoing transformations that obscure, though do not destroy, the underlying political and cosmological orders. At the risk of oversimplification, let me say what those orders are. In Southeast Asia, the prevailing understanding of the ideal-typical polity produced cities planned according to the cosmological model of the mandala. From Borobodur in Indonesia to Ayutthaya in Thailand, the same pattern prevails, mapping onto a symbolically royal and central territory a celestially ordained order of things, people, and powers. It is accompanied by an ongoing tension between hierarchical models of authority and legitimacy on the one hand and strongly egalitarian impulses on the other; it is that tension that generates the unstable ebb and flow of the central, royal power over the concentric spaces and identities of the mandala. It is a tension, moreover, that is as widely distributed in Southeast Asia as the mandala city plan (see Day 2002; Harms 2011; Herzfeld 2016).

In Mediterranean Europe, by contrast, cities, like churches and other religious buildings, were generally oriented toward the holy places, especially Jerusalem. Their logic often also centered around a royal power, and there were sharp differences between the forms of European and North African cities. From the Middle Ages on, Europe saw an emergent pattern of secular governance and military control that culminated in Baron Haussmann's redesign of Paris.

From the mid-nineteenth century on, moreover, that European model began to exercise ever stronger influence on the development of Southeast Asia cities. Most notably, perhaps, the deliberate imitation of Haussmann's Paris that we find in the reign of Rama V of Siam, otherwise known as Chulalongkorn, has led to a growing militarization of the city plan as a technique of urban control; and this example, with significant variation, has been imitated throughout the region. We are thus now in the later stages of a process whereby the physical manifestation of an older polity has been progressively overlain by the structures associated with the Western colonial powers; the people of Pom Mahakan may represent the dernier cri of the old *moeang*, or mandala-based polity, that was in fact the basis of Siamese royal power until it was systematically dismembered by Rama V as part of his program of national modernization—a change that is physically quite visible in the disjuncture between the road he had built in imitation of the Champs-Elysées in Paris and the original city wall at Pom Mahakan (see Herzfeld 2016; see also Rabinow 1989 on North Africa). While local protest has sometimes evoked the older model of the polity, as in the community of Pom Mahakan itself, it has become increasingly difficult to discern its traces in the everyday lives of most urban dwellers of the huge Thai capital city. It has become a distant echo of a lost past—evanescent, elusive, intangible, and deniable.

As with cities, so with another arena that is largely determined by cosmological conventions: the organization of esoteric (and sometimes not-so-esoteric) knowledge in the arena of craft production. I have expatiated on city form not only because it makes both the synchronic contrast and the diachronic of one system by the other rather explicit, but also because polities—whether urban in form or not—are the contexts in which craft production takes place. Following Barth's model, we might therefore expect that craft production in a southern European town would follow the pedagogical model of the old Ottoman guild (*esnaf*) with inflections derived from the Orthodox Christian tradition, perhaps enjoining brotherly love, or alternatively that it would entail upholding the honor of the family or clan and a high degree of open jealousy between artisans and their apprentices. We would also expect Thai craftspeople to teach their apprentices with the careful instruction associated with the religious teacher (*khru*, from Sanskrit *guru*; or *ajan*, from Sanskrit *acharya*)—that the Thai master craftsman would display the didactic propensities that one expects of a true guru, as Barth indeed demonstrated for the Balinese, and that the apprentices would reciprocally display the respect and loyalty that a guru expects as his due. The Greek artisan is a "master" (*mastoras*) and is so addressed, his authority recognized by customers and employees and apprentices alike; the Thai artisan is a *chang*, one who works with his hands and can demonstrate technical mastery, and for him "chang" can also be a respectful term of address to be coupled with his name: Chang Tao and so forth.

In reality, the Cretan small-town artisans with whom I worked (Herzfeld 2004) displayed more aggression than brotherly love to their apprentices, who, forced to "steal [the craft secrets] with their eyes" by their monumentally secretive masters, developed social craftiness more rapidly than knowledge of their artisanal crafts. Stealing secrets, after all, is not a long way from stealing sheep; and it aims at a similar resolution, in which only those who are sufficiently tough and rough will be acceptable as allies and friends. The Zoniana shepherds "steal to make friends"; the Rethemnos artisans' apprentices demonstrate their social mastery by stealing secrets from masters who become interested in co-opting them as business partners (in part to prevent them from becoming direct rivals). The Thai artisans do not have such a rural model before them, although many of them are of rural origin, hailing from the impoverished villages of the northeastern part of the country. Their interactions are instead verbal, respectful, and, for the most part, calm.

This comparison has something in common with the one that Barth conducted in his "guru and conjurer" article. Crete does in fact sometimes seem a bit Melanesian, in a way that would probably have amused Fredrik Barth: big men swagger about, they boastfully promote the interests of their respective patrilineal clans, and they engage in sometimes dangerous forms of violence, with blood feuds running through several generations. Even in the bigger towns, those features frequently surface in moments of tension, although usually with some degree of muting. Although the town of Rethemnos was famous for its gentility (Prevelakis 1972), for example, aggression among working-class people of recently rural origin was always palpable and stood out against the behavior of the elite minority. It is the working people of Rethemnos who continue to fly the banner of aggressive Cretan masculinity, while the educated elite delicately averts its collective nose.

Consistent with their self-image, these tough men in their stereotypically Mediterranean town also practice agonistic secrecy. While they may be sedentary workers rather than agile goat thieves, they continue to speak and act in the self-stereotype of the aggressive Cretan male (see Damer 1988), and this means displaying a kind of verbal continence that is certainly also considered by the shepherds in the mountains to be a paramount, and indeed necessary, virtue.

The goldsmiths in Ban Maw similarly seem to conform in certain ways to the expected model—expected, that is, of a Buddhist society in Southeast Asia—of the working artisan. Unlike their Cretan counterparts, they make few major distinctions between artisans on the basis of gender, although men may criticize women's craftwork as less well-sustained than their own. One aspect in particular sets them off from their Cretan colleagues and from artisans in many parts of the world: they teach by explaining carefully and patiently to neophytes all the fundamental secrets of the craft. Moreover, they treat those neophytes with friendly gentleness, albeit with a watchful eye lest these young people be too easily tempted by the precious metals and stones to be found lying all over every workshop (not to speak of all the gold and silver dust in the carpets and clothes).

On Crete, male performativity is easy to establish. For one thing, a large part of it is extremely noisy. Cretan men are generally given to highly visible demonstrations of their masculinity, twirling their whiskers and uttering dire threats as well as hearty welcomes according to the company that forms at any given moment. There is nothing secretive about that behavior; quite to the contrary, it is easily addressed through theories of performance (Bauman 1977), social poetics (Herzfeld 1985), and so on, precisely because it is so demonstratively a way of drawing attention to the social actors themselves. Even when they affect an air of slightly suspect modesty, the gestural equivalent of a "disclaimer" (Bauman 1977: 21–22), they know very well that such poses will be taken as ironic inversions of what they are really trying to say—namely, that in reality they are the greatest of the great. These are public displays of what J. K. Campbell (1964) rightly called "self-regard." Silence about their excellent qualities would do them no good at all. And sedentary artisans, who may worry that their masculinity does not compare so impressively with that of the goat thieves, are likely to be especially noisy in proclaiming their masculinity.

Noisy, yes—but also capable of silence: I have already mentioned the importance of verbal continence (which in Crete is understood to be analogous to sexual continence, once also viewed as a male virtue). In particular, and demonstrating the hierarchical nature of the relationship, they are secretive toward their apprentices; masters and apprentices are expected to adopt stances of mutual incomprehension, even though, if they are skilled, they understand each other very well indeed. By so acting, they test their apprentices' mettle. More than that, they show that they can manage their knowledge as well as they are able to manage the two other arenas in which they are expected to practice continence: the sexuality of their women, and the content of their spoken words. For all their boasting, they do measure their speech; those who talk too much come in for consistent ridicule, and every adult male walks a fine line between demonstrating his virility verbally and revealing instead a stereotypically "female" proclivity to talk *too much*—that is, to betray his own or his family's secrets. In their very reserve, they are also announcing something important about themselves: they know how to exercise self-control—because, moreover, they have something worth protecting from others. Just as I was instructed to display secrecy in showing that I was trying not to be seen recording laments at a village funeral (Herzfeld 2009: 147), these artisans try to look as though they are doing what in fact they are doing (but also to look as though they are not doing it!). In dealing with their apprentices, they therefore either bark gruff orders or say nothing at all, so that their speech, if it is heard outside the workshop, will be interpreted as a stylized assertion of authority, not as something that actually might have revealing content. People understand that such behavior means they actually do possess more or less esoteric knowledge but that they want passersby to understand that they are not going to teach their apprentices any of it.

As I noted in the original study, men assiduously avoid hiring patrilineal kin as their apprentices. They claim that to do so risks exposing the entire clan to ridicule at any point at which they are seen or heard to be abusing their young charges, verbally or physically; such abuse, if it occurs between agnatic kin, *must* be kept secret if ridicule is to be successfully avoided. Most of the time, the issue does not arise because, most of the time, agnatic kin simply do not get hired. The risk of ridicule is too great.

In practice, this means that the apprentices who do get taken on belong to potentially rival clans; they are not the kinds of people with whom one should share family secrets. They are called *parayi*, meaning "foster sons"—a term that suggests that they are like fake kin, potentially treacherous youngsters who ought to be grateful for being taken on at all but who might very well turn against the hand that feeds them. While the formal term *mathitevomeni* implies people who are in receipt of true instruction, it is rarely heard except in the speech of well-educated elite townspeople explaining the current situation to an equally well-educated visitor. The term *parayi* merely suggests a not-quite-real kinship connection, with implications of obligation but also of the fear that the specific obligation of loyalty will at some point be ruptured.

I would argue, however, that the artisans do in fact instruct these boys. They do so, however, not through verbal pedagogy, but by the example of the rough treatment they mete out to them—for what they are teaching the lads is not the craft itself, but survival in a tough, agonistic society, in which the ability to keep a secret—especially while stealing those of others—is a highly prized quality, and one that is especially appreciated in a potential future business partner. So there *is* a form of instruction here; it is not verbal and is therefore not easily identified *as* instruction. Cretan artisans are quick to point out that craft is not something that a school or university can teach; and in this, in fact, they are in agreement with their Thai colleagues in Ban Maw.

Because the apprentices are usually not agnatic kin, they can safely be allowed to work in socially visible spaces; there is no risk that a sudden altercation will attract the mockery of unrelated passersby. Indeed, this is an arena in which the artisan displays his masculine control over the entire workshop; his curses and kicks reinforce the image of the strong man. In that sense, the more visible the setting, the better: the master's capacity to act secretively is highly visible to the public eye. If he does speak to an apprentice, it will usually be in a few rough barks. Most of the time, he is very *demonstratively non-teaching*, as it were. His secrecy has value precisely because it is constituted by a consistent series of public acts. Secrecy has little value unless it is recognized in a public space (Herzfeld 2009; Simmel 1964).

But even if the concern with secrecy and the contempt for formal institutions of learning are common ground, the situation of the Ban Maw goldsmiths in Bangkok is significantly different in an important respect—namely, the social organization of secrecy and knowledge. Most of these Thai artisans operate in closed spaces, some of them sections of six-story buildings shielded from thieves by elaborate and impenetrable sliding grilles and from curious eyes by their sheer height. Some do work before an open door, especially in the oppressive heat of the day, but little interaction is visible from outside so that the social relations among the workers is not something a passerby would easily be able to assess.

When I first visited the district, I had the impression that the upper stories were teeming with eager youngsters, all bent on the pleasures and pains of practicing a craft that for some would represent a lucrative improvement on their lives of their provincial peasant parents. Imagine my astonishment, then, when I came back to Bangkok early in 2017, prepared to begin research on apprenticeship in these workshops, and found, in effect, that there seemed to be no apprentices anywhere! First of all, none of the people working seemed particularly young. In the end I found one young man who might have been seventeen, another of eighteen, but most were well into their twenties or older. Then, when I asked why there seemed to be so few apprentices, I was told that "there were no pupils [*luksit*]!" Here and there, to be sure, I espied someone who seemed young and junior enough to be at the receiving end of instruction—but that also surprised me: these young men were being quietly guided in their work by the experienced artisans, some of whom were clearly the owners or chief goldsmiths of their respective workshops. I had expected something analogous to the "stealing with the eyes" model I had encountered in Crete; there are ample examples of the same attitude in East Asia (e.g., Singleton 1992). So why not here?

These are not "foster sons." They are "child-artisans"—*luk chang*—and, as such, treated as real offspring. Nor are they "apprentices" (*luksit*), because, in the Thai context, apprentices are people who learn a craft but are paid while doing so. Since the owner of each workshop actually profits from the often very repetitive, simple, and boring labor of young would-be artisans while emphasizing their role as kin, appearing to exploit the relationship or to be claiming the moral authority of a teacher would risk a loss of face (*sia na*). This is a consequence of the goldsmiths' tendency to treat anyone they can trust enough to work in their workshops as real kin. It seems to be why I was told that there were no apprentices in the workshops: the owners would not classify as "pupils" young people who were by preference being treated as close "kin." Indeed, goldsmiths would airily claim that everyone in a given workshop was *yat-kan*, related to each other. When I asked *how* they were related, the answers were either a slightly embarrassed avoidance of the question itself or a rueful admission that, yes, well, some of them weren't actually kin (*yat*), but the sons of friends or the sons of someone who was more literally a kinsperson (often via the workshop head's wife—affinal relations count as *yat* in this setting).

Given, then, that there is a categorical assumption that those who work in one's atelier are by definition one's relatives, so that the work situation determines the attribution of kin status rather than the other way around, any attempt to be secretive with those who are learning the craft would look ridiculous; it would be a denial of the very intimacy and trust that define being relatives. Indeed, trust is a key notion in this context, doubtless in part because of the sheer monetary value of the materials lying around in every such workshop. When I asked one friendly atelier owner to introduce me to colleagues running other shops, he demurred, explaining that—while apparently he had no objection to helping me—he was concerned that they would all treat me as some sort of spy acting on his behalf. Then it emerged that one of the most important neighboring shops belonged to someone who happened to be his uncle (father's brother). But his uncle, he said, was very jealous of him, so he would be particularly careful not to take me there.

This is important because it shows that people in this community do not always, or literally, expect kin to be trustworthy and constitutes further evidence that it is the work situation that defines the affirmation of ties of kinship rather than the other way around. As we proceed in this argument, moreover, it becomes increasingly clear that secrecy is, as we so often find under an enormous range of circumstances, directly related to questions of trust; and trust is a key attribute of being kin. Just as the Cretan artisan would look ridiculous if he beat a young member of his own patrilineal clan, so, too, but contrastively, a Ban Maw goldsmith would look equally foolish if he refused to explain the work directly and patiently—because patience, too, is self-stereotypically defined as a Thai trait and especially as a characteristic every artisan must possess—to someone defined as a member of his *khreua yat* (kin group). The jealous uncle is described by a single kin term, not as the all-encompassing *yat*. The implication is clear: some residual respect may remain toward him because he is an elder blood relative, but, as the key social emotion of trust is absent, he is assumed to be concealing his knowledge behind the same wall of secrecy that my informant uses to keep him at arm's length as well—and that excludes him from the more generic label of *yat*. The *khreua yat* defines the limits of mutual comprehension, and this is metaphorically transposed to the workspace; those on the outside must be treated with a display of polite incomprehension lest they become too intimate—and, in stealing the workshop's best ideas, show that they have comprehended all too well.

When I inquired how the young goldsmiths had learned their trade, they all responded, without exception, that their masters had taught them, explained everything, and freely demonstrated the techniques. There was no withholding of comprehension or instruction there. The one element they held in common with Cretan goldsmiths was a period of training on cheap materials, as gold is increasingly expensive, but there was no hesitation about describing the relationship as usually a cordial and productive one. One man did recall how the old Chinese goldsmiths who had founded the majority of the workshops—and whose characteristic shrines, now electrically enhanced, still light up the dark interiors of the houses—would curse and swear and refuse to explain anything to the young provincial lads from the northeast of the country who had come to learn this trade.

But that phase was described contrastively, as something that real Thai people would not do. Whether the story is true or not, it speaks volumes about the idealized self-perception of the present-day goldsmiths as good Thais and good Buddhists. Kindly interaction and an open sharing of knowledge are the order of the day—but only inside each workshop. Outside, artisans rarely even socialize over food with colleagues from other workshops, so strong is the public display of mutual distrust. More generally, one sees unusually little socializing on the streets of the district. While there *is* a sense of community in respect of religious devotion and some new initiatives designed to encourage the elderly to occupy their time productively, everyday gossip is carefully channeled and, as far as I could tell, does easily not cross from one workshop to another.

Where would Barth's (admittedly much more ambitious) transactionalist interpretation in "The Guru and the Conjurer" lead us in my present discussion? I suggest that there is at least a plausible analogy, as follows. The Cretan master artisan, like the Melanesian officiant, holds knowledge in; thus, those who wish to gain that knowledge implicitly accept that they will in some sense become incorporated within him. Nothing is to leak to the outside. But in fact what does leak to the outside is the image of the tough male artisan who treats his young charges with appropriate disdain and suspicion, thereby at once protecting his own interests while also indirectly instructing the apprentices in the arts of survival in the tough male world they inhabit together.

The Ban Maw goldsmith, by contrast, heir to a grand tradition (and conscious of operating in a field that has royal sanction), zealously transmits a tradition that is laterally reproduced in a multitude of such workshops. This occurs in full awareness that competition between workshops can be quite fierce in this lucrative field. The commercial agents, jewelers with impressive storefronts in shopping malls and along main streets, will go to those who can complete tasks well and in timely fashion, and the workshops are mostly energetically competing with each other to show both mastery and reliability. As in Thai markets, people who do the same work and sell the same kinds of labor and products tend to cluster together. This is convenient for the buyers, but it produces an intensely involuted sense of competition. The artisans, however, who in this respect act much like market stallholders, mask their privately ad-mitted competitive attitude with an air of innocent disinterestedness, hiding social tension behind an officially sanctified and ever-intensifying traditional-ism that grants them special respect as its representatives.

Greece, too, went through a late twentieth-century paroxysm of craft mania based on the premise that the self-centered individualism of traditional arti-sans could, if it was not dismissed as a relic of Ottoman antisocial attitudiniz-ing, be represented instead as the highest expression of the Western (or at least European) self and its self-ascribed autonomy and creativity. But in the Greek case this means that indigenous craft practices have effectively been subordi-nated to a largely imported model of national identity, of Greekness. The trap for the Greek artisans, goldsmiths and all, is that whatever they do, they repro-duce both their own social immobility as picturesquely uncouth working-class ruffians and the beholden state of their country to the Western powers' cul-tural hierarchies—to what, in short, I have called the "global hierarchy of value" (Herzfeld 2004). Their secrecy forms part of the uncouth image; it may protect the immediate interests of artisans aware of the antics of their most jealous rivals who are trying to steal their trade techniques, but it also locks them into a situation in which they cannot afford to behave like the ordinary bourgeois teachers employed by the national state—such a move would lose them their one advantage, their one distinctive selling point, in the market. So their se-cretive approach to training contributes to their continuation in the same old status and working at the same old crafts, a situation further reinforced by the dominant classes' conviction that to allow these uncouth artisans to develop in new directions would be to pose a threat to their own hegemony.

In Ban Maw and throughout urban Thailand, however, we are looking at a tradition not only of respectful and fruitful teaching in the Buddhist tradition, but also of compromise as a tactic of survival. I have elsewhere remarked on how surprised I have been, on more than one occasion, to be actively encour-aged by local community leaders to speak with their tormentors and rivals in the bureaucracy and in factions opposed to their own. No Greek community head would strongly urge me to go and speak with a bitter rival who was sim-ply awaiting the chance to denounce the village leadership to the bureaucratic and police authorities or to discredit it in the eyes of other residents. In that context, conversation with the enemy means total rupture with one's erstwhile friends. The Thai community leaders, however, were not simply throwing up their hands and saying that they did not care if I had a friendly relationship with their foes. Quite to the contrary, they would themselves do everything possible to maintain at least the appearance of moral authority over their communities, even with people (and in this alone they resembled their Greek counterparts) with whom they "did not speak." Their displays of confidence were as much performances as were the displays of secretive behavior by artisans; they were devices for maintaining "face" (*na*) by avoiding anything that could be construed as disturbing communal harmony or as signaling fear on their part.

This contrast adds to the sense of regional difference between Southeast Asia and Mediterranean Europe, although we would need much more information about artisan-apprentice relations in *other* Southeast Asian societies (as we have already for Europe and the Middle East) to make the point effectively.[9] What I want to emphasize here is that we have strong evidence to support the idea that these two regions operate quite differently with the devices of silence and the refusal of communication, both in their dealings with the relatively new national bureaucratic offices in each area and in determining which demarcations of kinship and friendship make cooperation or social engagement with others dangerous and therefore undesirable.

The outcome is necessarily a provisional acknowledgment of a loose but palpable connection between geography and cultural specificity. Perhaps the most important aspect of this is that such connections traverse both the national boundaries that a methodological nationalism would impose and the ethnic boundaries that ultimately spring from the same nationalism-based model. As nationalism increases its hold, authoritarian or democratic as the case may be, across the entire world, it will be increasingly difficult to identify the "cultural stuff" that vast areas share; each nation-state guards what it sees as its own and, in many instances, simultaneously tries to filch cultural elements from its neighbors. But the model I am discussing here, which is itself something of a Barthian hybrid born of "ethnic groups" and the "guru and conjurer argument," acknowledges the forces that at other times and perhaps also in some respects today—perhaps through ASEAN and the European Union?—emphasize instead the sharing of cultural traits and attitudes on a regional basis. The problem with the ASEAN/EU model is that it simply reproduces methodological nationalism on a larger scale. And a comparison that emphasized Thailand and Greece, rather than Ban Maw/Southeast Asia and Rethemnos/Mediterranean Europe, could too easily be trapped in methodological nationalism engendered by the two countries' shared trajectories in the penumbra of the Western colonial project.[10]

I hope that the revisionary amalgam of Fredrik Barth's ideas that I have suggested here may help us to identify and avoid an insidiously easy "explanation" of similarities and differences. These can only be understood through the intensely local focus of ethnography, contextualized in the "big history" of long-term cultural exchange and contact and realized—as Ben-Yehoyada (2014, 2017) has argued for the Mediterranean—through models of kinship that acknowledge conflict and confrontation as much as the sharing of a common cultural heritage. It can also only be understood by acknowledging that cultural identities that stretch across regions are necessarily inchoate, evanescent, partial, provisional, and ambiguous. None of those adjectives mean that such identities do not exist. Treated with the respect and restraint of a Fredrik Barth, they can still emerge in the consciousness of local people who want to resist the closure of those more formal identities that governments and academics alike have all too often wished upon them.

Moreover, Barth's original insight was not only about regional commonalities. It was also, more importantly perhaps, about modalities of knowledge transmission. Awareness of a shared cultural pattern of social interaction—and thus of the consequences of departing too drastically or unthinkingly from its norms—must therefore feed back into the way in which even quite technical knowledge is presented during transmission. Ban Maw artisans, for example, as well as the protesting evictees of Pom Mahakan, are acutely aware of being Buddhists—and therefore of being part of something larger than the Thai nation-state. Patience and gentleness are virtues here. The very different artisans and shepherds of Crete are similarly aware of traits they share with neighboring peoples, even with those—notably the Turks—toward whom they profess unquenchable enmity. They, too, are constrained by such regional stereotypes—in this case, to the point of refusing to treat unrelated apprentices with too much soft kindness; true men cannot be made through mollycoddling. Different modalities of knowledge transmission and social value thus operate within generic geographies that lend them additional authority and stability without suppressing the capacity of socially skilled individuals to effect cultural and social change.

Michael Herzfeld is Ernest E. Monrad Research Professor of the Social Sciences in the Department of Anthropology at Harvard University and also holds visiting appointments and affiliations at several other institutions, including the Universities of Leiden and Melbourne and Shanghai International Studies University. Author of eleven books (most recently *Siege of the Spirits: Community and Polity in Bangkok*, 2016, and *Cultural Intimacy: Social Poetics and the Real Life of States, Institutions, and Societies*, 2016) and producer of two films about Rome, he has conducted extensive field research in Greece, Italy, and Thailand. His ongoing research focuses on craft production and apprenticeship, knowledge politics, the politics of heritage, nationalism, bureaucracy, and the social impact of historic conservation.

Notes

1. I would like to record here, with gratitude, grants variously awarded for the research presented here by Harvard University's Asia Center and Weatherhead Institute for International Affairs. Since the original formulation of this essay, the Bangkok community has disappeared, and I have become familiar with recent events in the Cretan village and their subsequent consequences; see Herzfeld 2019.
2. I used to call the village by the pseudonym "Glendi" (Herzfeld 1985, etc.), but the events of 2007, briefly mentioned elsewhere in this chapter, have rendered that option of dubious value, and the residents seem pleased that a sympathetic investigator is at last looking

at those events from their perspective—which is not to say that this anthropologist approves of the violence that was committed, any more than all of the residents do.

3. I have elsewhere (Herzfeld 2016: 91–94) documented the very effective ways in which the community leadership has employed formulaic politeness as a parodic device used to wrest initiative from the authorities even as the latter seemed to be gaining the upper hand.

4. I have maintained contact with the village since 1974 and have most recently conducted research there in 2019; I have spent a total of over eighteen months in the village.

5. I began research in Ban Maw in early 2017 and so far have conducted about nine months of fieldwork. Since I was mostly living nearby in a market community, I also had generous opportunities to observe market attitudes—which merge competition with a display of friendly camaraderie—and to ponder what made goldsmiths different and what features, instead, they shared with the merchants in the marketplace.

6. Barth 1969; on methodological nationalism, see Wimmer and Glick Schiller 2002.

7. See my afterword to the recently published compendium of Pitt-Rivers's essays edited by Giovanni Da Col and Andrew Shryock (Herzfeld 2018).

8. And indeed of Heine-Geldern and Tambiah; see below.

9. Strangely enough there is relatively little such information despite the varied and historically deep artisanal traditions of the area. This contrasts with the rich array of studies of apprenticeship in many other parts of the world, prompting the thought that perhaps the seeming straightforwardness of the didactic process among Southeast Asian artisans made their transmission process seem straightforward and unremarkable—and therefore not specifically worthy of careful study.

10. In other words, both are what I call "crypto-colonies." See, most recently, Herzfeld 2019: 31.

References

Barth, Fredrik. 1969. Introduction to *Ethnic Groups and Boundaries: The Social Organization of Culture Difference*, edited by Fredrik Barth, 9–38. Boston: Little, Brown.

———. 1990. "The Guru and the Conjurer: Transactions in Knowledge and the Shaping of Culture in Southeast Asia and Melanesia." *Man* 25(4): 640–53.

Bauman, Richard. 1977. *Verbal Art as Performance*. Rowley, MA: Newbury House.

Ben-Yehoyada, Naor. 2014. "Transnational Political Cosmology: A Central Mediterranean Example." *Comparative Studies in Society and History* 56: 870–901.

———. 2017. *The Mediterranean Incarnate: Region Formation between Sicily and Tunisia since World War II*. Chicago: University of Chicago Press.

Campbell, J. K. 1964. *Honour, Family, and Patronage: A Study of Institutions and Moral Values in a Greek Mountain Community*. Oxford: Clarendon Press.

Damer, Seán. 1988. "Legless in Sfakia: Drinking and Social Practice in Western Crete." *Journal of Modern Greek Studies* 6: 291–310.

Day, Tony. 2002. *Fluid Iron: State Formation in Southeast Asia*. Honolulu: University of Hawai'i Press.

Harms, Erik. 2011. *Saigon's Edge: On the Margins of Ho Chi Minh City*. Minneapolis: University of Minnesota Press.

Heine-Geldern, Robert. 1942. "Conceptions of State and Kingship in Southeast Asia." *Far Eastern Quarterly* 2(1): 15–30.

Herzfeld, Michael. 1985. *The Poetics of Manhood: Contest and Identity in a Cretan Mountain Village*. Princeton, NJ: Princeton University Press.

———. 2004. *The Body Impolitic: Artisans and Artifice in the Global Hierarchy of Value.* Chicago: University of Chicago Press.

———. 2009. "The Performance of Secrecy: Domesticity and Privacy in Public Spaces." *Semiotica* 175(1/4): 135–62.

———. 2014. "Po-Mo Med." In *A Companion to Mediterranean History*, edited by Peregrine Horden and Sharon Kinoshita, 122–36. Chichester: Wiley Blackwell.

———. 2016. *Siege of the Spirits: Community and Polity in Bangkok.* Chicago: University of Chicago Press.

———. 2018. "Grace and Insight: The Legacy of Julian Pitt-Rivers." In *From Hospitality to Grace: A Julian Pitt-Rivers Omnibus*, edited by Giovanni da Col and Andrew Shryock, 464–472. Chicago: Hau Books.

———. 2019. "What is a Polity? Subversive Archaism and the Bureaucratic Nation-State: The 2018 Lewis H. Morgan Lecture." *Hau: Journal of Ethnographic Theory* 9(1): 23–35.

Prevelakis, Pandelis. 1972. *The Tale of a Town.* Translated by Kenneth Johnstone. London: Doric Publications.

Rabinow, Paul. 1989. *French Modern: Norms and Forms of the Social Environment.* Cambridge: MIT Press.

Simmel, Georg. 1964. "The Sociology of Secrecy and Secret Societies." In *The Sociology of Georg Simmel*, edited by K. H. Wol, 307–76. New York: Free Press.

Singleton, John, ed. 1998. *Learning in Likely Places: Varieties of Apprenticeship in Japan.* Cambridge: Cambridge University Press.

Tambiah, Stanley J. 1976. *World Conqueror, World Renouncer: A Study of Buddhism and Polity in Thailand against a Historical Background.* Cambridge: Cambridge University Press.

Wimmer, Andreas, and Nina Glick Schiller. 2002. "Methodological Nationalism and Beyond: Nation-State Building, Migration and the Social Sciences." *Global Networks* 2: 301–34.

3

Cosmologies in the Remaking
Variation and Time in
Chinese Temple Religion

Robert P. Weller

One of Barth's most important contributions, extending in different ways through much of his work, was his attempt to press anthropology beyond a Durkheimian conception of society.[1] It is not simply that he gave more voice to strategizing and agentic individuals, although he certainly did that. He was always looking for alternative ways to conceptualize how social relations can form group identities and distinctions. He led us to focus less on fixed bodies of belief ("culture") or fixed patterns of social institutions ("society") and more on the processes of communication that foster different kinds of social connections and variations.

Barth's later books drew our attention to places where the amount of variation seemed truly remarkable: Bali, a complex society whose degree of microvariation had already drawn significant attention (e.g., Geertz 1959), and the Ok of mountain New Guinea, whose tiny, neighboring groups varied so much in religious life that they were sometimes shocked by each other's most sacred rituals (Barth 1987, 1993). Taken together, one of the morals of these books is that we should stop being so surprised at this level of variation. It seems remarkable to us only because ideas like "culture" and "society" imply that everyone involved is the same in some fundamental sense. Instead of starting from an assumption of cultural or social unity, however, Barth in these books starts from the idea of reproduction, of how similarities and differences are *generated* (to use a term he favored throughout his career) and transmitted. Variation thus seems less like a problem of how patterns are distributed over space than one of how knowledge (in its broadest sense) is produced, reproduced, and adapted over time, through quite different institutional and communicative forms. Variations in such knowledge are crucial because they provide the raw material for a sense both of personal identity and of group membership, that is, for the basic building blocks of social life.

The problem of variation has vexed China scholars as well, of course. Especially in the religion field, it has spawned several vigorous and unresolved debates. At the risk of oversimplifying, it seems to me that we have seen four main ways of approaching the problem. The first was Maurice Freedman's idea of an underlying religious structure that was the same for everyone (Freedman 1974). That is, in the style of French structuralism, he made the problem of variation disappear by considering it as a kind of froth on the surface of a deeper cultural unity. Second was Arthur Wolf's position, articulated in direct argument against Freedman, that religious ideas reflected people's social positions (especially the gap between elites and peasants) and therefore must vary significantly in a complex society like China (Wolf 1974). Both positions assumed a kind of group unity, but the nature of the group differed—all Chinese for Freedman, and all those sharing certain social characteristics for Wolf. Neither position explains how those group unities could be formed and reproduced.

The third intervention was the only one to deal directly with the kinds of geographical variation that seem so obvious to anyone moving around the country: G. William Skinner's analysis of regional systems (see his chapters in Skinner 1977). Skinner was not writing with religion in mind, but his innovative analysis helped shape our understanding of all kinds of variation along two lines: the differences between one geographical region and another, and the differences between cores and peripheries within each region. The key idea for both was that social and economic interaction was far easier over water than over land (until railroads and other more recent forms of transportation) and that the structure of watersheds would thus create cultural, social, and economic similarities (where interaction was easy) and variations (where interaction was difficult).

Finally, the fourth way of dealing with variation stems from James Watson's discussions of standardization and the related concept of orthopraxy (Watson 1985).[2] He argued that a powerful centripetal force, led by the state and local elites, counteracted tendencies toward local variation that were rooted in processes like what both Wolf and Skinner documented. Although his "orthopraxy" idea developed in the context of an argument about the relative importance of texts as opposed to rituals, the "ortho-" prefix itself already assumed that some process of standardization was at work, whether for text or for ritual action.

Each of these approaches began from somewhat different theoretical positions (central place theory, French structuralism, Durkheimian equation of religion and society, and so on). Each also inspired generations of further work, and generations of critics—too numerous even to mention here. That is, we still have no agreement at all on how to understand variation in China because none of these approaches seems sufficient to capture the richness and variability that we see in life on the ground. Perhaps part of the problem is that all of these theorists, like most anthropologists, have only the short time frames of fieldwork to think about the problem. They have thus imagined variation primarily as a problem in social and physical space, rather than as a problem of transmission and generation over time. This is where Barth's work suggests a helpful intervention.

In his analysis of the Ok, for example, Barth discusses variation in rituals for the highest initiation level that men can achieve. There are many such levels, each revealing vital secret information that leads to a total reconsideration of what people learned at their previous initiation (see also chapter 8 in this volume). These rituals often happen only once a decade or so, which means that the people achieving the highest level are typically already old and that the very senior men initiating them are even older. Given the very small size of these groups, there might be only one or two men qualified to lead the ceremony. They may never have led one before, and in any case after a decade-long time lag, much will have to be constructed. Barth shows how this structure of secrecy and age forces the old men to be active cosmologists, reconstructing and constructing the way the world works through ritual objects and techniques. These factors combine to foster an engine of innovation, where variations can easily multiply. While Barth of course recognizes that this situation is unusual, and while he also analyzes several other quite different mechanisms involved in creating Ok variants, it illustrates how he uses the flow of knowledge over time to reveal how individual agency and social institution combine to create variation.

Three Kinds of Time

This is the insight I will use to understand two recent ethnographic episodes of Chinese cosmologies in the remaking. Both took place in southern Jiangsu Province (in the center of China's booming east coast), both involved challenges over the significance of gods and temples, and both have helped to foster new forms of religious variation. Barth's general approach in both Bali and New Guinea, late in his career, was to examine how different institutional structures and historical conjunctures could foster (or discourage) variation by creating branches and alternate channels for the flow of knowledge. Mine differs somewhat in looking first at the distinctive ways in which that flow of knowledge over time can be conceptualized. In particular, I will focus on three ways of imagining time, which offer alternative mechanisms for the formation of variant social groups around flows of knowledge: continuous time, folded time, and emergent time.[3]

Continuous time invokes the claim that knowledge is passed down in a continuous stream over time, from parents to children, masters to disciples, or teachers to students. It can also be solidified into museums, monuments, ancestral halls, and much else. These are the processes usually called social or collective memory (see, e.g., Halbwachs 1980; Assmann 1995). I am not suggesting that such knowledge really remains unchanged in the process, but only that the construction of social memory relies on a *claim* of continuity. Real continuity is impossible for memory; my memory of Istanbul is certainly not the same as my experience of Istanbul. It is always constructed after the fact.

Memory as the construction of a continued inheritance over time creates a sense of identity through the sharing of the stories and memorials that materialize shared experiences. Continuous time as memory thus fosters delimited social groups (those who share the "memory"), just as those social groups foster the creation of their own memories and memorials. In Chinese families, we can see this clearly in the ancestral tablets that once defined every family and in the construction of written genealogies and communal halls that created lineages. Note that such materialized memories did not simply reflect an existing social organization; creating a genealogy or a lineage hall performatively marked the beginnings of the lineage as a group even as such objects hardened the group's boundaries by defining access to shared resources. Temples to deities often defined larger groups, which could be based on geography, kinship, place of origin, or any other kind of grouping. Until the twentieth century, most clearly defined groups—rotating credit associations, guilds, villages, and almost everything else—grounded the continuity of the group over time in an altar to one or more gods.

The second way of thinking about the flow of knowledge involves *folded time*. By this I mean the possibility of repeating "the same" event over and over, even though time may flow in other ways between the events. It is as if a sheet of paper were folded over so that two separate areas touch each other or like the expansion and contraction of the folded bellows of an accordion.[4] In the case of the temples I will be discussing here, the most relevant cases are the rhythmic repetition of rituals. Rituals of course draw boundaries, just as memories do, but in a significantly different way, because ritual boundaries are always capable of being crossed or transcended (Seligman et al. 2008). At the very least, they require crossing the boundary between ritual time and ordinary time. This is what I mean by folding time, so that the current ritual act counts as if it were the same as the previous one and the next one—as if time had been folded together to connect each event—even though we know there are a myriad of empirical differences in practice.

In the case of Chinese temple ritual, large events in particular encourage forms of border crossing. First, gods (and their followers) can visit other temples, crossing the boundaries between the groups that each temple defines by materializing continuous time. Such interactions are highly ritualized, often (though not always) occurring on set occasions, and always surrounded with elaborate conventions of courteous respect for the host god. Second, large rituals at community temples are typically open. Anyone can come, and anyone can share in the spiritual benefits. No one is limited by having to share an imagined continuous past (a "memory" in the broadest sense). Participation alone is enough to join in the ritual flow of folded time. In some cases, the ability to share folded time has been able to allow diverse communities to live together by sharing the repetitions of ritual without worrying about whether they also share interpretations. Michael Carrithers has theorized this process as "polytropy" or spiritual cosmopolitanism as it occurs in cross-religious ritual traditions in India (Carrithers 2000).

Finally, knowledge can be understood to have been transformed through *emergent time*, in the way that new properties can emerge from a system, as when crystals form or hurricanes take shape. The fundamental building blocks of this kind of time have not changed so much as they have reworked themselves into something quite new. For religion, this is most obvious with revealed knowledge, which in contemporary China takes place primarily through spirit mediumship of various sorts. Most often, of course, such transformations are minor things. For instance, they might lead to a diagnosis that sickness has been caused by an angry ghost and needs to be cured by exorcism. Such a ghost has broken the continuity of time by having a past event—perhaps an unfortunate and long-forgotten death—break into the present. At the same time, the boundary between the yin and yang worlds has been breached. Such small breaks are usually healed by a successful ceremony, and the system of transmission continues more or less unchanged.

Sometimes, however, the emergence of new properties in time can have long-lasting significance. In the 1840s Hong Xiuquan realized that he was God's younger son, and he was supported by mediums who spoke directly with the voices of the Christian God and Jesus. This ushered in the Taiping Heavenly Kingdom, a new era and a break in time from the Qing dynasty. Tens of millions of people died before time returned to something like its earlier forms. Some Buddhist-inspired movements have also led to large-scale rebellions, almost always described as emergent time—as the beginning of a new *kalpa* (cosmic age), which would usher in the time of the new Buddha. In such events, knowledge can flow in new and unexpected directions, marking itself off as a new beginning instead of a continuation or a repetition. Occasionally it can foster the formation of new social groups or the transcendence of old boundaries.

Each of these understandings of time has its own ways of producing and reproducing knowledge, and therefore of generating variation.[5] With the imagination of continuous time, knowledge moves through stories and their objects in an attempt to pin the memories down. The process emphasizes the continuity and the solidarity of those people with shared access to that continuity. In fact, however, historical change also creates gaps and divergences in practice. The tension between claims of continuous knowledge and the contingencies of history creates a constant evolution, so that ancestral altars are rather different in different parts of China or among different groups. Thus, the village where I did my first fieldwork typically featured two, three, or four different surnames highlighted equally on the altar. One could barely call the place patrilineal. Just down the road, however, another village insisted on patrilineal surname purity, and any other surnames that could not be avoided (like a wife's parents who had no one else to worship them) were relegated to dusty back rooms (Ahern 1973; Weller 1987). Without taking space to go into detail or to cite other examples here, I suggest that these differences represent adaptations to quite different environments, like the lack of landed property in the village that allowed multiple surnames.

Folded time also generates variation, especially because repeated performances are never precisely the same, but always contain an element of improvisation that can later be incorporated into what counts as "the ritual." Barth's description of the role of Ok cosmologists is something like this. In most cases, knowledge of the ritual forms of folded time is primarily embodied, passed along through direct participation and experience. There may be liturgical or textual guides, of course, but the text itself is never the performance.

Finally, the source of variation is most obvious for emergent time, where every revelation opens the possibility of novelty. In the cases below, this is especially clear for those spirit mediums who claim that all of their relevant knowledge comes from direct divine inspiration and never from any human institution like family members or temples.

These three forms do not represent differences in the nature of time itself, if there even is such a thing. Instead, we might think of them as three arguments about how time is imagined, about how knowledge can continue and be created over time, and about how to understand people's claims about their group identities. Any given case, any actual performance of knowledge, is potentially subject to reinterpretation. One could argue, for instance, that the Taiping Heavenly Kingdom was really no more than another dynasty in practice (continuity, rather than emergence) or that a ritual performance is really so improvised that it cannot be counted as repetition at all, but instead constitutes an unacceptable failure or a complete innovation (both forms of emergence, rather than folding).

The two cases I will discuss here involve situations of rapid change where the ways of framing time become open to argument, and so too do the forms of knowledge and the social groups associated with them. The first involves the reconstruction of temples to the goddess Tianhou (天后, or Mazu 妈祖) in Nanjing, in a kind of indirect dialogue with Taiwan, which opened a tension between claims of continuous time and those of folded time. The second case involves a temple to Suiliang Wang (随粮王), a very local deity not far away in Suzhou. There, rapid urbanization has undermined the place-based structure of local temples, and a newly emerged form of time is challenging the continuous time of memory and group identity.

Claiming Tianhou

The goddess Tianhou began life in northern Fujian, where she first saved seafarers in jeopardy. From there her temples multiplied mostly along routes of water transportation, both on the mainland and overseas. Emigrants from Fujian to Taiwan and around the world brought her along as they established new communities. Inland water workers carried her cult across many parts of the mainland, as did sojourning merchants from Fujian, for whom she served as the primary deity in their native place associations (*huiguan* 会馆) (Zhang n.d.).[6]

In every case, the new communities established in these ways regenerated Tianhou through a combination of the mechanisms I have called continuity and folding. Claims to continuity often happened tangibly, through images that people brought with them on their journeys or from incense ash carried from a mother temple at home to a newly founded temple elsewhere. The folded time of ritual life gave periodic social form to the new communities, especially through large annual celebrations like her birthday; it also allowed these communities to redefine themselves through the possibility of crossing boundaries. Thus, in parts of southern Vietnam, Tianhou has lost her ethnic affiliation with Chinese migrants and become a Vietnamese deity (Nguyen 2016). In Taiwan (where she is almost always called Mazu, in another example of how continuity can lead to variation), the boundary-crossing aspect of the ritual has gone so far that the cult has partially de-territorialized from its original separate communities of worship in small towns and villages. It now encompasses the entire island in overlapping spheres marked by various core Tianhou/Mazu temples (Chipman 2009), attracting even people whose ancestors had brought over quite different deities. The tie to a new sense of island-wide identity, partially transcending earlier senses of community identity and formed in the face of mainland China, is obvious. Note that while the social memories of continuous time are important for many Tianhou temples and their followers, this change in scale and in the nature of identity holds together almost entirely through periodic rituals—folded time. People learn these rituals above all by participating them, so that the knowledge is embodied through action.

The ritual aspects of these cults are thus crucial. Even though the temples I will discuss are in Nanjing, let me begin for a moment in Taiwan, because the situation there is crucial for the story I want to tell. The annual birthday festivals for Tianhou/Mazu in Taiwan can now attract tens of thousands of people, and even more in the case of half a dozen key temples. Local communities always controlled these temples and their rituals directly, generally through a committee of leaders chosen through divination (see, e.g., Chang 2003). The major social issues—how to provide housing, food, sanitation, and security for crowds that are often many times higher than the population of the towns housing the temples—are all handled directly by the community rather than the government or the priests (who are hired for the event on an ad hoc basis). Nowhere are these celebrations larger than in Taiwan, where a small number of Tianhou/Mazu temples have grown into an island-wide national cult over the last century and where the gathered crowds may well surpass anything in earlier Chinese history.[7]

A "hot and noisy" (*renao* 热闹) event is an index of a powerful and efficacious deity, and these rituals in Taiwan epitomize the phenomenon. They brim over with activity and noise—there are huge crowds, Daoist ritual performances, multiple operas (sometimes competing with each other on parallel stages), and parades through the streets where the deity would be mobbed by thousands of people. The teeming streets fill as well with the constant explosions of fire-crackers, their acrid smell combining with the sweeter odor of incense. Every-one wants to make the most of the opportunity to make offerings on this most auspicious of days. Each such event folds across time, making a claim of unity with last year's ritual and with next year's.

The reason I have been describing Taiwan is because the reconstruction of Nanjing's two Tianhou temples cannot be understood without considering Tai-wan. A deity like Tianhou and the community-based cults around her normally have no recognized legal standing in China today. Tianhou is not part of the Daoist or Buddhist hierarchy, and her temples typically housed no clergy. That is, they have no natural affiliation with the officially sanctioned Buddhist or Daoist Associations of China. Once condemned as "feudal superstition," such cults are now usually grudgingly tolerated at best. Both these temples had been shut for decades (with one having been destroyed since the 1930s) but were rebuilt in Nanjing with official state blessing (and funding) in the mid-2000s. One (now controlled by the Daoist Association) had been the local place asso-ciation for Qing merchants from Tianhou's home area in Fujian and the other (now controlled by the Buddhist Association) had been founded by Zheng He, to commemorate the goddess's help in his enormous voyages of ocean explora-tion and trade during the early fifteenth century.

To understand why they reopened with government blessing, we need to turn to China's idea of a united front. The united front has been a crucial con-cept in Chinese Communist thought about how to deal with diversity and plu-ralism. Especially during the anti-Japanese war and then during the early years after 1949, the Communist Party recognized that there were certain kinds of people who would never be proper Communists, but with whom the party could ally over the long term. The party set up the United Front Work Depart-ment to deal with such people, who included all overseas Chinese, people living in "national" territory that the People's Republic of China (PRC) did not control (Hong Kong, Macao, or Taiwan), ethnic minorities, religious believers, and ac-ceptable capitalists (Weller 2013). From this point of view, Tianhou combines religion with the possibility of shaping the relationship to Taiwan; it speaks to the core mission of the united front.

Nanjing is the capital of Jiangsu Province, which is home to many thousands of Taiwanese businesses. Establishing good ties to these businesspeople is eco-nomically important to the province and politically important to the idea of a united front. In the terms I am using here, we can see the temple reconstruc-tion as an effort to craft continuous time. That is, the two temples constitute a claim of communal memory: the people of Taiwan and those of Nanjing (and by extension, of all China) are parts of a single community of memory and thus share a single identity. The evidence for this, in this case, would be the commemoration of Tianhou through her temples.

When I first went to the old merchant association temple, I noticed a placard on the wall showing the names of major donors in the initial rebuilding of the temple. This is standard in many temples, but this particular one stood out because the first name on the list, having contributed 16,000 RMB, was the Nanjing United Front Work Department of the Communist Party and the Religious and Ethnic Affairs Bureau of the city government. Normally the party would not make contributions directly to a religious institution, especially to one with such a thin claim on being "religious" at all. Here, however, the united front mission had clearly outweighed the proper attitude of atheism. The other Tianhou temple did not show evidence of any direct contributions from the party or state, but their stone inscription of donors did include, listed in the first place, Lien Chan, who at that time was the chairman of the Nationalist Party in Taiwan. He was more willing than most Taiwanese politicians to promote the cause of reunification by visiting the mainland and would always be sure to visit Nanjing, the nominal Nationalist capital. This is exactly the sort of thing the united front was intended to foster. Both temples thus represent in part a conscious strategy by the provincial and metropolitan governments to reach out to Taiwan through the rather unexpected mechanism of temple-based religion.

With this background in mind, let me turn to Tianhou's birthday as it was celebrated in Nanjing on the twenty-third day of the third lunar month (April 22) in 2014. Both temples faced a set of problems quite different from what temples in Taiwan see. First, both were under the control of clergy who had no interest in Tianhou and saw her at best as tangential to their religious interests. Her rituals fell well outside of their liturgical worlds. The "Daoist" temple thus did not do anything at all on Tianhou's birthday.

The "Buddhist" temple, on the other hand, regularly hosts a birthday ritual, but the Buddhist monks who run it take no part. When I asked the monk in charge of the temple how he felt about the birthday ritual, he said that it was fine for people to do this celebration, but it had nothing at all to do with Buddhism or even with religion at all. It was just popular custom (*minsu*民俗). He would not try to change it, he said, but he also had no interest in taking part in any way. The local community did not organize the ceremony either, in contrast to the situation at similar temples outside of China or in rural areas. Instead, the chief organizer was the Nanjing Metropolitan Tourism Bureau, because it is in charge of the park in which the temple sits. No priests of any kind were involved.

This temple had reopened about eight years earlier, and in prior years it had carried the image of Tianhou on a tour of the local neighborhood, like a much scaled-down version of her territorial tours in Taiwan and elsewhere. When I watched in 2014, however, the government had decided to make the ceremony more austere (*jianpu* 简朴) by limiting the procession to the grounds of the park itself. This was an odd arrangement that involved a one-way journey from the temple to a pavilion elsewhere in the park, very different from the tour of the temple's territorial boundaries that deities usually take. Performance inside the park discouraged almost everyone from watching.

By the standards of Taiwan, the ritual aspects of the birthday had been stripped of all the life and effervescence that any event needs to be successful—it had very little of the quality of "heat and noise" that people so value. It began with formal speeches on a temporary stage set up directly across from the temple. This was the space where an opera should have been performed in other contexts. The speeches came from members of the city's Tourism Bureau and the local district government, who recited political chestnuts about cultural preservation. The closest model for those local officials seemed to be formal party meetings to disseminate new policies. Dragon dancers stood around looking bored through this. Facing the speakers stood a group of about a hundred people in yellow sashes—representatives of companies who had donated significant amounts of money for the ceremony. They chatted to each other during the speeches, looking equally bored. A few hundred local residents also watched from the sides; they were not allowed in the central area, which had been reserved for the donors. At last the speeches ended, and everyone turned to face the temple to offer incense.

With no priests to orchestrate the worship of the deity, the state organizers fell back on a Confucian ceremonial model that was just the opposite of the heat and noise of what most people would consider successful popular ritual. A convener speaking in a slow, deliberate monotone instructed people to bow once, and a second time, and a third time. Then some of the leaders were introduced to offer fruit and incense a first time, and a second, and a third. Finally, the people in sashes were given the opportunity to come up in orderly rows and offer their incense. The contrast to the atmosphere of Tianhou's birthday in Taiwan could not have been greater.

The lack of ritual leadership was even more obvious when the procession began, because it was clear that no one knew exactly how to do it. Various performing groups (the dragon dancers, some costumed women) had been hired to accompany the parade, but with no one watching they soon lost their enthusiasm and just trudged up the hill gossiping to each other. The low point came when the bearers of Tianhou's sedan chair realized that they had not rigged it properly for carrying and put her down on the ground to rework the straps. This was enormously disrespectful to the deity and marked a crisis point for the success of the ritual. The event simply petered out when the group reached the pavilion at the top of the hill.

Whether this counts as a "failed ritual" is in the eye of the beholder. It was not a failure for the government officials, who were able to show their preservation of popular custom and their ability to attract business donations. Above all, they could report to the United Front Work Department that they had helped foster a link to Taiwan. Perhaps it was also not a failure for the donors, most of whom represented businesses based in Fujian, for whom participation could help tighten their ties to local government. That is, in a partial sense, this temple had taken on the role that some Tianhou temples played in earlier historical periods, as the sacralized centers of native place associations for Fujian merchants based in Nanjing and many other cities.[8] Most striking, however, was the complete absence of anyone from Taiwan. No one took part, I was told, because the ritual was so badly done. To take part was to risk bringing bad luck, as when Tianhou's sedan chair was placed on the ground—just the opposite of what ritual should achieve.

Everything about the situation contrived to minimize ritual and especially to dilute completely the sense of wild excitement that proper Chinese temple rituals normally generate. Instead of unruly crowds elbowing each other to get to an incense pot so full of their offerings that it would burst into towers of flame, we had a few rows of wealthy donors offering incense on command. Instead of thousands or tens of thousands of people waiting for a glimpse of Tianhou as she toured her territory, there was a hot hike up a hill, witnessed by a few dozen people at most. This diminution and thinning out of ritual texture was the product in part of the government's anxiety about allowing an independent, popular, public expression of enthusiasm (religious or otherwise) and of a long-standing attempt to minimize and simplify all kinds of ritual, from funeral practice to etiquette. The attempt to de-ritualize life has been going on for over a century and shows clearly in China's constitutional guarantees of freedom of *belief* but not of practice. For Tianhou, a claim on continuous time and its unified sense of identity was exactly what the state wanted. The folded time of ritual, however, was largely unacceptable, especially in the ways Taiwanese assumed such rituals should be conducted.

The result was an ultimate failure of the "united front" effort to use the temple to build a bridge toward Taiwan. The underlying problem in this ritual was an unsuccessful attempt to replace Taiwanese ideas of folded time with PRC ideas of continuous time. The result was a mismatch between the intention to draw Taiwanese businesspeople into a sense of solidarity with Chinese identity by claiming a collective memory of Tianhou and the actual practice of ritual, which did not "fold" into Taiwanese ritual time at all and thus attracted only small numbers of people, and none from Taiwan.

If anything, the result reminded Taiwanese living in Nanjing and Jiangsu of just how different their social memories are from those of the PRC. The united front people hope to emphasize the continuities in how people remember Tianhou, but the Taiwanese see only differences. From the Taiwanese point of view, the chain of transmission of ritual knowledge through performance had been broken. The Taiwanese may hope to fold Tianhou ritually into their own chain of performances, but political control in China has many reasons for rejecting that model. The result so far, at least in Nanjing, is that the two ways of thinking about continuity over time remain separate, and so do the identities that those senses of continuity create. Both the Taiwanese and the Nanjing temples are celebrating Tianhou's birthday in her temples, but the variation fostered by the relevant contexts has already created two extremely different ritual traditions.

"The Yin World Is in Chaos"

Tianhou in Nanjing illustrates the interplay between continuous and folded time and the variant forms of identity that resulted. My second case centers on a different dynamic, where emergent time (and space) appear to be significantly "remaking the cosmology" or at least reshaping religious life. It takes place on the east side of Suzhou (not far from Nanjing on the high-speed train) in an area that was quite rural and agricultural until about fifteen years ago, when it was completely flattened to make way for the Suzhou Industrial Park—a highly planned, upscale urban development. The original population of about one hundred thousand is now close to a million. The old canals, ponds, and streams that were so typical of this area have been forced underground and covered with concrete; the villages and townships no longer exist as political or material objects; the social fabric of life has been transformed as the entire population moved into multistory apartment complexes; every village temple has been bulldozed; every grave has been uprooted or crushed under the weight of new high-rise buildings.

Somewhat unusually, the urban planners decided to build several Daoist temples to house the local gods of the villagers. There are a number of such temples around Suzhou, but the strategy seems rare almost everywhere else.[9] Two large and ornate temples have been built in the Suzhou Industrial Park and given to the Daoist Association of China (the officially sanctioned organization in charge of Daoism) to manage. Just as for Taiwan's temples to Tianhou, the older village temples were run by local people. The only priests involved would be hired as needed for ritual purposes. The new arrangement is thus a major change in scale and in the power of religious clergy and their associated bureaucracy over the temple. All of this has happened at great speed in the area around the temple I will discuss, beginning around 2005.

The old villages, now politically dissolved and materially shattered and buried, all had small temples of their own. Given the constant history of temple destruction in the area (going back well into the Qing dynasty), none of these temples were large or elaborate, because people knew they might have to be rebuilt at any time. Often they were difficult to identify as temples from the outside. The identities of the gods varied widely and ranged from very well-known deities like Sakyamuni, to some known mostly in the broader region (Mengjiang or the Wutong, for instance), to some known only very locally. Suiliang Wang—whose temple I discuss here—was among the most local of all. There were several temples to him in the township, but he was almost unknown elsewhere.[10] When the Daoists were charged with constructing the new temple to house all of these gods, they decided to declare Suiliang Wang as the major god of the temple because of his local importance, even though he is completely unknown in the Daoist pantheon.

Temples always feature a primary deity, and the one to Suiliang Wang is not unusual in that sense. In other ways, however, it is not at all ordinary. In most of the temple, instead of a major deity on the central altar and possibly some secondary deities in the lower positions to the left and right, we see instead image after image, each with its own incense pot and altar table. All have been newly carved and are the same size. The Daoists say that the order is random; almost none of the images represent gods the Daoists normally recognize, and so they discern no hierarchy. The only exception is for the Buddhist images, which have been confined to a basement room.

This new temple is the first of two aspects of remaking the cosmology that I will discuss: it represents an urban planner's world of the gods. This applies not just to the planners who made space for the temple, but to the attitude of the Daoists who run it. As the head Daoist explained, they have "standardized" (*guifanhua* 规范化) everything now. He used the word over and over, with an apparent sense of pride. They had standardized the general look of all the images, standardized the names of the deities by figuring out the proper name for each (because the villagers themselves often did not know), and standardized the placement on the altar into neat rows (see figure 3.1). The interior of the temple feels every bit as planned as the broad avenues and right angles of the newly built streets outside, drawn with rulers by experts in their studios.

This is very different from the continuous time that village temples had represented, where the deities—shabby and unstandardized as they may have been—shaped (and did not simply reflect) the social life of the village. The time could be continuous even though the temples had periodically been destroyed by warfare or government campaigns, because people understood replacement temples exactly as replacements. The physical space might have changed, but the social and cosmological spaces it created remained.

In the new temple, however, those connections are now impossible. When villagers demanded that their village god have its own image, the Daoists refused if there was already an image of the same deity from another village. The head Daoist scoffed at the very idea that the village temple was the relevant unit rather than the god: "Don't those people know that there is only one of each god? If two villages worship Suiliang Wang, there's still only one god!" People still know which of the many deities was associated with their lost village, but they also know that other people from other disappeared villages are worshipping in the same space. Instead of being the vital mechanism of the flow of knowledge over continuous time, those buried villages are now just spaces of nostalgia. Just as their political structures are now based on the urban mechanisms of districts and neighborhood committees, their temple structure now refers much more vaguely to some combined sense of cosmology with far looser ties to local life than before.

Figure 3.1. Re-carved deity images in the Suiliang Wang temple (author photograph)

Each of the old villages usually had at least one religious leader, locally called an "incense head" (*xiangtou* 香头), many of whom also served as spirit mediums. They remain important locally and often refer to themselves as the sons or daughters of a particular deity. In interviews, many of them claimed that after the destruction of the villages and the people's relocation into apartment complexes, the yin world had fallen into chaos (*yinjian luan le* 阴间乱了). They meant a wide range of things by this: the ghosts of the dead were attacking more people because their graves had been destroyed; the gods were taking less care of the community because their "homes" had been reduced to rubble; there were more arguments among incense leaders because thrusting them together in the temple and in the apartment complexes had fostered new kinds of competition. That is, breaking the yang world breaks the yin world as well.

These new kinds of competition lead to the second kind of remaking I want to mention. Just as with every kind of urban planning, real life tends to intervene as blueprints become reality, and so the urban planning cosmology is itself being remade constantly. We can see this in the space itself, both in the apartment complex and in the temple. As part of the planners' image of how modern dwellings should work, each of the apartments assigned to relocated people includes a basement storage area, which people call garages. These "garages" are perfect places for spirit mediums to place their altars—private and out of sight, but with easy access for all the neighbors. The space in the temple was perhaps even more unexpected. In addition to the "standardized" spaces I have described, the temple is riddled with smaller rooms housing quite different altars, which break all the Daoists' principles of organization. Most of them are small, incense-stained images or crude paintings moved in from elsewhere, and many of them are duplicates of deities that appear on the main altars (see figure 3.2). All of these altars belong to incense heads and in most cases represent deities that were housed in their old village temples. The Daoists are not very happy about these spaces, but they have compromised because if the incense heads do not bring people to the temple, then no one at all is likely to come.

These altars continue to attract followers of the incense leaders who construct them, which for now means mostly the residents of the destroyed villages. These groups become realized in other contexts as well—for example, in dragon dancing or something more like "ballroom" dancing (*guangchang wu* 广场舞) teams who perform in the temple under the leadership of these same incense heads. That is, even though the Daoists have consistently undercut the old local social structures in their standardization of the temple, the old bits of continuous time—of reproduction of local identity through shared altars and performances—still continue.

This is not to suggest, however, that nothing has changed in this respect for the villagers. Throwing the yin world into chaos means in part that the incense leaders are competing in quite new ways. For instance, even though the Daoists claim that the deities on their altars have been placed in no particular order, the local people conceive of temple space as always hierarchical, and they argue for better space for their own deities. One such event happened on Guanyin's birthday in 2016, when the temple was quite crowded. In the basement area where the Buddhist images have been exiled, a middle-aged woman was suddenly possessed by the Tathagata (*rulai fo* 如来佛, a reference to the historical Buddha), whose image was directly behind her. She/he began to sing (in the

Figure 3.2. Unofficial altar in the Suiliang Wang temple (author photograph)

fashion typical for spirit mediums in the region), but in a rather angry voice. "I am the Buddha! Why am I down in the basement? I am far more important than those little locality gods [*tudi shen* 土地神]. Why am I down here while they are up in the light?" The medium was eventually talked down, and the Buddha's demand to be moved was let go, at least for the moment.

In other cases, incense heads have fought over the more desirable spaces for their personal altars in the temple—not coming to blows (to my knowledge) but occasionally enlisting some threatening thugs. This happened, for instance, when a successful incense head discovered some images from one of his competitors in his altar space. He was convinced that the Daoists had been bribed to allow this and so organized some young toughs to threaten them. The situation was ultimately mediated without violence, and the images were removed. The lack of fit between the old, very local-based temples and the new, urban temple has created this new space of competition. Much the same happens in the apartment complexes, where an ambitious spirit medium can now easily poach the clients of mediums who once had their own relatively safe village turfs. That is, the annihilation of the villages as physical spaces has deep implications for how their deities can foster both social worlds and communities of memory.

In the terms I have been using here, time has taken on new emergent properties by undergoing what we might think of as a phase transition. Agricultural time, around which the ritual life of temples and the personal lives of farmers were organized, has suddenly become irrelevant with the paving over of the entire region. The transformation of space is even more obvious, although we should remember that it really also represents another transition in time, between the agricultural space of the past and the urban space of the present. Those disappeared physical spaces of fields and canals, of private houses and village temples, fostered the continuous time of memory in a way that has now been broken.

Spirit mediums are one way that people are filling the gap created by these transitions. Many of the spirit mediums report that the numbers of people getting possessed have increased twice in living memory: during the early years of the Cultural Revolution in the late 1960s, and during the village destruction and resettlement of the past decade or so. The reasons were the same both times. The gods, as people described it, had no more homes, because temples had been destroyed on a large scale. The gods thus had no choice but to take people's bodies. In this area with a long history of temple destruction, it is perhaps no surprise that spirit mediums are able to step quickly into the breach.

It might be tempting to think of those mediums as reservoirs of social memory, who are able to reconstruct continuous time when temples are destroyed. Instead, however, it may be more useful to think of them as potential agents of change who thrive most exactly at periods of emergence. All spirit mediums are potentially capable of radical innovation, because they speak directly with the voice and authority of the gods. And unlike the situation in some other parts of China, mediums here are eager to claim that their powers come because the gods have chosen them personally. They say that one cannot learn to do this from parents or family traditions, cannot disciple oneself to a master, and cannot undergo the kinds of formalized training we see elsewhere in China. In this region in particular, mediums thus imagine themselves as resisting pressures toward institutionalization. Here, knowledge is constructed as flowing directly and only from the deities, which makes it easy to innovate away from past practices.

Before the twenty-first century, we could see how the system of very localized temples and deities was reconstructed, albeit with changes, after periods of destruction. This time is surely different, however. People's physical villages, graves, and temples have been destroyed before, but this is the first time that the village as a way of life has been destroyed. The emergent time and space are interacting with patterns of religious life, but it is far too early to see clearly how things will end up. It is difficult to imagine that the locality-based forms of earlier worship can be reconstructed, but it seems equally unlikely that the urban planners' version of religion will fully succeed either. For now, we have a space of innovation and flux—chaos in the yin world—so that future patterns for the flow of knowledge and the crafting of identity are not yet clear, and new variations pop up continually.

Conclusion

"Repetition exists," wrote Gabriel de Tarde, "for the sake of variation" (1903: 7). That is, the very acts of transmitting and reproducing knowledge generate change. Seen this way, we should no longer feel surprised or frustrated by the huge amounts of variation we see in a place like China or even in tiny groups deep in the mountains of New Guinea. We have normally tried to understand these processes in China as questions of variation over space or social position. We have always known, however, that such broad-brush variants barely scratch the surface of what we can see in a place where villagers often delight in pointing to how different they are from the village next door. Here, following Fredrik Barth loosely and from well behind, I have tried to suggest that looking at questions of transmission over time may provide a useful supplement to such approaches. Repeating "the same" ritual or building "the same" temple is never a simple reproduction, but is itself an engine of change. "Imitation," after all, "is generation at a distance" (Tarde 1903: 34).

I have suggested that there are multiple ways in which people can understand these processes of transmission over time and that each has somewhat different implications for how people form group identities. Claims of continuous time foster communities of memory and clearly bounded groups; claims of folded time can instead allow certain kinds of boundary crossing; and claims of emergent time open up possibilities for a more radical reimagining of identity. Note, however, that emergent time is not the only way to generate variation. Because imitation or reproduction is never perfectly mechanical, each kind of time fosters variation.

These notions of how knowledge (in its broadest sense) can move over time are not given in the nature of the transaction, but always have the potential to be negotiated, and this process can create further variation. Both the examples I have discussed involve the interplay of different frames for conceptualizing knowledge transmission over time, and both are actively producing new religious variants. Tianhou's birthday in Nanjing involved an implicit argument between continuous and folded time, and thus about shifting identity. So far at least, it has done little to accomplish its political goal of attracting Taiwanese businesspeople, but it has led to innovation in Nanjing's religion, not least including the opening of the two Tianhou temples and the invention of a ritual to accompany the birthday, quite different from the traditions in Taiwan. The more radical disruptions of the yin world in chaos in Suzhou still include a kind of dialogue with the older traditions of continuous and folded time that had centered on village-based practice. With the villages gone, however, there can be no simple reproduction of the old practices transferred to the new temple. A new and less localized form of practice is being made through an unexpected and indirect dialogue between urban planners and spirit mediums. It seems likely to continue to generate new variants, at least until some point when the yin world has returned to some kind of order.

Cosmologies are always in the making. Looked at through the lens of Barth's anthropology of knowledge and his emphasis on generation through transmission, we can no longer be surprised to find the high levels of variation that exist even in a place like China that had significant political and cultural pressures toward standardization. The Ok, as he describes them, are thus not really unusual in their constant remaking of the cosmology. Our job as anthropologists, which he does so clearly in his later books, is not just to clear the theoretical space to let us see these processes, but to understand the socially, historically, and politically unique situations that shape such remaking for particular people, places, and times. I have tried here to provide the beginnings of a rough sketch of what such an analysis might look like for parts of Chinese life.

Robert P. Weller is Professor of Anthropology at Boston University. Most of his work concentrates on Chinese societies in a comparative context. His early work began with the problem of religious meaning and authority. His most recent book is *How Things Count as the Same: Memory, Mimesis, and Metaphor*, co-authored with Adam Seligman (Oxford University Press, 2019). He is currently working on urbanization and religious change.

Notes

1. I am grateful to the Guggenheim Foundation and the Fulbright Program, for grants that enabled me to pursue the research in Nanjing, and to Nanjing University, which made most of the Suzhou research possible. Thanks also to Keping Wu, who has been a universal sounding board and a research partner for the Suzhou portion of the research, and to Merav Shohet for a generous reading of an early draft.
2. The standardization discussion itself harks back to the much earlier work of M. N. Srinivas (1956) on "Sanskritization," which was a way of thinking about similar problems of variation in India.
3. For a related analysis, see Seligman and Weller (2019).
4. Unlike the concept of cyclical time, which appears more commonly in the anthropological literature, the idea of folding insists less on symmetry and more on variety in how things can be folded.
5. For reasons of space, I will not try to develop each of these three modes in more detail here. A related and more nuanced discussion appears in Weller and Seligman (2014).
6. See also the map redrawn from Cheng (1955) in Tufte (1990: 76).
7. Chipman (2009) attributes this change especially to improved transport, wealth, and media promotion, although a sense of general Taiwanese identity in relation to the mainland is also part of the picture.
8. The "Daoist" Tianhou temple in Nanjing had historically been the base for the Fujian association (*huiguan* 会馆), but was no longer serving that function at all, and indeed seemed to have little public support from any group.
9. Suzhou may have done this more than other areas in part to avoid having temples become centers for protest against urbanization, as has sometimes happened in other parts of China. The policy speaks as well to the flexibility of the Religious Affairs Bureau in Suzhou and to the creative opportunism of some of the Daoist leadership.

10. The name means "the king who accompanied grain." He was supposedly an early official with responsibility for moving grain up the Grand Canal (which passes nearby) to the capital in Beijing. During a famine, according to the stories people tell, he diverted grain to feed the local people, even though it meant defying the rules. He was thus deified after his death.

References

Ahern, Emily M. 1973. *The Cult of the Dead in a Chinese Village*. Stanford, CA: Stanford University Press.

Assmann, Jan. 1995. "Collective Memory and Cultural Identity." Translated by John Czaplicka. *New German Critique*, April, 125–33.

Barth, Fredrik. 1987. *Cosmologies in the Making: A Generative Approach to Cultural Variation in Inner New Guinea*. Cambridge: Cambridge University Press.

———. 1993. *Balinese Worlds*. Chicago: University of Chicago Press.

Carrithers, Michael. 2000. "On Polytropy: Or the Natural Condition of Spiritual Cosmopolitanism in India: The Digambar Jain Case." *Modern Asian Studies* 34(4): 831–61.

Chang, Hsun. 2003. *Wenhua Mazu: Taiwan Mazu Xinyang Yanjiu Lunwenji*. Nankang, Taiwan: Institute of Ethnology, Academia Sinica.

Cheng, Dacheng. 1955. *Matsu Chuan*. Min su wen yi cong shu di 1 zhong.

Chipman, Elana. 2009. "The De-territorialization of Ritual Spheres in Contemporary Taiwan." *Asian Anthropology* 8 (September): 31–64.

Freedman, Maurice. 1974. "On the Sociological Study of Chinese Religion." In *Religion and Ritual in Chinese Society*, edited by Arthur P. Wolf, 19–42. Stanford, CA: Stanford University Press.

Geertz, Clifford. 1959. "Form and Variation in Balinese Village Structure." *American Anthropologist* 61(6): 991–1012.

Halbwachs, Maurice. 1980. *The Collective Memory*. Harper & Row.

Nguyen Ngoc Tho. 2016. "Mieu Tho Thien Hau Cua Nguoi Viet Vung Tay Nam Bo [Vietnamese Thien Hao Temples in the Mekong River Delta]." Paper presented at the conference on Economic Networks, Social Organizations, and Popular Culture in Vietnam, Vietnamese Academy of Social Sciences, Hanoi.

Seligman, Adam B., and Robert P. Weller. 2019. *How Things Count as the Same: Memory, Mimesis, and Metaphor*. New York: Oxford University Press.

Seligman, Adam B., Robert P. Weller, Michael J. Puett, and Bennett Simon. 2008. *Ritual and Its Consequences: An Essay on the Limits of Sincerity*. New York: Oxford University Press.

Skinner, George William. 1977. *The City in Late Imperial China*. Stanford, CA: Stanford University Press.

Srinivas, M. N. 1956. "A Note on Sanskritization and Westernization." *Far Eastern Quarterly* 15(4): 481–96.

Tarde, Gabriel de. 1903. *The Laws of Imitation*. Translated by Elsie Worthington Clews Parsons. New York: H. Holt.

Tufte, Edward R. 1990. *Envisioning Information*. Cheshire, CT: Graphics Press.

Watson, James L. 1985. "Standardizing the Gods: The Promotion of T'ien Hou ('Empress of Heaven') Along the South China Coast, 960–1960." In *Popular Culture in Late Imperial China*, 292–324. Berkeley: University of California Press.

Weller, Robert P. 1987. *Unities and Diversities in Chinese Religion*. Seattle: University of Washington Press.

———. 2013. "Chinese Communist Thought on Religious Diversity." In *Religious Diversity in Chinese Thought*, edited by Joachim Gentz and Perry Schmitt-Leukel, 171–86. New York: Palgrave-Macmillan.

Weller, Robert P., and Adam B. Seligman. 2014. "Pluralism and Chinese Religions: Constructing Social Worlds through Memory, Mimesis, and Metaphor." *Review of Religion and Chinese Society* 1: 29–47.

Wolf, Arthur P. 1974. Introduction to *Religion and Ritual in Chinese Society*, edited by Arthur P. Wolf, 1–18. Stanford, CA: Stanford University Press.

Zhang, Xiaojun 张小军. n.d. "天后北传与漕运贸易 : 一个文化资本的视角 [The northern spread of Tianhou and the water transport trade: A view from cultural capital]." Unpublished paper.

4

Building Infrastructure and
Making Boundaries in Southwest China

Keping Wu

Infrastructure seems to be the least obvious place to start thinking about Barth's relevance in today's anthropology because of his focus on "actual people doing actual things."[1] Yet, it is actually a straightforward one—infrastructure occupies space and organizes people's lives, thus creating boundaries and social organizations. Moreover, the building of new infrastructure involves the interaction of various stakeholders and sometimes transforms people's behaviors significantly (see, e.g., Anand 2011). During my fieldwork in Southwest China bordering Tibet and Myanmar, Barth's work was always on my mind, not only because it was a highly diverse region with astonishing variation both biologically and socially, but also because of changes that were happening daily in front of my eyes. How to grasp such changes and the individuals' world-making in the process? More importantly, I ask the same question Barth asks, "How might small but cumulative changes reshape the face of vast collective institutions?" (Barth 1987: 84).

Infrastructure building has been an ongoing reality and daily experience for the people in Southwest China for over a decade. As early as 2008, when I first entered upper Gongshan County[2] through the newly paved road that connected it to the provincial capital Kunming, I was shocked to see how much active construction there was in this seemingly remote and forgotten part of the world. It took me about twenty-four hours riding the bus from Kunming along the only road that was chiseled out from the formidable mountains, winding along the treacherous waters of the Nu River (literally meaning "angry river") to reach Bingzhongluo, the periodic market town that met every Tuesday. On this day, people of Nu, Lisu, Tibetan, and Dulong ethnic groups came from surrounding villages and shopped for daily necessities (often from Han and Bai merchants). Locals also sold their finds—a couple of mountain rats, a handful of truffles, a pile of matsutake mushrooms, and so on. The market was just one narrow street less than half a mile long. Old pictures from the 1980s and 1990s showed no multistory buildings and only a handful of shops. In 2014, the street has stretched to one and a half times its earlier length, with many buildings over four stories high, dotted with shops, hotels, and restaurants. Much of the infrastructure, however, is not built for the local people. Instead, it is built for tourists and traders to have better access to their resources. Hence, the easiest job for a local villager to find has been in the construction or service business.

The largest and most controversial infrastructure in upper Gongshan is the hydroelectric dam. Though the national plans of building thirteen giant dams on the Nu River were never carried out, over 80 percent of the branches of the Nu River is already dammed by less efficient small dams (Tilt 2014). This chapter, however, does not focus on this kind of infrastructure, for the simple reason that those dams have not closely and directly reorganized people's interrelations and interactions. Most of the smaller dams involve the relocation and compensation of several households only. The biggest dam-related relocation concerned the administrative village of Dimaluo. According to Liu Jianqiang, a long-term observer of environmental issues in Nujiang, the hydroelectric plant built in Dimaluo resulted in the relocation of about one hundred people to the New Socialist Countryside Housing that was built near the river banks.[3] Those individuals' lives were changed—many complained of the poor quality and unfriendliness of the housing—but the organization of the life in the region has not been affected. Therefore, not all infrastructure is the same. Only when infrastructure projects constitute "interactional events" (Barth 1987: 83) do they become significant in reshaping "the face of vast collective institutions."

My thesis is that the building of certain infrastructure leads to changes in actors' interactions, which has fortified ethnic and religious boundaries in the local context of a previously pluralistic area with fluid boundaries. Infrastructure is not just a concrete architectural blob. Instead, it shapes ways, especially the younger generation's ways, of seeing, experiencing, and interacting with the material and social world. It is world ordering.

Plastic Pluralism: Ethnic and Religious Diversity in Upper Gongshan

As oral history has it, the Nu were the "aborigines" in this land. The Tibetans came from the north to establish the first and only Tibetan Buddhist temple in Nujiang in the eighteenth century. Five Tibetan families came with the monks to serve their needs and intermarried with local Nu people. The Nu and Tibetans both proudly announce themselves to be the valley people. The Lisu were migrating people from the eastern part of the province, mainly Weixi County. They occupied mostly the higher mountains and practiced slash-and-burn agriculture. The Dulong were mostly native to the Dulong River valley, toward the northwestern part of Gongshan County; this area was shielded from the outside world by mountains that until recently were inaccessible over six months a year. They were also hill people and practiced hunting and gathering. Though there is one "Dulong village" in Bingzhongluo, individuals with Dulong origins live in many villages through migration and marriage.

Despite the government's promotion of tourism in branding a few villages to be exclusively "Nu" villages, intermarriages are very frequent, and most people are of mixed ethnic origins. This seems so obvious to local people that they do not even think it is worth mentioning. After three years of knowing my host family, my "Lisu" host mother randomly mentioned as chitchat, "My father is Lisu, and my mother is Han." She married a Bai schoolteacher (who changed his ethnicity to Han on his ID card after obtaining a formal education among other Han people), and her older son married a Nu woman. Two of her grandsons are registered as Nu. Another means of ethnic boundary crossing is through political campaigns. One Lisu family told me that their grandfather was a Dulong from the Dulong River. He accidently took up residence in one hilltop village in Bingzhongluo by chasing his hunting prey. However, the village leader was Lisu, and in a report to the local government during the late 1950s, he made everybody's ethnic identification to be Lisu. Since then their family has been identified as Lisu.

It is not so much the plasticity of ethnicity that is worth noting, but more people's attitudes toward it. Though ethnic prejudices abound—the Lisu are supposedly drinkers and daughter-sellers (due to their high bride price), the Nu are considered slow and lazy, the Dulong not so clever, and the Tibetans fierce—those are "cultural intimacies" that never stop them from intermarrying or interacting with one another. One easily crosses over to the other side, even in the face of the hardest boundary, that between Han and other. I met an old blind man in a government-constructed nursing home. He played traditional Lisu tunes but spoke to me in Mandarin when he heard my broken Lisu. Curious that any Lisu of his age would speak Mandarin so well, I asked him where he had learned it. He replied, "Oh, my parents were Han soldiers on duty in this border region, so I grew up with Lisu neighbors in these villages. [That's why] I am Lisu." It turned out that he became blind when the neighborhood kids played tricks on him, the outsider, and it got out of hand. But it did not prevent him from identifying with the Lisu. The fluidity seems to go against the grain of most studies on ethnically diverse regions. Barth's seminal essay on ethnic groups and boundaries shifted our attention from cultural content to boundary-making as the ways ethnic groups come into being (1969). In the present case, it seems that ethnic boundaries have not been culturally significant in most instances. Nevertheless, these ethnic markers—Nu, Lisu, Tibetan, Dulong, and so on—become significant boundary-making *material* at "interactional events." And I will argue that the building of certain infrastructure such as roads has elicited boundary-making by invoking those previously nonsignificant cultural markers.

The second set of cultural markers employed locally to make boundaries is religion. People of all ethnic groups in upper Gongshan once practiced or have some knowledge of some form of animism. Each group had its own healer/ medicine man and its own spirits. However, with the arrival of institutionalized religions (Tibetan Buddhism in the eighteenth century, Catholicism in the late nineteenth century, and Protestantism in the early twentieth century) and political campaigns against superstition in the 1950s and 1960s,[4] the animistic practices are hard to find nowadays. The religious boundaries are less porous than ethnic ones, since each institutionalized religion comes with a corpus of texts, ideas, and practices that draw boundaries between the self and the other. However, local villagers find themselves crossing religious boundaries frequently too. The Protestants, for instance, are the most exclusive and individualistic. Their missionaries saw that drinking was a big problem in this region and decided that Protestants should not drink or smoke. This has become the most significant way one is identified as Protestant. If one starts drinking, one would become "embarrassed" to participate in any church services. Hence, that person is not considered a "Waku ma/pa" (literally, "a woman/man who sings," meaning, churchgoer or believer) any longer. However, if one stops drinking or smoking again, one is welcome to go back to the church anytime. In a rare case, if a family makes a living through entertaining tourists, it is only considered hospitable to drink with their guests. In one such family I know, the husband took up drinking (and thus quit going to the church), while the wife continued serving the church by not participating in the entertainment of the guests. The church leaders fully understand the difficulty and are confident that the husband will return to the church once he retires from serving the guests. Though not encouraged by church leaders, local people do go back and forth all the time without being discriminated against.

Marriage is one other way of crossing religious boundaries. Though marriages within the church are encouraged, most marriages do not happen within the church. There are numerous instances of changing one's religious affiliations to follow the husband's or wife's religious practices. There are almost no rules to this, except if one person is Catholic from one of the big Catholic families and wants a Catholic wedding, then it is usually the other person who will convert to Catholicism. In other cases, one marrying into the family would normally change one's religion to the religion of the family one is marrying into. But even that does not apply to all the situations. In an extreme case, one Lisu Christian woman from Myanmar married into a Buddhist household in an upper Gongshan village. She converted her husband to Christianity and raised her kids that way. Unfortunately, the mother-in-law was then diagnosed with stomach ulcers (probably from excessive drinking), and she blamed the daughter-in-law for her disease, because she stopped the family from making offerings in the Buddhist temple. In a different scenario, a Christian woman married her brother's Buddhist friend and gradually stopped going to the church, since drinking and making alcoholic offerings to the temple was part of the family's daily routine. Though her brother is church leader, he does not blame his sister, and the families remain very close.

Thus, marriages create webs of connections that cut across ethnic and religious boundaries, making it hard to divide the people up according to one standard. In most rituals of weddings, funerals, childbirth, and house construction, families and neighbors are required to contribute their labor, despite their ethnic or religious differences. In most rituals I went to, Protestants were given soda or tea instead of alcohol (and they were not given food with animal blood in it), but they were never excluded from such collective activities. Friendships between people of different religious backgrounds were frequent, especially among the younger generation, who found companionship in one another when they took up migrant work in the cities. Like ethnic markers, religious markers are not significant in people's daily interactions and only become available as material of differentiation when situations arise. Local lives have until recently been completely intertwined along those lines, crossing boundaries at ease, but changes are happening right before our eyes, and ethnic and religious identities are now more frequently brought up as significant boundary-making and group-differentiating markers.

In the following pages, I will demonstrate how infrastructure fosters different kinds of interactions among individuals, producing consequences that are unintended by the governments that initiated and sponsored those projects. Like Barth, I will pay attention to the context and to individuals "embedded in social relations engaged in producing his particular expression or representation" (Barth 1987: 87). In other words, the unintended consequences of infrastructure must be analyzed in the local context through individuals in relationships to one another.

Roads to Tibet: Boundary-Making through Connection

Consider the recent complaint of a Catholic Tibetan named Jose from a remote village in Nujiang Prefecture of Southwest China:

> When I lived in the big city of Beijing, sometimes officials would identify me among the crowds and demand to check my ID. At that time, I thought I had the looks of a bad guy. Now I am back to my hometown in the deepest mountains, but I am still stopped at the doorstep of my home for ID checks. I realize that my looks are not the issue. . . . From now on, I better carry my ID while drinking tea by the fire pit in my own house.[5]

Jose's home village Dimaluo is a critical point between Deqin County—the central part of Diqing Tibetan Autonomous Prefecture—and Gongshan

County, the Nu Autonomous County of Yunnan Province. Though it has a large Tibetan population, over half of the population in Dimaluo is Nu, with a small percentage of Lisu and Han people.[6] Due to the visibility of Tibetans (for reasons I will explain below), Dimaluo has acquired an image of a "Tibetan village." Most Tibetans from Dimaluo are Catholics who have families from Deqin County. Jose belongs to the largest three Tibetan families in Dimaluo, and all three families maintain active kinship relations with families in Deqin.

Despite the close proximity between Dimaluo and Deqin, to go from one place to the other normally took two days in the treacherous paths of the Biluo Mountains. The hardest part is called the Peacock Pass. At 3,882 meters above sea level, the Peacock Pass is covered by snow year-round. Relying on horses and human power, this path is only accessible to locals who are familiar with the routes. For outsiders, the only route available is a 1,000-kilometer detour via Lijiang.

As part of the 2006 decision of the Yunnan provincial government to build "eight roads and one bridge" to promote tourism, the Deqin-Gongshan Road began construction in 2008. Though it was only ninety-five kilometers, it was one of the hardest roads to build due to the mountainous surroundings. By 2016, the road was "near completion" until a big snowstorm caused mudslides that destroyed the road near the Peacock Pass. By April 2018, the accessibility was still on and off depending on the snow situation.

Numerous roads to Tibet have been built since the entrance of the People's Liberation Army (PLA) in 1951; the Sichuan-Tibet, Qinghai-Tibet, Xinjiang-Tibet, and Yunnan-Tibet motorways are famous entryways to Tibet. The ultimate "road," however, is the 3,757-kilometer railroad that connects Beijing and Lhasa. Since its completion in 2006, it has brought more people and goods to and from Tibet than at any other time in history. Yongming Zhou (2010: 72–73) characterizes three stages of Sino-Tibetan road construction. The first stage was in the 1950s and 1960s, when roads were built to connect Tibet with central China and other ethnic minority regions as ways of nation building. In the 1970s and 1980s, roads served as channels of both civilizing projects and natural resource extraction from Tibet. The third stage was after the 1990s, when ethnic tourism became the main developmental strategy of Tibet and roads became part and parcel of the central planning of a regional transportation network salient (conceivably) to economic globalization. The Deqin-Gongshan Road is definitely the result of an imagined network that is meant to enhance economic development in the region. Roads, however, have unintended consequences.

Criticisms of these roads often highlight environmental damage, destruction of ethnic culture, and draining of resources in Tibet. The consequences of the roads on ethnic relations on the local level are, however, under-examined. The Deqin-Gongshan Road provides an opportunity to examine the subtle changes it brings to the interactions of local people affected by the road. Besides an obvious sense of "developmentalist rhetoric" (Joniak-Lüthi 2016: 119), the state also foresees ethnic integration in the planning of those roads (Juean et al. 2010). I argue, however, that the roads, as symbols of communication and exchange, have become a mechanism of boundary-making processes between the two ends that it tries to connect. In other words, the roads separate more than integrate.

"Infrastructures are built networks that facilitate the flow of goods, people, or ideas and allow for their exchange over space" (Larkin 2013: 328). All the roads connected to Tibet are important channels through which "goods, people, or ideas" flow. The number of tourists exceeded the entire population of Tibet for the first time in 2007, one year after the completion of the Qinghai-Tibet Railway. On the other hand, "Tibetan peasants did not benefit from the tourist development," and some Tibetans feel that "Lhasa feels like a little town outside of Chengdu" (Juean et al. 2010: 32–25). Similarly, in Xinjiang, "new roads increase connectivity, as well as the circulation of *some* people, *some* goods and *some* capital" (Joniak-Lüthi 2016: 120). Therefore, there is often inequality in this flow, and the "exchange over space" is unbalanced. The Deqin-Gongshan Road is another example of this unbalanced exchange. This unbalanced exchange is not just experienced in economic aspects of life,[7] but has more dire consequences in the area of ideas. Roads are infrastructure that are "matter that enable the movement of other matter" (Larkin 2013: 329). The Deqin-Gongshan Road not only enables the movement of "other matter" such as tourists and goods, people and capital, and concepts such as "civilization" and "modernity," but also ideas of "us versus them."

One of the key sites of contestation is the checkpoint. A regular sight in China's borderlands, checkpoints come with roads and become markers of state power. When I inquired, the local government officials adopted the usual discourse of "maintaining stability" (*weiwen* 维稳) to justify the installation of three checkpoints around March 2017 within Gongshan County. All of them are along newly constructed roads: one by the Gaoligongshan Tunnel toward Dulong Autonomous Township (recently completed); one close to the Myanmar border; one at Qiunatong, the last village before the Tibetan border and the beginning of the 280-kilometer "New Yunnan-Tibetan Road";[8] and one at Dimaluo, at beginning of the Deqin-Gongshan Road. Before March 2017, there were only two major checkpoints: one in Huaqiaoba, upon entering Nujiang Prefecture, which is considered "a border region," and the other one 330 kilometers away in Chawalong Township, the first entry point into Tibet and the township after Qiunatong. The close proximity of two of the three recently installed checkpoints to Tibet marks the making of an internal border, with all its tensions. The Tibetan border shows both religious and ethnic complications, which have now become historically enduring and politically sensitive.

Two months after his first WeChat post about checkpoints, Jose posted another WeChat moment, this time about selling his house in Dimaluo. He cited reasons of "unbearable inconvenience" and the "feeling of living in a prison" that the checkpoints have caused him. Jose might be a bit extreme in his outspokenness, but his feelings were shared among Tibetans living in the same village: the fact that there was a checkpoint has something to do with them being Tibetans.

Non-Tibetans from other villages thought that the government put those checkpoints near Dimaluo because those Tibetans were greedy and unruly: "They need to show some color to those Tibetans [*gei dian yanse kankan* 给点颜色看看], because the Tibetans are too fierce [*lihai* 厉害]." "Showing some color" is to deter someone. *Lihai* in Chinese can be both positive and negative, meaning powerful and capable or fierce and not easily appeased. The Tibetans, being the dominant group in this area, were thought both positively to be the capable and "culturally advanced" group (i.e., emulated) and negatively as fierce and intimidating (and therefore feared and avoided). However, as shown in the aforementioned narrative, the latter discourse has come to dominate in recent years.

Before the construction of this road, a hydroelectric plant was built on the Dimaluo River. Villagers were compensated by the size of the land they gave up for the power plant. One plot of land that was previously unclaimed came under dispute. An armed feud took place between two factions in the village, among mostly all Tibetan villagers. This feud ended with many wounded bodies and the arrival of the local police. This event reinforced the perception of the fierceness of the "Tibetans from Dimaluo" by both the government and the people around them. One day a Tibetan from Dimaluo was taking me to see a remote village high up in the mountains where one could see the construction of the Deqin-Gongshan Road at work. As we were walking down the Dimaluo River, we saw a man coming toward us. Pointing at him, the Tibetan friend said to me, "Look at him! That's a Lisu. Look how he is dressed—adorned with a Tibetan hat and Tibetan dress, trying to be like us. They [the Lisu] can try all they want—speaking Tibetan, drinking yak butter tea, and eating *Zanba* [糌粑, a typical Tibetan food made with barley flour], but they can never be us, because we are fierce!" The boundary between a Tibetan and a non-Tibetan, according to this Tibetan, is not relevant to language, clothing, or cultural habits, but hinged upon how fierce one is. Both sides thus augment this "Tibetan" characteristic of fierceness.

The boundary this man tries to maintain, however, was hardly as fixed as imagined today. Instead, it was much more porous than my friend would like to claim. I was invited to a Tibetan family for a meal of wild mountain rats one day. During the meal, I was introduced to the oldest man in the family. Because he worked for horse caravans and traveled around when he was young, he was esteemed as one of the most learned men in the area. Toward the end of the meal, I asked him about the family history, expecting the same story about migration from Deqin. To my surprise, he winked at me and said:

> None of us are "real" Tibetans. In the old times, the Tibetans were powerful. They were landowners and took slaves. Many Nu were slaves. Others scrambled to live

at the margins of the Tibetans. Then, the Nu learned to speak Tibetan, eat like them, dress like them. [We were the descendants of those Nu.] When outsiders came, they thought we were Tibetans and were afraid of us. Some of us gradually passed as Tibetans and even married Tibetan women. So, we became Tibetan. . . . We still know this because when we were still Nu, we were not allowed to hunt in the Tibetan land. Some Nu came here [to the Dimaluo area]. It was close to Tibetan territory but not owned by anybody yet at that time. The Nu brought buckwheat seeds and planted them while they hunted. So, next time they came back, there would be buckwheat waiting for them. They don't have to carry so much food while hunting. This is why there are still buckwheat fields here.

Later he revealed to me that it was a common practice: "During the horse caravan days on the Tea Horse Road, many Nu people worked for the horse caravans whose owners were often Tibetans.[9] After living with the Tibetans days and nights for years on the road, they just become indistinguishable from each other. So, they become Tibetans too." Like the Basseri who became peasants with the change of their economic situation (Barth 1961), the Nu became Tibetan when they adopted the Tibetan livelihood. Though the crossing of ethnic boundaries did not challenge the ethnic categorization system, it provided a basis for flexibility and creativity for individuals. However, the space for this kind of fluidity is shrinking through the construction of roads, checkpoints, and many other changes. The boundaries between a Tibetan and the other have become more fortified.

Since the beginning of the Deqin-Gongshan Road construction, many Dimaluo families have tried to raise the price of compensation they receive by various protests. Their fierce reputation has also earned them much leverage. Other villagers from Gongshan believe that Tibetans got unjustifiably rich from the compensation because the Tibetans were good at ganging up and making trouble (*naoshi* 闹事). A Lisu woman from a neighboring village said, "Those Tibetans are lucky to get so much compensation for their land. Our land is still worth nothing. But we are not as fierce as the Tibetans. If their needs are not met, they will gang up and make trouble. Even the government officials are afraid of them." Indeed, many Tibetans used the compensation money to buy a motorcycle, a car, or a house in the market town. This kind of "conspicuous consumption" confirmed the perceived profits Tibetans have received and their power, though the money hardly lasts them long enough. Many of their young men died from motorcycle accidents and heavy drinking. The Tibetans are far from simply being beneficiaries of the road construction.

With the construction of the road, more village land has been cashed out. One villager, who spent years investigating and planning the cultivation of medicinal plants on his family land to generate income, had to give up that idea, since the road went through his family land. Though the compensation was considered hefty by local standards, it was not sustainable. Entrepreneurial as he was, the only way he could conceive of was to use this money to invest in a hostel. But since the tourist flow was relatively small and was getting smaller due to the construction of the road, building a hostel in the village was not worthwhile any more. In addition to the land the actual road has now taken over, much farmland has been rendered useless during the construction. Another villager asked me to write an appeal letter to the local government asking for compensation for his land that was not used by the road (hence not compensated) but ruined by the construction team's recklessness. Furthermore, many villagers complained that the mudslides caused by the construction washed out their crops, but nobody was compensated for that loss. Despite all the rumors of Tibetan aggression in getting compensation, this was a losing game for the villagers across the board. Even though some villagers who had ties with local government officials seemed to be well compensated, the money went quickly, without sustainable ways of making a living. Therefore, feelings of resentment flew high. With the installation of checkpoints, both well- and under-compensated families felt that they were exploited and terrorized because of their ethnic identity.

"It's just because we are Tibetans!" one villager exclaimed. "They do that to all of us Tibetans. They single us out and check us everywhere. I was denied a hotel in Kunming after the '314 event' because my ID read Tibetan.[10] Now the checkpoints are at our doorstep. Who knows what they are going to do [to us] next!" Another Tibetan villager who has a milder attitude told me how the road destroyed a sacred forest in the Biluo Mountains: "There is a part of the forest where the Tibetans from Deqin go for celebrations. That forest is sacred for the Buddhists, and there are many beautiful Buddhist flags hanging around the trees there. It is very important to us Tibetan people." "But you are a Catholic!" I asked. "Yes, but we are all Tibetans," he answered. Many Tibetans from Dimaluo consider Deqin to represent more authentic Tibetan-ness. The road shifted the allegiance from a location-centered Bingzhongluo identity to an ethnicity-centered "Tibetan solidarity" with the rest of the Tibetan world.

Consequently, the ease of ethnic boundary crossing in the past was getting increasingly difficult today. A schoolteacher of Nu ethnic identification introduced me to his family, who were quite entrepreneurial. They operated a small store in the village, selling daily necessities. Soon, they expanded their business to town and opened a restaurant there. In many ways, they were like the Tibetans in town—operating their own business, fluent in Tibetan, and even converted to Catholicism. The owner of the restaurant, father of the schoolteacher, told me:

> My older son married a Tibetan woman from Dimaluo. She introduced us to the [Catholic] church. We went a few times and thought it was good. Then we converted to Catholicism. The Tibetans at the church also helped us with the setting up of the business. We are very grateful. We have a lot to learn from them.

However, when I asked if they could become Tibetan, he smiled and said, "No. Becoming Catholic is one thing, becoming Tibetan is another." When I asked some Tibetan friends if this family would be considered Tibetan someday, they vehemently denied it: "No they are Nu. We are Tibetan. Although they are hardworking Nu and learned a lot from us, we Tibetans are fierce."

The construction of roads is certainly not the only factor that has led to this solidification of ethnic boundaries. However, as an important form of infrastructure, the roads' impact on the ways ethnic groups interact is clearly observable during a very short period of time. If the old road, the Tea Horse Road, which transported goods by horse caravans, served as a channel of ethnic interchange, the new road, which transports goods by cars, impedes it. What leads to this difference? A crude answer would go as follows: Roads can be both a channel of connectivity and a concrete form of state power. The Tea Horse Road was a network of paths that were developed primarily by its local users who relied on it. The current roads, however, are state projects that benefit outsiders more than the people who live by the roads. Though one can argue that the Tea Horse Road was probably in the hands of powerful merchants or elites, it was still an organic part of the local society. The new road, on the other hand, is a pure insertion of state power that is external to local life. That results in the boundary-making instead of its previous boundary-crossing role. However, this argument does not explain *how* state involvement produces hardened boundaries.

Here is when a Barthian perspective that is process-oriented and local context-specific bears more fruit. The context of the road construction is one in which the entire country of China is going through an infrastructure building craze in the name of modernization and development. This craze is mainly state initiated and often involves forced relocation and imbalanced compensation (see Ho 2015). In addition, the specific processes through which those roads are built in Bingzhongluo, a "border town," result in shifting power relations among various groups vis-à-vis the Tibetans. First, many Tibetan families happen to be the ones that are compensated with cash, the amount of which is considerable by local standards. Second, however, the roads come with checkpoints that mean tightened control of local residents, especially Tibetans. Third, the particular history and unrest in the past decades have rendered the ethnic category of "Tibetan" a politically sensitive one. The combination of those conditions led to the Tibetans being singled out and treated with envy and fear by other groups. Therefore, like Todorov's infrastructure that trains "subjects in a particular relationship to state power" (Todorov 1994: 10), the roads constructed here have unintended consequences of producing subversive relationships to the state, even as they sharpen ethnic boundaries.

Basketball Courts: Boundary-Making through Association

On Christmas eve 2008, I was invited to attend celebrations in the Catholic church in Zhongding hamlet, part of Jiasheng village. After a short service inside the church, everyone moved to the courtyard, where a big bonfire was built. Others—villagers and tourists, Catholics, Buddhists, and nonbelievers alike—started filling the courtyard. In what appeared to be a basketball court, people danced, sang, and drank all night long. Later I found out that this was nothing special. During six years of research in the upper Gongshan region, we have celebrated numerous occasions on the basketball courts: Peach Blossom Festivals,[11] Fair Lady Festivals,[12] Chinese New Year, Chongyang Festivals,[13] and so on. Many couples have come to know each other on the basketball courts during those occasions and subsequently gotten married. Moreover, important political events also take place there, such as village elections, political mobilization meetings, and policy briefs. The basketball courts are thus not just for playing basketball. They are also important sites of public events and the material setting in which many *interactions* among people take place.

If the roads sharpen ethnic boundaries through connection, basketball courts have come to solidify religious boundaries though association. Through different ways of associating with various forms of authorities, it forges power relations among them. Basketball courts have gone through stages of development. Due to the limited amount of flatland in this mountainous region, basketball is one of the most popular sports among the village youths. In the 1980s only schools had basketball courts. When village schools were replaced by centralized schools in town, the old village schools and their basketball courts ceased to be in use, but many young people still played the game in the deserted schools. In the late 1990s and early 2000s, a few Catholic churches were rebuilt. Some young people took the old school basketball poles and installed them inside the church courtyard to provide easy access to entertainment in their spare time. Though some church elders complained about using church space as a sports facility, these simple basketball courts provided much entertainment to Catholics and non-Catholics alike.

An interesting turn of events occurred when the local government started building basketball courts in the villages outside of the churches in the name of promoting "healthy competition and stronger bodies" in the mid to late 2000s. Local government-sponsored festivals also include basketball competitions among villages, in addition to singing, dancing, and weaving performances. Each village is required to put together a basketball team that competes with other villages. The final game in the township elementary school basketball court normally marks the finale of the festivities.

When I spoke with the township government officials about the basketball courts, they were clear about the government's role in "cultural and sports affairs" (*wen ti shiye* 文体事业), and the basketball courts were part of their effort to "improve the quality of cultural life" and "build up stronger and healthier bodies" (*qiang shen jian ti* 强身健体). Sports and a certain kind of body produced by sports have been an important concern in the nation-building process of modern China (Brownell 1995). In contemporary China, recreational sports facilities installed in many communities are seen as forms of cultural governance (Oakes 2017). In other parts of the world, for instance, sports have been related to forms of development, such as a kind of investment in tourism in Poland (Hadzik and Małgorzata 2014) or as "institutionalized notions of modernity" in the Solomon Islands (Mountjoy 2014: 326). In this context, encouraging sports competition among ethnic minorities is an important form of "civilizing projects" (Harrell 1994) by the state. The infrastructure that comes with sports is thus a state apparatus to govern ethnic minority bodies. The financing and placing of these sports infrastructures reveal crucial decision-making processes but, in this case, yielded unintended consequences.

"Cultural and sports facilities should benefit everybody," one village cadre explained when I asked him why the township government spent money on building basketball courts. He continued, "The government thought it was inappropriate [*bu heshi* 不合适] that basketball courts were all inside churches." As a result, many township governments financed and built "public" basketball courts in the mid-2000s. The location of these basketball courts was strategically planned. Often they were built either next to the village government office (*cun wei hui* 村委会) or next to a Buddhist stupa, where villagers gather during festivals. Among the four villages in Bingzhongluo township,[14] every village government office now has a basketball court built next to it. Take Qiunatong village as an example. One of the hilliest villages, Qiunatong is the last stop before reaching the Tibetan border. There are about nine hamlets in the village. In the mid-1990s, a Catholic church dating back to the late nineteenth century was rebuilt in one of the hamlets. The young people converted the open flat space in front of the church into a basketball court, using deserted basketball poles from the local school that was no longer in use. It has since then become the meeting point and gathering space for all the major village affairs, festivals, and even meetings called upon by the local government to disseminate official messages. In 2006, the village committee was given a sum of money to rebuild a basketball court as part of the cultural and sports program. This time, the village government chose the open space right next to it to be the location of the "official" basketball court. However, this has never fully become the preferred meeting place for the villagers, since the majority villagers, being Catholic, still find it convenient to gather near the basketball court outside of the church.

A similar story took place in Jiasheng village. In 1996, a famous Catholic church was rebuilt in the Zhongding hamlet (part of Jiasheng village), and two basketball poles were installed on both sides of the courtyard, without accurate dimensions measured out. This provided the only space for the young people of the surrounding villages to play their favorite sports. As mentioned in the beginning of the section, even non-Catholics come to celebrations in this basketball court. Wuli hamlet, about seven kilometers away, got subsidies from the township government to build their own basketball court in 2006. It was built next to the Buddhist stupa, where villagers gather for important holidays, including Buddhist and non-Buddhist festivals. In Bingzhongluo village, half of the hamlets built their basketball courts near Buddhist stupas, because people have gotten used to gather around the stupas for festivities, and there is often flat space right next to it.

The location of basketball courts brings unintended consequences. First of all, Protestants are isolated from the center of power as a result of such infrastructure building despite the fact that Protestants are about 20–30 percent of the population. Very few Protestant churches were able to afford a space for basketball courts. Though there are seven Protestant churches in the township, only two of them have a basketball courts adjacent to them. However, neither of them are gathering places for the entire village. One of them has a closed courtyard that makes the basketball court not accessible by non-Protestants. The village government built another court next to its office as the meeting point for the villagers. The other one is in a tiny hamlet that is quite isolated. Originally called Leprosy Village (*mafeng cun* 麻风村), this hamlet was used as a quarantine place for people with leprosy. Gradually the survivors and their offspring formed this hamlet. Now it is part of the Bingzhongluo administrative village. When I talked to the young men playing basketball there, they said, "We don't celebrate holidays here. We go to the adjacent village. They have a bigger basketball court, next to the stupa." The basketball courts, therefore, are associated with the center of power and village life. The Protestants, however, are sidelined from this power center because they are separated from the basketball courts, the sites of both abstract state power and concrete political message distribution. As a result, Protestants became the least visible group in the villages.

The second unintended consequence of basketball courts involves the symbolic power given to Buddhist spaces. Though there is only one Buddhist temple in the township, there are many white stupas scattered in the villages, demonstrating the influence of Tibetan Buddhism in this region. The Buddhist temple Puhua Si, the Temple of Universal Salvation, has been undergoing recovery, renovation, and reconstruction since the 1990s, heavily subsidized by the provincial and prefecture government, especially the tourism department. However, it does not mean that the government promotes "Buddhism" or "Tibetan Buddhism" in any explicit way. Buddhist temples in other parts of China are also important tourist sites, providing significant revenue for the government. The building of basketball courts around Buddhist stupas is purely an accident—normally the stupas are built in a location with some flat land that would provide space for holiday gatherings and some worship services. Therefore, it seemed logical to build a basketball court there without sacrificing other flat land, such as farmland or land for housing. As previously emphasized, the basketball courts not only are used for recreational purposes but are imbued with political power, since it is the center of village political life and state presence. Consequently, the building of basketball courts next to Buddhist stupas associates the stupas with the political center of the village and accidently provides legitimacy for Buddhism in the local context.

There are two unintended consequences that result from building basketball courts. First, the location and usage of the basketball courts create a subtle shift of power relations away from religion to the state. Such a recreational sports infrastructure unintentionally draws boundaries between those spaces that were previously fuzzy: the Catholic church courtyard that was also used as a semi-public square became clearly separated from the nonreligious "public" that is designated by the state. Second, the association of such sports infrastructure as basketball courts to political and public life creates the context within which significant public interactions take place and establishes power relationships among various religious and political authorities. In due course, the Protestants were marginalized from political power and isolated from village public life. All of the unintended consequences result not from the infrastructure itself but from the *interactions* (Barth 1993) that happen among people in the public square. This draws our attention not only to the content of interactions (e.g., casual socialization, discussion of political decision-making) but also to the entire *context* in which the interactions take place. Every time people play basketball or gather at the basketball courts for important public events, a new world order is created. In this new world order, ways of associating and the corresponding power relations are established.

New Socialist Countryside (NSC) Housing Projects: Boundary-Making by Reorganization

The world-ordering of infrastructure is even more clearly shown in the case of the construction of the New Socialist Countryside (*shehuizhuyi xin nongcun* 社会主义新农村) housing. The "Building of New Socialist Countryside" is a slogan and policy that was introduced in 2005. Under Hu Jintao, this policy focused on rural infrastructure and housing projects (Looney 2015: 909–10). Translated into the local situation, especially for ethnic minority areas such as in the current study, this often means the building of paved roads within villages, construction of public bathrooms, and, most important of all, the building of new housing projects. The NSC housing is especially marked by its particular aesthetics—it is uniform, orderly, made of bricks and concrete, and (often) bright-colored. The village officials often emphasize one more important feature: the NSC housing separates living quarters for people and animals, posing a big contrast to traditional housing, which put humans and their animals in close contact. "That was very unsanitary and backward," the officials would emphasize. This reorganization of people's lives in order to promote modern standards of living is very much embedded in the entire NSC project.

The "Digital Countryside" project is part of Yunnan Province's effort in building the New Socialist Countryside.[15] Besides providing survey data on demography, infrastructure, and economy, every village in Bingzhongluo has posted pictures of its achievement in the NSC project. Not only are orderly organized rows of brick housing with metal windows showcased, but also the concrete paved roads, as well as the neat pig pens separated from spaces of human dwelling.

Von Schnitzler's (2016) study of the installation of water and electricity meters in South Africa demonstrates how such basic service infrastructure aims at creating a new kind of citizen—responsible, self-motivated, and rational, and yet the struggles of residents and activists against the constraints those meters impose suggest material ways of how democracy works. The NSC village housing certainly calls for a new kind of "peasant," who is orderly, sanitary, and modern. The ethnic minorities in China are especially characterized as dirty, disorganized, and backward/primitive. In contrast to the old (often Nu style[16]) wooden houses scattered randomly in the villages, the NSC housing neatly lines up the houses, installs paved roads, and separates the living quarters of human and animals. Instead of a traditional fire pit (for cooking and heating) and a sacrificial pole in the middle of the main room, the NSC housing has a kitchen area with a stove and no open fire. The living area is separated from the bedroom. The dirt floor is replaced by concrete. Furthermore, the Nu houses often had very low door frames and tiny windows to prevent unwelcome spirits from entering. The new houses, instead, have high door frames and big bright windows that have metal frames.

When the NSC housing was introduced to the region, villagers considered it completely undesirable, citing several reasons: (1) the houses have no fire pit, which is very important not only for cooking, socializing, and serving as the privileged space for family elders to sleep by, but also for ritual purposes related to the health and well-being of the family members; (2) the concrete floor is cold, and the big windows and door openings do not help; (3) the houses are too close to one another, so that if one family has an argument, everybody can hear it and that is very embarrassing; (4) it is inconvenient to feed the animals, since they are separated from the human living quarters; (5) the smell is bad because the garbage piles up everywhere, instead of being burned or buried by individual households in their backyards as was practiced before; (6) the houses are too close to the river (bringing the possibility of insects and infections) and too far from their farmland (which is often uphill). The list could go on. For the above-cited reasons, most villagers are unwilling to live in the NSC housing. It has been one of the hardest tasks for the local village cadres to persuade villagers, especially those who live higher up in the mountain, to move down to the water level. Many older people also refuse to move. In some cases, the earliest ones willing to move are the ones who lost their homes due to fire or natural disasters such as mudslides. However, in two of the four villages, something quite unexpected took place.

The Protestant church leaders in Nidadang (a hamlet in Qiunatong village) and Xingta (a hamlet in Jiasheng village) decided to mobilize their people to move to the NSC housing: "We Protestants do not drink or smoke, but other villagers do. It's more convenient if we all live together [in the NSC housing]."

When probed further, the church leader explained, "[If the Protestants all live together in the NSC housing], the young people will not be tempted to drink or smoke when their non-Protestant neighbors or relatives do." Furthermore, the Protestants do not mind the high door frames, big windows, and the lack of a fire pit, because they are not concerned with spirits and the religious functions of the house, as the other villagers are. Some other Protestant villagers told me that it was easier for Protestants to live together because they did not have many arguments in their families, and if they did, the church leaders would help them solve those problems. Therefore, for social and religious reasons, the Protestants were more willing to move to the NSC housing than the other villagers. In exchange for the cooperation from the Protestant community, the Nidadang village got permission to construct their own small church right next to the NSC housing. Though it was constructed on less desirable land by the water right next to the road, it was a good enough incentive for Protestants, especially the elderly members of the church, to move to NSC housing. The Xingta hamlet did not get this treatment because the nearby Dongfeng hamlet already has a church. It takes the villagers fifteen to twenty minutes to walk uphill to reach the church for services. After the Protestants moved into some of the NSC housing, some other villagers followed suit, though they tend to live in separate rows or clusters.

In both hamlets, the Protestants are proud to be good citizens. One township government leader commented, "In comparison to Protestants in other parts of China, the ones in our township are easy to manage [*hao guanli* 好管理]." This is not necessarily a compliment, but it explains the relatively tolerant control over religion, especially Protestantism, in this region. In a sense, Protestants are rewarded for being docile citizens. Protestant leaders often proudly remind me that the crime rate is next to zero in villages where there is a high percentage of Protestants, citing no drinking or smoking as the major reason. In villages where Protestants live with non-Protestants, furthermore, I have never heard of any conflict (based on religious difference) between those two groups during my six years of research in the region. Though there are more and more non-Protestants moving to the NSC housing when the old village becomes increasingly dilapidated due to the lack of people, a "Protestant versus non-Protestant rows/quarters" pattern now occurs within the villages, instead of the pluralistic living situation previously. In Nidadang, people were quick to point out which rows of housing were inhabited by Protestants. The neat rows create a visible line of division based on religious affiliation, especially between Protestant and non-Protestant, creating an interesting unintended consequence of the NSC housing in the specific local context.

In this religiously pluralistic region where the religious affiliation was not used as a primary index of division among people, therefore, the consequence is dire. In contrast to the fluid boundaries mentioned earlier between Protestants and non-Protestants, when the mere act of drinking can take a person from one side of the boundary to the other, the boundary crossing becomes much harder when they move into the NSC housing. If this fluidity was the social mechanism of loosening tension produced by the closely knit pluralistic society, this mechanism is now replaced by the increasing authority of religious leaders within the kind of community they intend to create. Some families where not all members are Protestant have to make a hard decision about whether they would move to the Protestant side of the NSC housing or not. Moving to either side draws boundaries within the families. It is quite common that the younger generation has converted, but the older generation kept the habit of drinking and smoking. It was not only acceptable but considered laudable for the Protestant and non-drinking children to make alcohol for their non-Protestant drinking parents. But when the question of moving to the new village arises, the older generation often prefer living by themselves in the old village, making it harder for their non-drinking Protestant children to take care of their drinking needs. A few others who have been frequent boundary crossers are also forced to make a commitment. One of them, Ade, told me, "Before, I would drink and feel embarrassed to go to the church. Then I would go back to the church when I was clean. Nobody made a fuss about it. Now that the pastor has persuaded me to move to the new village, where I am surrounded by the singing people [Wakupa, i.e., Protestants], drinking is not so good." I asked him if he has drunk since he moved to the new village. He told me, "I haven't. . . . Now I go to the church every time. I used to drink with my non-Protestant friends in the village, but now we do not hang out any more." These instances show that the unintended consequences of NSC housing have to do with the local context of previous pluralistic living and the fluidity of boundaries.[17] Such infrastructure results in the hardening of boundaries established by religious differences and among people through reorganization. Specifically, the NSC housing sharpens the boundaries between Protestants and non-Protestants through the reorganization of people and space, which leads to the further marginalization of Protestants.

Conclusion

This chapter has drawn attention to the unintended consequences of infrastructure in the context of a previously pluralistic region with very fluid boundaries. Contrary to the intention of all levels of government that initiated and sponsored those infrastructure projects, whose purposes include encouraging more ethnic integration, economic justice, and cultural pluralism, these concrete structures build "internal borders" of ethnicity and religion in this previously pluralistic region with plastic boundary-making mechanisms.

Previous studies on infrastructure (and related developmental projects especially in the ethnic minority regions) emphasize the presence of state power and the forceful insertion of the state into the most local level of the society and the intimate lives of individuals. This has definitely been the case for all three types of infrastructure I have mentioned above: the roads, the basketball courts and the NSC houses. Though Barth did not focus on large state societies such as China, his transactionalist model is nonetheless helpful here. Not only are those projects state-sponsored, but the state is also propagated as a patron of development in this process. If we regard the state as an actor (a powerful one at that) in the transactions, it can help us understand the process of knowledge making: the state, through all its local actors, dramatically transforms the ways of interaction among local groups by demonstrating its power through infrastructure building and inserting itself into the negotiations in the local context. No one else is capable of building at such a scale and speed. The roads, for instance, were financed by the central government and carried out by provincial government, constructed by Han companies with formidable machinery that produces infrastructure that is considered impossible by the local standard. The establishment of the checkpoints is just one other example of such demonstration of state power. The NSC is a national project, and its housing program that ambitiously provides such a large number of people with houses at almost no cost is itself a miracle. Even for the basketball courts, though the villagers were scrambling to recycle deserted ones and building their own, the ability of the local government to make it the center of social and political life cannot be matched by any single actor. By presenting itself as an indispensable and undisputable patron, the state is able to change the interactions among other actors, who are from various ethnic and religious groups.

Therefore, this chapter goes beyond the state-power analysis of infrastructure, by focusing on the less visible, unintended, and longer-term impact of such state insertion of power through the exercise of strategy making of the individuals. The three cases presented—roads, basketball courts, and NSC housing—though they are of different scale, come to represent three ways through which boundaries are made: connection, association, and reorganization. Each situation fosters different kinds of interactions between actors who are embedded within the local context, reshaping the lifeworlds they live in. These unintended consequences are far more intimate and transforming than the intended consequences the state or various levels of governments had in mind. As Barth remarks, "We need to focus on the communicative *consequences* of events" (1987: 78, emphasis his). Infrastructure projects in this local context have become the loci of such events, and their consequences may reshape the ethnic and religious relations among the people forever.

Keping Wu is Associate Professor at the Department of China Studies in Xi'an Jiaotong–Liverpool University. She held previous teaching and research positions at Sun Yat-sen University, National University of Singapore, and the Chinese University of Hong Kong. Her research interests are ethnic and religious diversity, urbanization, and gender. Her recent publication includes a coauthored book (with Robert Weller and C. Julia Huang), *Religious Charity: Social Life of Goodness in Chinese Societies* (Cambridge University Press, 2018).

Notes

1. I am grateful to the Chinese University of Hong Kong for providing initial funding for this research and to Professors Tan Chee-Beng and Yang Hui for providing guidance and support during the fieldwork.
2. Here I use "upper Gongshan" to include the northern tip of Gongshan Nu Autonomous County in the Nujiang Autonomous Prefecture in Northwest Yunnan Province, Southwest China. It includes the township of Bingzhongluo and the adjacent administrative village of Dimaluo. Though Dimaluo belongs to a different township (Pengdang) in Gongshan County, it has more interactions with the villages in Bingzhongluo through market, migration, and marriage. Due to its proximity to the Tibetan border, upper Gongshan also has a more Tibetan presence than the rest of the Gongshan Nu Autonomous County. In fact, the name Bingzhongluo is from Tibetan, meaning "a Tibetan village." Therefore, I analyze Bingzhongluo and Dimaluo together in this chapter and use the phrase "upper Gongshan" to refer to it.
3. Liu Jianqiang, "Nu River Lessons," Chinadialogue, 28 March 2007, https://www.chinadialogue.net/article/show/single/en/885-Nu-River-lessons (accessed 28 September 2017).
4. To this day, the villagers call it "doing superstition" when they engage in any healing practices based on animism.
5. Jose posted this complaint on his WeChat moments. WeChat is the most popular social medium in contemporary China.
6. According to the village record dated in 2010, there were 873 Tibetans, 1,050 Nu, 18 Han, and 168 in other ethnic groups, making up its total population of 2,109.
7. The research in both Tibet (Juean et al. 2010) and Yunnan (Zhang and Gao 2015) has shown that local people often do not benefit economically from the roads.
8. There has been an unpaved road from Qiunatong to Chawalong (a township in the Chayu County of Tibet). This road was very important for transporting matsutake and other Chinese medicinal herbs from Chawalong and commercial goods from Bingzhongluo to Chawalong. The construction of a paved 280-kilometer "New Yunnan-Tibetan Road" (*Dian Zang xin tongdao* 滇藏新通道) that starts from the village of Qiunatong began in May 2015 and by 30 March 2017, the 27 kilometers around Qiunatong was completed. This part alone cost 36.2 billion RMB (about 87.1 percent of the total construction). Upon completion, this road will be a three to four grade road.
9. The Tea Horse Road, or Chamagudao, refers to the paths among Tibet, Sichuan, Yunnan, and Guizhou and extended all the way to India from the tenth to the early twentieth century. It is sometimes referred to as the Southern Silk Road. The Tea Horse Road transported tea from Yunnan to Tibet and horses from Tibet to the rest of China, along with many other goods that were exchanged, including salt, medicinal plants, yak butter, gem stones, and so on.
10. The "314 event" refers to a riot that happened in Lhasa on 14 March 2008. This event led to the tightening of control of Tibetans in other parts of China.
11. A festival that involves the celebration of female and male deities that are supposedly indigenous to the Nu people during peach flower seasons on alternating years.
12. A local festival that involves worshipping in a sacred cave when azaleas are blossoming. Sometimes called Flower Festival (*xianhua jie* 鲜花节), the Fair Lady Festival (*xiannü jie* 仙女节) is now promoted as an official festival in the upper Gongshan Region.
13. A Chinese festival that pays respect to the elderly in society. The Society for the Elders (*laoren xiehui* 老人协会) is an official organization at the village level in China. It organizes group dancing parties and offers free drinks on the Chongyang Festival at the basketball courts in this region.
14. The four administrative villages are: Bingzhongluo, Shuangla, Jiasheng, and Qiunatong. Under those administrative villages, there are thirty-two hamlets.

15. The "Digital Countryside" project started in 2007, and in recent years the Yunnan provincial government invested over 5 million RMB to update and maintain it. It showcases the work of the NSC (http://www.ynszxc.gov.cn/S1/S1506/S1525/, accessed on 15 August 2017).
16. Despite the diversity of ethnic groups, most people adopt Nu style housing in this area. The Nu style housing is low and dark, made up of stacked logs with few windows. In the main room, there is usually a fire pit that is used for both cooking and heating and a middle pole (*zhong zhu* 中柱), which is considered one of the most important religious features of the house. On festivals, people gather and dance around the fire pit and the middle pole.
17. The NSC project is a nationwide campaign, and its manifestation and consequences are by no means the same everywhere. Emily Yeh (2013) has shown that the NSC housing creates an indebtedness that Tibetans owe the Chinese government, which expects loyalty in exchange.

References

Anand, Nikhil. 2011. "PRESSURE: The PoliTechnics of Water Supply in Mumbai." *Cultural Anthropology* 26(4): 542–64.

Barth, Fredrik. 1961. *Nomads of South Persia: The Basseri Tribe of the Khamseh Confederacy*. Boston: Little, Brown.

———. 1969. Introduction to *Ethnic Groups and Boundaries: The Social Organization of Culture Difference*, edited by Fredrik Barth. Boston: Little, Brown.

———. 1987. *Cosmologies in the Making: A Generative Approach to Cultural Variation in Inner New Guinea*. Cambridge: Cambridge University Press.

———. 1993. *Balinese Worlds*. Chicago: University of Chicago Press.

Brownell, Susan. 1995. *Training the Body for China: Sports in the Moral Order of the People's Republic*. Chicago: University of Chicago Press.

Hadzik, Andrzej, and Małgorzata Grabara. 2014. "Investments in Recreational and Sports Infrastructure as a Basis for the Development of Sports Tourism on the Example of Spa Municipalities." *Polish Journal of Sport and Tourism*, 21(2): 97–101.

Harrell, Steve. 1994. *Cultural Encounters on China's Ethnic Frontiers*. Seattle: University of Washington Press.

Ho, Cheuk Yuet. 2015. *Neo-Socialist Property Rights: The Predicament of Housing Ownership in China*. Lanham, MD: Lexington Books.

Joniak-Lüthi, Agnieszka. 2016. "Roads in China's Borderlands: Interfaces of Spatial Representations, Perceptions, Practices, and Knowledges." *Modern Asian Studies* 50(1): 118–40.

Juean, Lamu, Agui, Zeyong, and Zeren Zhuoma (觉安拉姆, 阿贵, 泽勇, 泽仁卓玛). 2010. 青藏铁路对西藏民俗文化旅游的影响及对策 [Impact of Qinghai-Tibet railroads on cultural tourism in Tibet and its reactions]. 西藏大学学报 [Journal of Tibet University],第一期 1: 31–35.

Larkin, Brian. 2013. "The Politics and Poetics of Infrastructure." *Annual Review of Anthropology* 42: 327–43.

Looney, Kriten E. 2015. "China's Campaign to Build a New Socialist Countryside: Village Modernization, Peasant Councils, and the Ganzhou Model of Rural Development." *China Quarterly* 224: 1–24.

Mountjoy, Tom. 2014. "Playing with Knowledge: Sport and the Paradox of Development in Solomon Islands." *Contemporary Pacific* 26(2): 324–45.

Oakes, Tim. 2017. "Happy Town: Cultural Governance and Biopolitical Urbanism in China." *Environment and Planning A: Economy and Space*, 14 February. https://doi.org/10.1177/0308518X17693621.

Tilt, Bryan. 2014. *Dams and Development in China: The Moral Economy of Water and Power*. New York: Columbia University Press.

Todorov, Vladislav. 1994. *Red Square, Black Square: Organon for Revolutionary Imagination*. Albany: State University of New York Press.

Von Schnitzler, Antina. 2008. "Citizenship Prepaid: Water, Calculability, and Technopolitics in South Africa." *Journal of South African Studies* 34(4): 899–917.

Yeh, Emily T. 2013. *Taming Tibet: Landscape Transformation and the Gift of Chinese Development*. Ithaca: Cornell University Press.

Zhang, Jinpeng, and Mengran Gao (张锦鹏, 高孟然). 2015. 从生死相依到渐被离弃:云南昆曼公路沿线那柯里村的路人类学 [From interdependence to desertion: The anthropology of the Keli Village along Kunman Road]. 云南社会科学 [Yunnan social science], 第4期 (4): 98–104.

Zhou, Yongming (周永明). 2010. 道路研究与'路学' [Road studies and "roadology"]. 二十一世纪 (Twenty-first century), 第120期 (120): 71–79.

5

On *Nomads of South Persia*

Thomas Barfield

Fredrik Barth's *Nomads of South Persia* (1961) has proved to be the most influential work on pastoral nomadism in the twentieth century, and its impact remains strong sixty years after he did the research. No studies done afterward escaped its influence, and almost every earlier book on nomads (even those almost contemporaneous with it) now appeared obsolete. As the first example of modern anthropology on Iranian pastoralists and one that immediately became the "classic ethnography" in the field (Bradburd 1992, 315), it inspired both a generation of scholars who later studied nomadic pastoralists and attracted the attention of comparatists keen to add nomadic pastoralists to their mix. As with many of Barth's other books, it was short and focused on the implications of his fieldwork rather than on debates in the published literature. Its fresh observations, models, and conclusions were presented concisely and clearly, each chapter providing some new insight as if it were obvious to anyone.

In Barth's words, "my project became an argument to reevaluate both the economic contributions of pastoral nomadism and the cultural value of a nomadic lifestyle within a modern state" (Barth 2007: 6). Previous studies of pastoral nomads had largely ignored the state framework and set nomads apart from their sedentary neighbors, contrasting the desert and the sown as different worlds. Anthropological typologies typically focused on movement itself rather than the reasons why pastoralists moved, and gave pride of place to the "pure nomads," people who subsisted entirely on meat, milk, or blood without resort to agricultural products (Bacon 1954). The study of pastoral nomads also had to overcome the legacy of nineteenth-century evolutionists who defined them as a primitive type of society that emerged after hunters but before farmers and cities, a view that relied heavily on armchair theorizing rather than on any data (Dyson-Hudson and Dyson-Hudson 1981: 15–16). It should also be said that existing histories of pastoral nomads produced by their literate sedentary neighbors were very negative, a view still held by contemporary government officials in many countries today. These descriptions asserted that the nomadic way of life was hostile to sedentary people and that their presumed lack of culture could only be cured when they stopped moving around and settled in one place. Although the fourteenth-century Arab social historian Ibn Khaldūn wrote an excellent and generally sympathetic description of how such nomadic people were organized based on firsthand knowledge, he still saw them as the inherent enemies of sedentary societies.

> The very nature of their existence is the negation of building, which is the basis of civilization. . . . Furthermore, it is their nature to plunder whatever other people possess. Their sustenance lies wherever the shadow of their lance falls. They recognize no limit in taking the possessions of other people. Whenever their eyes fall upon some property, furnishings or utensils, they take them. (Ibn Khaldūn 1969: 118)

Barth, without making much of an issue about it, revolutionized the field by taking the natural linkages between nomads and sedentary societies in Iran as his central focus. *Nomads of South Persia* set the Basseri within a larger ecological, economic, and political context—one that was not only contemporary but interactional. Yes, they were pastoralists, lived in tents, and made long-distance migrations, but they were also integrated into the sedentary economy as sheep-raising specialists. They sold animals and pastoral products and used the proceeds to purchase the wheat that was their staple food. They had always dealt with the Iranian state and its officials, and their political organization reflected this. While Barth thought that a thorough quantitative study would certainly document the flow of goods and services, resources, and population dynamics he was observing, the short period of time he had available for his research (set by the Iranian government) pushed him to look at processes that likely created the patterns, a methodology he had used effectively when studying the Swat Pathans and had recently demonstrated in his then just published monograph (Barth 1959a).

> This model can frame a comparison with other pastoral nomadic regimes and can be tested by more precise demographic and sustainability analyses, as has indeed now been done. My Basseri materials further served to strengthen my own trust in a focus on processes rather than on descriptions of mere patterns and functions. As in my analysis of politics in Swat, it also recognizes that both the sought purposes and the unsought, indeed unseen, consequences of practices must be included in any systematic analysis of culture and society. (Barth 2007: 7)

It was these sets of regularities that gave his *Nomads of South Persia* such power because they forced anthropologists to view pastoral nomads as parts of a complex system that produced predictable outcomes. Unlike earlier functionalist anthropologists, Barth used these regularities to create testable models that could be used comparatively. While Barth did not pursue them himself, others did. Indeed, one acerbic French anthropologist who also worked in southern Iran, Jean-Pierre Digard, complained that North American anthropological theory appeared to consist of nothing more than a constant reworking of *Nomads of South Persia* (Ganzer 2006: 565).

Responses to *Nomads of South Persia*

While practically all of Barth's work on the Basseri elicited overwhelmingly positive commentary, at least two aspects have attracted critical debate. The first came from those who took issue with his assertion that the Basseri had a "ritual life of unusual poverty" because their migration filled the role of ritual in a very satisfactory manner for them and for other nomads (Barth 1961: 146). On this issue, some critics questioned whether the Basseri truly lacked a ritual life while others doubted the applicability of migration as ritual to other nomadic societies. The second, and much larger debate, revolved around his model of how the dynamics of private ownership of sheep by individual families led to the maintenance of pastoral economic stability over time. The most cited aspect of this model was that the sedentarization of both the very rich and the very poor left the number of people in the pastoral economy relatively constant and relatively equal in the number of sheep they owned. All of this took place within a larger Iranian market economy in which the Basseri were pastoral specialists. While Barth's model has been widely admired, later ethnographic research in southern Iran found some very different patterns, and the question arose as to whether Barth's model was flawed or if the dynamics he described had been transformed by economic and political changes in the years that followed his research.

Migrations and Their Meanings

In the 1950s the Basseri had a population of about sixteen thousand and inhabited the area in and around the Zagros Mountains of southwestern Iran, stretching 450 kilometers from the city of Lar in the south to the Kohi-i-bul mountain massif in the north. Like other nomads on the Iranian Plateau that specialize in sheep raising, they maximized the number of animals they could support by moving them through a sequence of seasonal pastures throughout the year on a fixed migration route. Making such a large number of moves required an infrastructure of mobile black goat-hair tents and the baggage animals (camels and donkeys) to transport them and other property. In the winter, the Basseri inhabited foothills at lower elevations (600–800 meters) in semi-arid areas along the Iraqi border. Such areas were relatively warm at that time of year and had poor but extensive areas of pasture. In late March, they began their main forty- or fifty-day migration into the Zagros range, moving ever northward into the higher mountain pastures that lie between 1,800 and 4,000 meters. These areas were snow covered in winter but produce grass in abundance during the summer. The return migration began in August or September and followed the same track but in the opposite direction. As one nomad told me about a similar pattern of migration in northern Afghanistan, "We chase the snow up the mountains, and then it chases us back down." While conflicts with farmers could arise over damage to growing crops in the spring (their fields lay at the midpoint of the migration at around 1,500 meters in elevation), these same famers were happy to have sheep graze the stubble in the fall after the harvest to fertilize the land. Barth noted that Basseri sheep were well adapted to this migratory cycle. Larger and more productive than breeds raised by local villagers, they could not withstand extreme temperatures (hot or cold) and suffered a 70–80 percent mortality rate if their owners kept them in one place year-round (Barth 1961: 6). It could be said that this failure to adapt well to extremes applied to the black goat-hair tent that each family owned. While remarkably easy to set up, take down, and pack compactly, such tents provided little protection against cold, wind, or heavy precipitation (Feilberg 1944).

All nomadic pastoral peoples engaged in some type of seasonal migration, but the regularity of these movements and the distances they covered were determined primarily by resource availability. The first rule of thumb was that pastoral nomads did not seek to travel any farther than they had to. The second was that migration routes tended to follow annually fixed routes only in areas where the quality of pasturage was high and its appearance dependable. Where pasturage was of poorer quality, highly scattered or undependable, seasonal migration patterns displayed more year to year variation (Johnson 1969). For example, the camel-raising nomads in the deserts of Arabia to the west not only migrated within much larger areas than nomads in Iran, but the location of their winter pastures changed each year depending on which areas had received rain most recently (Lancaster 1981; Cole 1975). By contrast, high-altitude pastoralists in Tibet and Central Asia far to the east of Iran managed to raise very large numbers of sheep and yaks while only moving camp a few times a year over sometimes surprisingly short distances (Goldstein and Beall 1990; Ekvall 1968; Shahrani 2002).

The Basseri followed a migration cycle that was much more tightly fixed in time than elsewhere, so regular that Barth likened the movements of the groups within it to a well-ordered train schedule (Barth 1959b). This migration route (*il-rah*, tribal road) was so consistent that nomads melded time and place. Since they arrived and left places at the same time each year, they had no experience at what local conditions there were like before or afterward. Nor was the thought of staying put to find out very attractive. Their winter camps were infernos in the summer, while their green mountain summer camps were buried under meters of snow in the winter. During the migration, camp groups had the right to use particular pastures only at set times and then were expected to move on until they reached their final destinations. The most powerful groups had the best pastures at the best times, while those with fewer numbers or less political clout preceded and followed them. One reason for this high level of coordination was that while groups like the Basseri and their Qashqai nomad neighbors reserved the use of their winter and summer pastures to their own people, the migration route between these pastures was for transit and shared with many different groups. Setting an overall schedule reduced conflict and eased the flow of traffic. This train-like schedule of the overall migration flow did not stop local camp groups from deciding whether they would break camp on a daily basis where no one seemed to be in charge. When a consensus emerged, they moved—nobody wanted to be striking out alone or be left behind. The overall schedule was therefore maintained not by commands from the top, but from the daily pressure exerted by camp groups moving up from behind against the resistance from those ahead of them perceived as not moving on fast enough.

The overall scheduling and coordination of the migration was historically overseen by powerful tribal khans, although the Iranian army took control of that task a couple of years before Barth began his research. Before that time the government in Tehran often had little control over these regions, so it was the heads of the tribal confederations who maintained law and order locally. Barth summarized the roles of the Basseri khan as three: "allotting pastures and coordinating the migrations of the tribe; settling the disputes that are brought to him; and representing the tribe or any of its members in politically important dealings with sedentary authorities" (Barth 1961: 76). The khan's allocation of pasture was particularly important because access to summer pastures was ensured by his protection of its collective (tribal, *il*) ownership, which he administered. Where pasturage was owned by mountain villages, the khan would negotiate its rental from the absentee landlords who controlled it (Amanolahi 2003: 273). We will return to the issue of pasture rights in later years when looking at changes in the pastoral economy that transformed the system after Barth completed his work.

Migration was the aspect of pastoral nomadism that attracted the most attention because the ability to move was what made a nomad a nomad. The nomadic migrations in the Zagros were particularly striking because they covered long distances through difficult and often dangerous terrain—crossing spring flooded rivers, transiting snowfields to reach lofty mountain passes, and taking vertiginous trails where animals and people sometimes fell to their deaths. The spectacular nature of the journey was captured in a classic silent film that documented the Bakhtiari migration through the Zagros Mountains, *Grass: A Nation's Battle for Life* (Schoedsack and Cooper 1925; Cooper 1925).

As mentioned above, Barth (1961: 146) observed a "poverty of ritual" that appeared to characterize the Basseri. He suggested that the migration itself might serve as a substitute for it, providing the psychic benefits filled by ritual activities in other societies. Barth's speculation has provoked considerable debate. Critcis like Daniel Bradburd (1984) contended that, based on the book's mention of them, the Basseri did have rituals and pointed to rites held at weddings, circumcisions, funerals, and their participation in broader Shiite Muslim religious events. He mounted a more detailed critique along these lines by comparing his own study of Komachi pastoralists with other Iranian nomads.

> The Komachi are members of a larger society that supplies them with ritual as it supplies them with their language, national identity, and religious dogma. Our task in regard to Persian pastoralists and their rituals is not to explain why tribes have them but, where necessary, to explain why they do not. Moreover, if most pastoralists' apprehension of ritual is like that of the Komachi, then I suspect that as more is published about ritual and southwest Asian pastoralists, we shall find that an absence of meaningful ritual among them is very rare. (Bradburd 1984: 392)

It may well be that anthropologists had not looked hard enough for ritual events among nomads in this region, but in other pastoral societies, like the cattle keepers of sub-Saharan Africa, ritual life was rich and obvious and did not need extra observation to find it (Herskovits 1926). The dispute appeared to be more about what type of ritual Barth appeared to say was missing—rituals whose common observance gave solidarity to all Basseri as a corporate group. They did have life-cycle rituals celebrating weddings and circumcisions, but these were family or small community events (and Barth argued that they were not very elaborate). Anthropologists who looked at sacred places among nomads in Iran (Khosronejad 2003) encountered a similar problem—beliefs might be commonly held, but rituals surrounding them were limited to small groups or were individual affairs.

If the question of existence of ritual was at least partly definitional, the question of whether the migration was a type of ritual and whether it was characteristic of all nomads in the region was more observational. Barth had seen it as a ritual and one that reinforced solidarity in three ways:

> 1) that Basseri migration isolates and emphasizes both the significant groups in the society and the mechanisms of group maintenance; (2) that Basseri migration orders and organizes Basseri notions of time and space; and (3) that the Basseri are emotionally engaged in their migration—that they are excited about it, rejoice in it, sing (most uncharacteristically) on it, and reflect their tension and excitement by rising ever earlier during its duration. (Bradburd 1984: 387–88)

Richard Tapper supported Barth's contention with his work among the Shahsevan nomads in northwestern Iran, where he also found that the migration itself created a special time when "spring is a party and the migration itself is the height of the party" (1979: 181). Following van Gennep's classic model (1960: 11), Tapper argued the migration could be seen as a particular type of ritual—a rite of transition in which the migration was a liminal stage where people felt more freedom from the ordinary strictures of daily life that applied at either their summer and winter quarters, the respective and more stable end points of the migration. Like Barth he saw it as reinforcing group bonds that help build solidarity within their descent groups (Tapper 1979: 17).

By contrast, Bradburd argued that the Komachi pastoralists he studied in southeastern Iran perceived their migration as a difficult time full of work. It had some high points, but by the end of it people were tired, irritable, and definitely not in a mood to sing. They welcomed the arrival of new roads that enabled them to move their families to the mountains by truck with only one or two days of travel (Bradburd 1984: 387–88). He went on to argue that the difference in the way they looked upon the migration was because it was independent travel by casually organized groups. Unlike more powerful nomadic confederations elsewhere in Iran that had strong identities and corporate resources to protect—including rights to pasture and migration routes—Komachi pastoralism was more individualistic with only weak identification to any larger community based on descent. The loss of corporate identities appeared to be a common development in places where descent groups no longer controlled vital assets. In a wide-ranging survey of Turko-Mongolian nomadic societies, Lawrence Krader (1963: 333, 369–70) observed that when links with corporate descent groups no longer validated rights to pasture or provided group protection, nomads might maintain a tribal or clan name for themselves but lose knowledge of the genealogies that originally produced it.

I observed a similar situation in my own work with the Central Asian Arabs in northern Afghanistan during the mid-1970s (Barfield 1981). As with the Komachi, the migration was viewed as work rather than ritual. When I first asked my wealthy herd-owning host about going on the migration to the mountains, he suggested I fly with him because "only poor people walk." Tellingly, the migration route itself was named after the animals (the sheep road, *gusfand rah*) rather than the people who used it (the tribal road, *il-rah*). And no one organized the move, government or khans, at a higher level. Choosing when to start and stop was more akin to deciding how best to drive to a holiday resort when everyone else was planning the same trip, braving heavy traffic on limited routes and taking bypasses where that was possible. Ritual events were all at the family or small community level, except for those they shared with the larger sedentary community whose religious belief, language, and culture were the same. Unlike Iran, where tribal organization and pastoral nomadism was often presumed to be synonymous, in Afghanistan, tribal groups (Pashtuns, Aimaqs, Uzbeks, Turkmen, Arabs) had both sedentary and nomadic components. This debate about ritual poverty among nomads was never really resolved satisfactorily. Since Barth (1993) later published extensively on cultures renowned for their richness of ritual, such as Bali, it is unfortunate he did not return to the topic. But it is also possible, as with the debate on sedentarization we will explore next, that his observations only occurred in certain types of nomadic contexts.

The Pastoral Economy and Models of Sedentarization

The most lasting contribution of *Nomads of South Persia* was Barth's model that addressed a series of questions that looked at the ecology of pastoralism, the pastoral economy, and population growth. The first was how the Basseri managed to stay in long-term balance with their environment, because the animals were privately owned but their pasture was held in common. Since each Basseri family was attempting to maximize its own production, it would appear that they could have very easily exceeded the carrying capacity of the land and thereby destroyed the very grasslands on which they depended. This turned out to be relatively easy to answer: pastures were not really common to all but historically redistributed by the khan to match their carrying capacity. At the local level a series of camp groups might claim that pasture was open to all, but their definition of "all" was restricted to a finite number of people. But this left open a second problem: why did not the internal population growth among the Basseri themselves upset the people-animal balance, since the number of sheep was largely independent of the size of the human population? That is, if the Basseri population size doubled but the total number of sheep remained the same, then each household would fall below the number of animals needed for its subsistence. But if each additional Basseri family maintained the same number of sheep, then the total number of sheep would soon exceed the carrying capacity of the pasture and collapse the whole system. Barth argued that since the Basseri had historically maintained a balance both in terms of the number of animals they grazed and the size of their total population, this "long-term balance between pastures, herds, and people and consequent stable pastoral population can only be maintained if the rate of *sedentarization* is sensitive to the population pressure of *animals* on the pasture" (Barth 1961: 126 [original italics]). In other words, some Basseri families had to leave the pastoral economy if the population was to remain stable and reduce the pressure to increase the number of livestock beyond its sustainable carrying capacity.

Barth's model of this sedentarization process was elegant, and the dynamic of the process lay in the symbiosis of villager and nomad. Although they raised sheep for a living, the Basseri diet was predominantly wheat based. The nomads acquired the wheat they needed in trade with "village friends" on credit, with the expectation the debt would be repaid at the end of the annual pastoral production cycle. Lambs born in the spring would grow and fatten during the summer, for sale in the autumn. Since Basseri pastoral products (live animals, wool, skins, milk products) had a relatively high exchange value in comparison with grain, the sale or exchange of pastoral products in a normal year should easily cover the advance and produce a surplus as well. The larger the number of sheep a household possessed, the more solvent it was. Barth estimated that a household required a minimum flock of sixty sheep to make ends meet and that more prosperous Basseri owned between one and two hundred animals.

He noted that few had flocks over that size because the family labor needed to herd them was limited.

Households that fell below this minimum flock size soon found themselves in a debt spiral. If unable to pay for the grain advanced during a previous year, they were forced to roll over ever larger debts each succeeding year, until they could no longer get new credit. Since their sheep were good collateral, they could continue a pattern of borrowing for quite some time. However, at some point, the number of sheep a family owned might approach or exceed the value of the debts they needed to pay. This was likely to happen if a family experienced a pastoral disaster in which a large number of animals died at once. Such disasters were rarely evenly distributed, and one family might lose half its stock while a nearby one remained unscathed. Losses of any kind had the greatest impact on those who were already vulnerable, and a bad year increased their rate of sedentarization, as they were then forced to sell off their remaining animals to pay their creditors and had to abandon pastoralism. Barth noted that there was no safety net. Since each family was responsible for its own economic fate, and no help could be expected even from close relatives, pastoral households were economically isolated, creating a situation where "the population becomes fragmented with respect to economic activities, and economic factors can strike differentially, eliminating some members of the population without affecting other members of the same population" (Barth 1961: 124). Because opportunities for contract shepherding were limited, destitute nomads entered the peasant labor force and from that point on were no longer considered members of the Basseri tribe.

The road to sedentarization through poverty involved the largest number of people, and its dynamics were clear. There was, however, a second route to sedentarization at the opposite end of the economic spectrum by those whose flock's growth rate exceeded the norm. Sheep pastoralists could ideally experience a doubling of their flock in three years, which was more than twice the reproductive rate of cattle and three times that of camels. However, these regular gains were normally offset by large periodic expenses that drain a household's income. A man may have acquired a large number of sheep as he matured and his flock grew, but they might be needed to meet expensive life-cycle obligations, particularly when it came time to arrange for his sons to marry. Among the Basseri, bride-price payments often required the sale of animals to raise cash for these marriages. However, unlike many other sheep-raising nomads, it was anticipatory inheritance that drew down even large holdings significantly because it was based on a percentage of the total livestock holdings at the time of marriage.[1] These inheritances at marriage created new independent households (or better, tent-holds).

If the forced settlement of poor nomads was so common, Barth wondered why the nomads remaining in the Basseri pastoral economy were not more highly stratified by wealth. To explain this, he posited a second path to sedentarization: wealthy pastoralists who put their profits into land purchases eventually and voluntarily chose to leave the pastoral economy. As their land investments grew over time, such families stopped migrating in order to better manage them and entered the Iranian provincial landowning elite, abandoning their former nomad identity. Barth claimed the cost of hiring shepherds to care for their sheep once a family stopped migrating reduced profits too much to encourage any absentee ownership.

The process may not have begun with the goal of leaving the pastoral no-madic economy, but rather in hopes of buying insurance against the unpre-dictable catastrophic disasters inherent in their livestock production regime. By converting their pastoral surpluses into landholdings, wealthy Basseri could in theory buy replacement animals after a disaster. But purchasing agricultural land along their migration routes also had three other advantages that eventu-ally pushed them toward settlement. First, Basseri families who invested in land diversified their economic base and gained better long-term stability. While no-mads might have had little desire to be farmers themselves, they appreciated the productive value of irrigated agricultural land. As a nomad in northern Af-ghanistan explained to me, "land never dies" and was therefore the most secure long-run investment. Second, such land could be farmed by sharecroppers and the grain it produced used to meet household needs. A nomad family with land was thus relieved of the need to purchase grain, a major annual expense. Finally, landownership in Iran historically brought prestige and social advancement re-gardless of the owner's origin, because elite status was based on it and the con-trol over the farmers who worked the land as tenants. In any event, Barth did not observe any really wealthy nomads among the Basseri, except for the tribal khan, who managed political affairs for the group but was not himself a nomad.

While this model was highly regarded, at least one critic took substantial objection to it. Jacob Black-Michaud, who worked in neighboring Luristan a decade later, found a thriving pastoral economy in which the rich pastoralists exploited the poor ones through shepherding contracts that put much of the risk on the caretakers while delivering the profits to the owners. In a polemic, he accused Barth be being bamboozled into accepting a type of nomadic false consciousness in which nomads like the Basseri maintained a cultural ideal of equality that did not really exist (Black-Michaud 1972). Why should the rich leave the profitable sheep-raising sector when so many destitute skilled herders were eager to take any available contracts herding other people's animals rather than sedentarize? The error, he claimed, was the product of poor fieldwork. Later studies also found more economic stratification among Iranian nomads and different patterns of sedentarization than Barth's model would have pre-dicted (Bradburd 1980, 1989). If Barth had an opinion on these critiques, he did not respond directly. Once he had shifted to another set of ethnographic issues, it was his practice to let his original work speak for itself. As an old Central Asian saying has it, "The dogs bark but the caravan moves on."

As one among those dogs still chasing the caravan at that time, I wondered how to reconcile these divergent accounts when I began my own research among nomadic pastoralists in northern Afghanistan during the 1970s (Barfield 1981). As good chance would have it, the Central Asian Arabs I worked with had undergone an economic change that appeared to answer at least part of the question. Originally engaged in what might be called subsistence pastoralism, which provided a good standard of living but offered less in the way of cash profits, they sold their sheep to urban meat markets and bought grain to feed themselves. To the extent possible, they employed their own family labor, but if they needed to hire shepherds to tend their flocks, they paid them in ewes (one per hundred sheep herded for six months). Paying in reproductive stock slowed the rate of growth for wealthy sheep owners and over time permitted a shepherd to build his own independent flock.

Like the Basseri, the Central Asian Arabs were pastoral specialists who serviced the larger sedentary population in a market economy. The profitability of being a pastoralist in such an economic system was changeable rather than fixed and depended on the rate of exchange for pastoral products (and the cost of producing them) compared to other goods, particularly grain (Bates 1973: 4; Bradburd 1996). In northern Afghanistan, the price of sheep in Kunduz province, where the pastoralists had their winter quarters, was historically low because this was an area of agricultural surplus with few export opportunities. In the mountains where they summered, there were no markets at all, and it was the nomads who brought in cash to purchase wheat from alpine farmers there. In the nineteenth and early twentieth centuries, the Central Asian Arabs had not bothered to market their sheep on the Afghan side of the border at all, but instead took them to more profitable markets in Bukhara, now in Uzbekistan. This business ended when Stalin fenced off the border between Soviet Central Asia and Afghanistan in the 1930s and began a policy of collectivization that was hostile to private ownership and trade. Afghanistan could not replace this market because it had no national economy—each of its regions had its own set of prices for livestock and grain, because the country's poor transport infrastructure did not permit the transport of bulk goods profitably. Prices for grain or livestock might be simultaneously high in one part of the country and low in another (Fry 1974: 56). Being a pastoralist in northern Afghanistan at this time provided a good living if you had enough animals and used family labor, but it was not a very profitable cash economy investment.

This changed in the 1960s when the Soviet Union and the United States completed a set of paved roads that linked the regions of Afghanistan together. What had been isolated provincial markets were now integrated into a national one, and products flowed to those with the highest returns. This had a big impact on pastoralists, because not only could livestock be shipped to new markets in Kabul, but the demand for mutton and the prices paid for it rose sharply. Pastoralists told me the price of sheep doubled within one year of the opening of the Salang Pass through the Hindu Kush Mountains in 1964 (at the time the highest road pass in the world), and prices doubled again over the next ten years. Flock owners, arguing that sheep had become too valuable to be used as

payments for labor, replaced their traditional in-kind wage payments for shepherds with cash salaries. Wealthy pastoralists quickly gave up on using family
labor and replaced it with crews of shepherds, which were now relatively much
cheaper since the price of sheep kept rising while wages remained stagnant.
Economic stratification increased rapidly, and both rich and poor sedentarized.
The rich stayed in the sheep-raising business but stopped migrating. Poor men
who took on shepherding jobs to support their families now left them in their
winter villages year-round. Some families still maintained traditional familial
pastoralism, aided by the fact that pastoralists here had exclusive rights to particular pastures on the steppe and in the mountains.

These exclusive pasture rights, *qawwalla*, were granted to individual people
rather than to groups and were registered in documents issued to the nomads
by the Afghan government beginning in the 1930s (Patterson 2004: 7–8). These
rights were reinforced when their validity was recognized by the *Afghan Pasture Law 10 March 1970*, which also legally protected their migration routes
and banned the transfer of customary pasturage to agricultural use (Barfield
2004: appendix). Merchants seeking to enter the now more lucrative pastoral
economy needed to rent pasture from pastoralists who had rights to it or contract for the care of their sheep with nomad families who were compensated
for the task by both a cash payment and the right to keep the wool and milk
products the sheep produced. As we will see, this recognition of rights to pasture granted to individuals in the north by the Afghan state (most of whom
were pastoralists) protected their customary rights far more strongly than in
Iran, where the state claimed ownership of all pasture in the 1960s and abolished tribal rights to resources. Despite more than three decades of war and
the collapse of the central state power in remote regions, these titles mostly
retained their validity when actively used and new ones were issued (Patterson
2004: 10–13).

What I concluded from the Central Asian Arab case was that when sheep
provided subsistence but relatively little cash profit, there was less reason for
the wealthy (who had invested in land) to remain in such a high-risk business,
where small annual profits could not offset the periodic catastrophic capital
losses endemic to this form of pastoralism. Unlike the Basseri, however, there
was evidence that a number of rich families with very large herds did exist.
They too had used familial labor to the greatest extent possible in herding, but
also so that women in the family could maximize the production and storage
of milk products. When shepherd crews replaced families, milk processing was
abandoned as a significant economic activity. When I visited their shepherd
camps in the mountains, however, the remains of low walled stone enclosures
that had formerly sheltered their family summer tents could still be seen.

The highly stratified Lurs examined by Black-Michaud appeared to be the
product of economic changes similar to those I had observed in Afghanistan,
although among the Lurs family groups took care of the sheep so that the poorer
nomads continued to migrate, taking care of other people's sheep. As in Afghan-

istan, when sheep moved from being a subsistence commodity to a valuable "cash crop," the economic dynamics changed even though the animals remained the same. I believed that this, rather than false consciousness or ethnographic error, better explained the differences in their cases. What I had not paid enough attention to at the time was the profound changes in state policy in Iran that occurred in the decade between Barth's research and that of Black-Michaud. As new studies came in over the years, it was clear that Barth was documenting a system that may have been quite old but was on the brink of dissolution and that Black-Michaud was looking at the adaptation to these changes.

Nomads in Iran have always had to deal with state policies. Sometimes it was their confederations that called the shots; at other times the state had held the upper hand (Barfield 2002). In the 1930s, the Iranian government forcibly settled all the nomads in Iran in the name of modernization, a destructive policy that collapsed when Reza Shah was overthrown in 1941 (Bayat 2003). Pastoral nomads returned to their old way of life, although as Barth documented, the Iranian army put state power at their doorstep. As destructive as the forced settlement policy had been, it was the Iranian government's "White Revolution" that proved to be the greater threat. Beginning in 1963, the Iranian Land Reform Program declared that the country's pasturelands were state property and abolished the tribes' exclusive right to use them. As Sekandar Amanolahi's follow-up study of the Basseri found, the finely tuned system that Barth had described had collapsed.

> Overall, the reforms resulted in tribal disintegration. Prior to the Land Reform Programme the majority of the tribesmen depended on the chief for pastureland. They either used the tribal pastureland controlled by the chief, or the pastureland owned by the sedentary communities, which the chief negotiated and allocated annually among the tribal members. However, as the land reforms were implemented, the chief could no longer function his traditional responsibilities. As a result, the tribal sections and subsections were left alone and each had to take care of its own affairs. Those sections and subsections that used the pastureland owned by the settled communities did not benefit from the reforms; hence they were forced to become dispersed among the sedentarised communities. The chief could no longer negotiate on their behalf and, more important, the landlords, who rented their pastureland to the nomads, also lost control over their villages as their agricultural lands and pastures were divided among the peasants. In short, the Land Reform Programme resulted in sedentarisation and tribal disintegration among the Basseri. (Amanolahi 2003: 273)

Iran's economic growth also provided new opportunities for seeking jobs in the country's growing cities. But one of the biggest factors in bringing about the end of the old system was education, so that a new generation of Basseri had no desire to return to a pastoral nomadic way of life. Amanolahi concluded:

> These changes have led to the tribal disintegration. The Basseri no longer exist as a unified tribal entity. As a matter of fact, political changes have led to detribal-

isation of the Basseri. ... This circumstance forced the Basseri to become integrated into the national state, although without effective political participation. (Amanolahi 2003: 276–77)

Conclusions

After more than fifty-five years, *Nomads of South Persia* still stands the test of time in spite of the many monographs about Iranian pastoralism that came in its wake. If anything, the greatest criticism that can be made today is that its models were applied too casually in contexts where the conditions that produced them were absent. Though elegant, Barth's model of sedentarization assumed that impoverished nomads could be easily absorbed by the surrounding agricultural societies. In other parts of the world, this was not the case. In areas where they could not, anthropologists found much more in the way of safety nets that included the redistribution of livestock by leaders to keep people within the pastoral economy because they constituted their political and military base. Before the expansion of stronger state control, resources could also be acquired by raiding or extortion to make up for deficiencies in the livestock economy, an avenue now largely closed. Or, as noted above, poor pastoralists could remain pastoralist by raising livestock they did not own, a type of ranching long common in Western Europe and the Americas (cf. Barfield 1993).

If Barth did not anticipate that the world he was describing was threatened with destruction, he certainly knew the Iranian government and international agencies were keen to see this way of life disappear. The UNESCO Arid Zone Project, which sponsored his research, had tasked him with reporting on how nomads could best be settled, and they were surely disappointed with his conclusion that "the way Barth viewed it, there were no good reasons for the Basseri to settle and become farmers, as the Iranian government wished" (Eriksen 2015: 62). Although Barth no longer continued to write about the Basseri, it is clear that this study was close to his heart, and he returned to visit them over the years. When Barth was interviewed about his many fieldwork experiences, he often mentioned his long trek with the Basseri as the most fulfilling one at a personal level. He also spoke of the Basseri as the happiest people he studied. They lived uncomplicated, independent lives close to nature, placed a great value on hospitality, and had strong family ties (Eriksen 2015: 61).

Readers come away from *Nomads of South Persia* not only with a far more profound understanding of pastoral systems than they had before reading his work, but with a sympathy for the people as well. It was what made all of Barth's work so distinctive.

Thomas Barfield received his PhD from Harvard University in social anthropology and is Professor of Anthropology at Boston University. He is author of *The Central Asian Arabs of Afghanistan* (1981), *The Perilous Frontier: Nomadic*

Empires and China (1989), and *Afghanistan: An Atlas of Indigenous Domestic Architecture* (1991) and was executive editor of *The Dictionary of Anthropology* (1997). In 2006, he was awarded a Guggenheim Fellowship to complete *Afghanistan: A Cultural and Political History* (2010). Barfield has also served as president of the American Institute for Afghanistan Studies since 2005.

Note

1. The flock was divided into shares, one for each unmarried son and a share for the father. If three sons, then the first received one-quarter of the flock at marriage, the second one-third, and the last got his and his father's share in return for taking care of the aged father or (more likely) mother. The number of animals these shares represented changed depending on whether the remaining flock size increased or decreased in the intervening years.

References

Amanolahi, Sekandar. 2003. "Socio-Political Changes among the Basseri of South Iran." *Iran & the Caucasus* 7: 261–77.

Bacon, Elizabeth. 1954. "Types of Pastoral Nomadism in Central and Southwest Asia." *Southwestern Journal of Anthropology* 10: 44–68.

Barfield, Thomas. 1981. *The Central Asian Arabs of Afghanistan: Pastoral Nomadism in Transition.* Austin: University of Texas Press.

———. 1993. *The Nomadic Alternative.* Upper Saddle River, NJ: Prentice Hall.

———. 2002. "Turk, Persian and Arab: Changing Relationships between Tribes and State in Iran and along Its Frontiers." In *Iran and the Surrounding World: Interactions in Culture and Cultural Politics,* edited by Nikki Keddie, 61–88. Seattle: University of Washington Press.

———. 2004. "Nomadic Pastoralists in Afghanistan: Reconstruction of the Pastoral Economy, with Appendix: The Afghan Pasture Law 10 March 1970." Washington, DC: Bank Information Service.

Barth, Fredrik. 1959a. *Political Leadership among Swat Pathans.* Monographs on Social Anthropology 19. London: Athlone Press.

———. 1959b. "The Land Use Pattern of Migratory Tribes of South Persia." *Norwegian Journal of Geography* 17: 1–11.

———. 1961. *Nomads of South Persia: The Basseri Tribe of the Khamseh Confederacy.* Boston: Little, Brown.

———. 1993. *Balinese Worlds.* Chicago: University of Chicago Press.

———. 2007. "Overview: Sixty Years in Anthropology." *Annual Review of Anthropology* 36(7): 1–16.

Bates, Daniel G. 1973. *Nomads and Farmers: A Study of the Yörük of Southeastern Turkey.* Ann Arbor: University of Michigan Press.

Bayat, Kaveh. 2003. "Riza Shah and the Tribes: An Overview." In *The Making of Modern Iran: State and Society under Riza Shah, 1921–1941,* edited by Stephanie Cronin, 213–19. London: Routledge.

Black-Michaud, Jacob. 1972. "Tyranny as a Strategy for Survival in an 'Egalitarian' Society: Luri Facts Versus an Anthropological Mystique." *Man* 7(4): 614–34.

Bradburd, Daniel. 1980. "Never Give a Shepherd an Even Break: Class and Labor among the Komachi." *American Ethnologist* 7(1): 603–20.

———. 1984. "Ritual and Southwest Asian Pastoralists: Implications of the Komachi Case." *Journal of Anthropological Research* 40(3): 380–93.

———. 1989. "Producing Their Fates: Why Poor Basseri Settled but Poor Komachi and Yomut Did Not." *American Ethnologist* 16(3): 502–17.

———. 1992. "Territoriality and Iranian Pastoralists: Looking Out from Kerman." In *Mobility and Territoriality: Social and Spatial Boundaries among Foragers, Fishers, Pastoralists, and Peripatetics*, 309–27. New York: Berg.

———. 1996. "Toward an Understanding of the Economics of Pastoralism: The Balance of Exchange between Pastoralists and Nonpastoralists in Western Iran, 1815–1975." *Human Ecology* 24: 1–38.

Cole, Donald. 1975. *Nomads of the Nomads: The Āl Murrah Bedouin of the Empty Quarter*. Chicago: Aldine.

Cooper, Merian C. 1925. *Grass: An Account of the Migration of a Bakhtiari Tribe in Search of Pasture*. New York: Putnam.

Dyson-Hudson, Rada, and Neville Dyson-Hudson. 1981. "Pastoral Nomadism." *Annual Review of Anthropology* 9: 15–61.

Ekvall, Robert. 1968. *Fields on the Hoof*. New York: Holt, Rinehart and Winston.

Eriksen, Thomas. 2015. *Fredrik Barth: An Intellectual Biography*. London: Pluto Press.

Feilberg, Carl. 1944. *La Tente Noire, Contribution Ethnographique à l'histoire Culturelle des Nomades*. Copenhagen: Gyldendal.

Fry, Maxwell J. 1974. *The Afghan Economy: Money, Finance, and the Critical Constraints to Economic Development*. Leiden: Brill.

Ganzer, Burkhard. 2006. "Power vs. Consent in Tribal Political Systems in Iran: Salzman on the Basseri Khan; Comments on an Extreme View." *Anthropos* 101: 564–70.

Goldstein, Melvyn C., and Cynthia M Beall. 1990. *Nomads of Western Tibet: The Survival of a Way of Life*. Berkeley: University of California Press.

Herskovits, M. J. 1926. "The Cattle Complex in East Africa." *American Anthropologist* 28: 230–72, 361–88, 494–528.

Ibn Khaldūn. 1969. *The Muqaddimah: An Introduction to History*. Edited by N. J Dawood. Translated by Franz Rosenthal. Abridged ed. Princeton, NJ: Princeton University Press.

Johnson, Douglas L. 1969. *The Nature of Nomadism*. Chicago: Department of Geography, University of Chicago.

Khosronejad, Pedram. 2003. "Reflections on the Diversity and Religious Functions of Holy Places and Sacred Stones among Bakhtiari Nomads." *Anthropology of the Contemporary Middle East and Central Eurasia* 1(2): 143–69.

Krader, Lawrence. 1963. *Social Organization of the Mongol-Turkic Pastoral Nomads*. The Hague: Mouton.

Lancaster, William. 1981. *The Rwala Bedouin Today*. Cambridge: Cambridge University Press.

Patterson, Mervyn. 2004. "The Shiwa Pastures, 1978–2003: Land Tenure Changes and Conflict in Northeastern Badakhshan." Kabul: The Afghanistan Research and Evaluation Unit (AREU). https://ageconsearch.tind.io/record/14636/files/cs04pa01.pdf.

Schoedsack, Ernest B., and Merian Cooper. 1925. *Grass: A Nation's Battle for Life.* Silent film. Los Angeles: Paramount Pictures. Reissued by Milestone Film & Video.

Shahrani, M. Nazif. 2002. *The Kirghiz and Wakhi of Afghanistan: Adaptation to Closed Frontiers and War.* Seattle: University of Washington Press.

Tapper, Richard. 1979. *Pasture and Politics: Economics, Conflict, and Ritual among Shahsevan Nomads of Northwestern Iran.* London: Academic Press.

Van Gennep, Arnold. 1960. *The Rites of Passage.* Chicago: University of Chicago Press.

6

The Language of Trust and Betrayal

Gunnar Haaland

We human beings are vulnerable to many kinds of affliction and most of us are at some time afflicted by serious ills. How we cope is only in small part up to us. It is most often to others that we owe our survival, let alone our flourishing, as we encounter bodily illness and injury, inadequate nutrition, mental defect and disturbance, and human aggression and neglect.
—Alasdair Macintyre, *Dependent Rational Animals*

Introduction

Since the Neolithic there has been an enormous expansion in the scale, content, and dynamics of interaction systems (economic, political, and informational) that people participate in. Dunbar has formulated an important dimension of this change in scale:

> We have lived in villages only for the last ten thousand years, and cities the size of Bombay or Rio de Janeiro only for the last century at most. These are novel innovations, a product of our capacity to invent new ways of making do. Yet, at the same time, our social world is still what it was several hundred thousand years ago. The number of people we know personally, whom we can trust, whom we feel some emotional affinity for, is no more than 150, Dunbar's Number. It has been 150 for as long as we have been a species. And it is 150 because our minds lack the capacity to make it any larger. (Dunbar 2010: 4)

However, between the small-scale world of 150 people, which our mind has the capacity to know personally and trust, and the large-scale world of states, global markets, and communication networks, where we interact with people without ever seeing them, there is a world of intermediate space of interactions based on cultural constructions derived from ideas anchored in experiences harvested in small-scale community life. In this chapter, I shall focus on this intermediate level of community life and on cultural constructions relevant for coping with the universal problem of vulnerability and dependence. I shall particularly focus on symbolic imagery that expresses and fosters "trust" cementing social dependence. Trust in fellow humans is precarious and particularly vulnerable to changes occurring in the politico-economic domain. Such changes may have far-reaching consequences for the afflictions we are exposed to and for our dependence on others, not the least on the tension people experience between individual benefits and moral commitments.

My analysis of trust probes two major issues that Barth only emphasized well after his pioneering studies of ethnicity and of the Fur in Sudan, whom I also discuss here (Barth 1967, 1969). First, there is the issue of scale, where he insisted that large-scale social groups are not fundamentally different from small-scale ones (Barth 1978). They are not, for instance, aggregates of a set of small-scale groups. Instead, he insisted that anthropologists should focus in the relations between people that take place at all scales. To explore this issue, I build beyond Barth's work on the Fur to examine a problem of scale that became clear only after his field research there. In particular, the grounds on which people could build trust changed considerably as new, large-scale Islamizing movements tied to the central state grew increasingly important.

Second, I draw on Barth's insistence that we go beyond the sorts of explanations rooted in what informants tell us during formal interviews. Instead, as Wikan's essay also discusses, he urged us to attend always to the unspoken acts of life, which can reveal quite different processes from what formal statements tell us. This point is clearer in his later works than his earlier ones. In his early works Barth focused on the way human consciousness and purpose shaped social life: "Since social acts are thus not simply 'caused' but 'intended' we must consider these intentions and understandings of actors if we wish to capture the essential contexts of acts" (Barth 1981: 4). Actors' intentions involve purposeful husbandry of a wide variety of concerns. Whatever the concerns (e.g., material wealth and political influence, honor and respect), they had to be husbanded in the context of culturally constructed and socially sanctioned ideas of moral obligations. However, it was especially after his New Guinea works that Barth focused on conceptualizing the primarily nonverbal symbolic imagery that served to make moral ideas convincing and compelling.

Verbal language has great limitations for construction of such compelling messages. As Rappaport has pointed out:

> When a sign is only arbitrary or conventionally related to the signified it is possible for it to occur in the absence of the signified and for it not to occur in the presence of the signified. Thus, the very freedom of the sign from the signified that permits discourse to transcend the here and now, if it does not actually make lying possible, facilitates it enormously and may encourage it as well. (Rappaport 1979: 180)

This implies that verbal language has limitations as a medium to sustain and transmit trust in interpersonal relations, because lying about trust may allow individuals to derive individual benefits by betraying others. A long time ago Bateson pointed out that stability in human relations could not have developed unless evolution of verbal language occurred in the context of the growing importance of nonverbal languages: "The discourse of nonverbal communication is precisely concerned with matters of relationships—love, hate, respect, fear dependency, etc.—between self and vis-a-vis or between self and environment and that the nature of human society is such that falsification of this discourse becomes pathogenic" (Bateson 1975: 412).

The problem is to say something about the messages communicated in nonverbal languages in an anthropological text that must be written in a verbal language. This was the problem Barth confronted in his work on Baktaman cosmology:

> The rituals which we treat here contain and articulate precisely such wordless conceptions. Even where they are associated with words—spells, myths, or verbal explanations—we can have no assurance that these words capture the depth and dignity of the conceptions. So our task still remains: to put words to them which capture their genuine character and the knowledge they impart. (Barth 1987: 47)

I confronted a similar problem when I did fieldwork among the Fur of western Sudan in the 1960s and 1970s. My field project was focused on economic anthropology and human ecology, but by living in villages and participating in daily activities, I became increasingly fascinated by activities that I could not see served any practical purpose. Inspired by Bateson, I started to look at them as symbolic imagery that expressed and fostered "hard-wired" ideas about "taken for granted" content of social relations—a content that can be summed up in the word "trust." During the period of my fieldwork I found significant time and space variations in the symbolic imagery through which this theme was expressed.

Most importantly I found that these variations seemed to be influenced by the extent to which communities were involved in extra-local interaction systems (i.e., large scales), and maybe even more significant, some forms of imagery showed a "family resemblance" with cultural traditions I had read about in ethnographic studies from village communities in East Africa, while others were clearly linked to cultural traditions current in the large-scale civilization of Islam.

The nonverbal expressions of African traditions I assume constitute just fragments of much larger corpuses of signs. When it comes to traditions connected to the large-scale Islamic traditions, I am confronted with great problems because my knowledge of the sacred written sources and their various interpretations is limited. Before I get into presentation of the events on which I shall base my discussion, I find it necessary to give a summary sketch of the ethnographic context in which they were played out. The first part of the chapter will concentrate especially on how trust was formulated at small scales and typically at earlier times among the Fur. The second part then moves to the changes that occurred when contact with the much larger-scale flows of Islamizing movements began to alter the possible grounds for trust.

An Ethnographic Sketch

The westernmost part of Sudan, Darfur, covers an area roughly the size of England, ranging from desert in the north to high rainfall savanna in the south. The dominant traditional subsistence activities were camel nomadism (primarily in the northern part), transhumant cattle husbandry (primarily in the south), and millet/sorghum cultivation (primarily in the mid-zone). In Darfur, these subsistence activities were associated with different ethnic groups. The Fur was the largest ethnic group in Darfur, numbering in 1965 about five hundred thousand people. The Fur language is the only member of the Fur subfamily of the Nilo-Saharan language family (Greenberg 1966).

The area inhabited by the Fur is made up of two main subareas: the volcanic ranges of Jebel Marra and Jebel Si, and the surrounding undulating savanna. Sorghum and millet are the main staple crops, with vegetables like tomatoes, chili, sesame, okra, and fruit trees like mango and citrus fruits as the main cash crops. In the dry season, Baggara Arab and Fulani cattle herders migrate into the lowlands.

The Fur sultan was once ruler of the greatest empire in western Sudan, which periodically included several other groups of the region. Growth of the sultanate cannot adequately be understood unless seen in the context of politico-economic processes of global scale—primarily the trade of valued items (e.g., ivory, slaves, ostrich feathers, copper) from areas to the south of Jebel Marra to demand areas along the Nile valley and in the Mediterranean world. In 1596 Suleiman Solong (*Suliman* means "Arab" in the Fur language) became the first Islamic ruler, but the main Islamization process started about one hundred years later. During the Turco-Egyptian occupations of Sudan (1821–85), the Fur sultan maintained independence until 1874. In 1880 a local *faqih* (religious teacher), Muhammed Ahmed, established a religious order with his followers (Ansar) on Aba Island on the Nile and declared himself a Mahdi (the awaited guide from Allah). He declared jihad against Turkish-Egyptian rule and its European staff (including General Gordon). The Ansar order gained large support among the Baggara tribes of southern Darfur, and in 1884 they had conquered most of Sudan, including the Darfur Sultanate. Remnants of the Fur dynasty did however manage to hold out in the Jebel Marra region. With the Anglo-Egyptian conquest in 1898, one of them (Ali Dinar) managed to re-establish an independent sultanate that lasted until 1916 when the British invaded Darfur allegedly because Ali Dinar had conspired with the Turkish government during the World War I (O'Fahey 2008).

With the growth of urban centers (e.g., El Fasher, Nyala, Zalingi) that accompanied the integration of the region into the larger economy of the Anglo-Egyptian Condominium, there has been a marked increase in a number of the so-called Jellaba—traders of different Arab and Nubian groups from the Nile valley. Darfur was linked to the Nile valley by a railway over one thousand kilometers long and by truck transport across the savanna. Improved communications have since the 1950s increased external demand for agricultural crops from Darfur, at the same time as the supply of externally produced manufactured goods increased in local markets. Increased demand for imported market goods has made farmers significantly reorient their cultivation toward cash crops or alternatively stimulated them to migrate to urban areas or to the cotton-growing schemes along the Nile in search of wage employment.

A particular feature of Fur family organization was that husband and wife operated as separate management units—having individual access to communal land and being individually responsible for cultivating grain to fill grain stores kept in their individual huts. Both spouses geared their production toward sorghum to satisfy basic consumption food requirements (porridge and beer). Wives were responsible for their own and their children's food requirements as well as for cooking and brewing (her husband provided the grain required for his share), while husbands were responsible for providing wives and children with a certain amount of imported market goods. This required him to cultivate more vegetables for sale at local marketplaces. There were important institutional restrictions on investment in the agricultural sector— land was communal and could not be transacted for money; certain activities (wage work and sale of basic food items like beer and porridge) were codified as shameful (*ora*), similar to prostitution. The only investment opportunity was to make sorghum beer and invite neighbors to beer work-parties (*tawisa*) to help in the weeding activities (Barth 1967).

That form of family organization seemed strange because the Fur for centuries had embraced Muslim identity. To become a Muslim requires that a person declares his faith by stating in Arabic the *shahada* ("There is no God but Allah and Muhammad is his prophet"). From that moment, one is considered to have converted to Islam. Although the convert should express the *shahada* with sincerity of intention, this formula would leave "them free to live as before and practice their old customs, short of actual worship of idols and natural objects" (Trimingham 1965: 78). In Darfur people distinguish between *din* (an Arab concept designating the sacred beliefs and rituals of the religious books of Judaism, Christianity, and Islam) and *adat* (an Arab concept covering beliefs and ritual falling outside these books). By declaring the *shahada*, one embraced Muslim identity but might continue to practice *adat* not prescribed in the Qur'an. Embracing Islam did however serve as a stimulus to increasingly adopt prescribed Islamic practices. Ramadan was generally observed in the 1960s, a few people had been on hajj to Mecca, alms were given to Qur'an schoolboys, but the five daily prayers were far from generally observed.

Serendipity and Curiosity-Driven Research

The serendipity pattern refers to the fairly common experience of observing an unanticipated, anomalous and strategic datum which becomes the occasion for developing a new theory or for extending an existing theory.
—Robert K. Merton, *Social Theory and Social Structure*

An important aspect of anthropological research is the ability to pay attention to unexpected chance events we are exposed to in fieldwork. As Walters and Vayda have expressed it, we should use models and theories learned beforehand

as potential aids for drawing alternative working hypotheses to interpret findings of interest. In this case, the greater array of theoretical tools at one's disposal, the better, but researchers in the field should strive to be open and willing to adapt to findings that are surprising or contrary to expectations and they should resist the temptation to jump uncritically to conclusions when observations appear initially to conform to such expectation. (Walters and Vayda 2009: 544)

In 1965 I followed up Barth's studies in Darfur with fieldwork among Fur living in different ecological zones. (Barth had mainly worked in isolated mountain villages of Jebel Marra; I mainly worked in the lowland savanna regions toward the Chad border.) I could recognize many sociocultural similarities between what Barth had described from the mountain villages and what I observed in lowland villages where people had been much more affected by nationwide political and economic processes for a longer period. My curiosity about signs and their symbolic associations started when I attended a circumcision ceremony in the Fur village of Amballa in the lowland of western Sudan. At circumcision, while the boy was waiting in his mother's hut before the operation, a group of relatives entered the hut with a calabash filled with a mixture of grain flour and water and sprinkled the contents over him while exclaiming, "*Bora fatta*" (milk white).

The circumcision ceremonies that followed involved consumption of large amounts of local beer and performance of festive activities with dancing, most importantly girls running forward and backward alongside the camel on which the boy was riding to the place of circumcision. During the dance (called *ferangabie*, "dance of the gazelle"), the girls were singing songs with very explicit references to female genitalia and to the sexual pleasures awaiting circumcised boys, that is, after transition to manhood (see figure 6.1).

As the boy was circumcised, I noted that women were splashing millet flour mixed with water from a calabash while they rather ecstatically exclaimed, "*Bora fatta, bora fatta*," which literally means "white milk"—mother's milk. I don't know why the events of the circumcision stimulated my curiosity—initially I think it was the rather explicit reference to women as sources of sexual enjoyment that fascinated me, but as my fieldwork progressed I was exposed to

Figure 6.1. The dance of the gazelle (*ferangabie*) (author photograph)

a variety of occasions where the phrase *bora fatta* was uttered, occasions that I could not see had any connection to the sexual aspect of womanhood.

Let me sketch a few such occasions. In Amballa the traditional rain ritual was described to me as follows: Early in the rainy season (about July) some old women of the village go to a big *Gimmeiz* tree (a *Ficus* species) located in the fields between the village and the Azum wadi. A snake was said to live in the tree, and informants stated that it was important to prevent the snake from getting out of the tree during the day, because this would keep the rain away. This prevention was said to be accomplished by performing a ritual that the women carried out near the tree. First, they take some boiled grain and mix it with blood from a ram slaughtered by a man from the village. One of the women sprays this mixture in a big hole in the trunk of the tree while all of them say, "*Bora fatta, bora fatta, allasin kwei ell*" (White milk, white milk, God make rain come). Afterward the women crawl on their knees to a mound that is about fifty meters away while they continuously make sweeping-like movements with their hands on the ground as they utter the words "*Bora fatta, bora fatta, allasin kwei ell.*" At the mound (which is called *gubba*, i.e., the burial place of an Islamic saint), they splash a mixture of flour and water on the top of the mound while they continue to say "*Bora fatta, bora fatta, allasin kwei ell.*" The Islamic elements—Allah, *gubba*, and, probably, the slaughtering of the ram— do not change the basic association between use of millet products and use of the verbal expression *bora fatta*.

In Jebel Si, I observed activities directed toward curing an elderly lady who suffered from dysentery. Millet-flour paste was smeared around her navel. A small calabash of the kind used for drinking beer was then filled with straws from birds' nests. The straws were lighted, and when the contents of the calabash were burning, its open end was pressed against the paste smeared around the navel. After a few minutes, the calabash was pulled away. It looked like sticking to the paste and the act of pulling it away gave the impression that one was extracting something out from the navel. This was repeated three times, and afterward the rounded end of the calabash was used to massage the stomach while the words *bora fatta* were repeatedly uttered and the ancestors (*wouonga*) were addressed.

In 1969 the daughter of my host in the village of Umo in Jebel Marra came down with smallpox (*abo*—literally "grandmother"). The evening before the girl died, her mother's sister and her mother's mother "did" (this is what my Fur interpreter called the activity they performed) *bora fatta*. Both women crawled on their knees around the hut where the mother was with the sick girl while they swept the ground with their hands, all the time saying, "*Bora fatta, bora fatta*," and sometimes adding, "*Kwasi djundi dien tong na kien filo kal*" (as far as I was able to make out, this seemed to say something like "People leave this home and do your work").

I also frequently heard the words *bora fatta* uttered in a spitting-like fashion as way of expressing well-wishing or blessing. The words *bora fatta* were also said to be part of sequences of ritualized activities connected with warfare. These activities would fall into the category of *adat*. It is important to emphasize that these actions did not constitute a corpus of standardized ritual procedures—it rather seemed that people used *bora fatta* as one standard component that they combined with other components in a bricolage-like fashion that might make the ritualized activities effective in coping with vulnerabilities.

Bora Fatta as Metaphors of Trust

> Metaphor [is] a pervasive mode of understanding by which we project patterns from one domain of experience in order to structure another domain of a different kind.
>
> —Mark Johnson, *The Body in the Mind*

Obviously, it was not the concrete object "mother's milk" that they wanted to understand when the words *bora fatta* were uttered. I therefore thought that *bora fatta* referred to a domain they had a good understanding of and that this understanding was projected to another domain where their understanding was less clear.

It did not require much imagination to guess that mother's milk is a convincing metonym for the mother-child relationship (Haaland 1990, Haaland

1998). Neither did it require much imagination to guess the metaphoric association between motherhood and items connected with making food (e.g., pots were frequently referred to as *eja*—mother). Qualities like trust, nurturance, support, and solidarity are generally experienced as inherent in the mother-child relation—experiences that are strengthened by the close bodily contact as babies are carried on the mother's back during her daily chores virtually the whole day.

The mother is the nourisher par excellence, providing milk from her breasts and porridge and beer from her cooking and brewing pots. Beer and porridge are metaphorically associated with motherhood, and to subject these items to market transactions is like selling sex—both are considered *ora* (shameful). Activities and objects associated with motherhood are "set apart" as something associated with a "sacred-like" quality inherent in motherhood. Understanding of "trust" as a quality experienced in the domain of mother-child interactions makes acts and objects associated with this relation particularly convincing as metaphors fostering this quality in other domains where vulnerability is at stake.

From my observation of *bora fatta* it was obvious they were words uttered in situations characterized by vulnerability, such as life crises, diseases, droughts, conflicts, and warfare—situations where survival chances depend on others.

We may have genetic dispositions for construction of such beliefs in trust and "solidarity," but such dispositions have to be expressed in symbolic constructions giving concrete content about how to cope with afflictions we are exposed to in our social and natural environment.

Belief in solidarity is, however, vulnerable to doubt, and its maintenance has to be continually communicated by symbols that people experience as "true." It is difficult to think about signs more apt than metaphors based on the mother-child relation to express the quality of solidarity in wider social relations. While solidarity is highly resistant to doubt in the mother-child relation, this is not so obvious in wider relations. Solidarity in such wider relations cannot be "taken for granted" as it can in the mother-child relation, and it is therefore sensitive to lingering doubts about possible betrayal. Among the Fur, such doubts are conceptualized as witchcraft, with the male witch (*kar*) as the prototype for betrayal.

As Evans-Pritchard pointed out in his study of witchcraft among the Azande, afflictions like human health, crop failure, and other natural accidents are not understood as chance events, but as caused by bad feelings between people, particularly between those to whom one may be closely related. Bad feelings have causal consequences brought about by the mystical influence of witchcraft. Belief in witchcraft operates as a sanction on people who act in ways that may make people doubt whether they can rely on them (Evans-Pritchard 1937).

Among the Fur, a person who keeps to himself risks being described as having a black heart (*kilma dikko*). Keeping to oneself is also said to be a characteristic feature of a witch (*kar*). The observable characteristic of a *kar* is thus his unsociability. His power, the witchcraft, is said to work unconsciously in the dark when he is asleep. A black bird will come out from his heart and suck blood from its victims so that they get sick. Thus, the color black (*dikko*) is associated with unsociability and mystical forces emanating from the heart. The color white (*fatta*), on the other hand, is clearly associated with sociability and mutuality (*kilma fatta*) experienced in the mother-child relationship. Millet beer (*kira*) is also clearly conceived as white (in fact my English-speaking Fur interpreter invariably talked about it as "white stuff"). *Kira* also provides the occasion for a main expression of Fur sociability, namely beer drinking, which usually takes place in groups. The institutionalized work-party (*tawisa*) requires a supply of beer for participants. Participation is open and is a major manifestation of neighborly solidarity. The association between the color white, millet flour, *kira*, and sociability thus seems highly plausible. If we look at the consumption of porridge (*nung*), this, too, is clearly associated with solidarity and mutuality. In their traditional form the two daily meals of porridge are consumed at specific places (*darra*), usually in the compound of a person who is said to be the head of the *darra*. The participants in the meal are neighbors (all male), whose wives place the dishes of porridge in the middle of the *darra* group, where participants share the food their wives brought. A person who eats individually is considered to be a miser, and this exposes him to suspicions of being a witch (*kar*). Commensality among *darra* members serves as metaphor that simultaneously expresses and fosters mutual trust.

Let us now turn to relations in which the contrasting qualities are seen to operate on a more conscious level. Here the contrast is between relations that are "believed" to be solidary versus relations that are "known" to be competitive.

In its most extreme form competition is manifested in killings. The relation between a killer and the victim's relatives (bilaterally traced, though I never received a specification of any limitation on distance) is expressed by the statement that there is blood (*kewa*) between them. Where a *kewa* relation exists, food sharing should not take place. If it does, the sanction is leprosy, which is also called *kewa*. A leper is thus understood to be a person who has eaten from the same porridge as a killer of one of his relatives, but he may never know when that event took place or who the killer was. Active unsolidarity (as differentiated from the passive unsolidarity of the witch) is thus in its extreme form of killing described by the term *kewa* (blood). Envy of other people's possessions or position is also considered an active form of unsociability. Its unsociable consequences for the victims (loss of objects, sickness) work through the conscious influence of the envious person's evil eye (*nungi toké*—hot eye). Such a person is described as having a *kilma fokka* (red heart). The association between active unsociability, blood, and the color red seems reasonable. Consistent with this, the utterance of *bora fatta* on ceremonies like circumcision or marriage is said to mean "removal of the evil eye."

The communicative universe of *bora fatta*, *kar*, and *kewa* is not symbolic of Fur solidarity in contrast to other groups. The "others" who are a threat are one's neighbors, even one's relatives—it is among them that the suspicion of witchcraft arises, and it is among fellow Fur that conflicts over land, women, and so on is most likely to arise. *Bora fatta* symbolism serves to establish a precarious order in social relations in the limited intermediate space of social relations, while *kar* symbolism is conceptualized as the threat of disorder in this social space.

Symbolic imagery constructed around the mother-child relationship does not have attributes that make it a convincing prototype for construction of metaphors fostering solidarity within larger social units. In other words the pre-Islamic beliefs and rituals I observed among the Fur served to counteract threats to solidarity coming from people within local groups, not threats coming from outsiders.

The Islamic Cultural Tradition in Darfur

Threats from outsiders were tackled by the military power of the Fur sultans, and this power was not legitimized by articulation of mother-child based symbolism. Social order within the sultanate was based primarily on control of trade in concrete material resources and on an administrative/military apparatus strong enough to extract a food surplus from the cultivators large enough to maintain the military/administrative organization.

Most importantly the Fur sultans encouraged proselytization by wandering teachers who established Qur'anic schools in villages. These schools played a very important role in connecting males in interaction systems of a scale covering large parts of Darfur and even to centers of Islamic learning in the urban centers of the Islamic world. At the age of six to eight years, boys were sent to Qur'anic schools, where they were instructed by local teachers (*faqihs/fugara*) to write and recite verses from the sacred Qur'an (see figure 6.2). During a four- to six-year period, the Qur'an schoolboys (in Darfur called *Muhagerin*—the term used for the followers who fled with Muhammed to Medina) attend schools led by different *faqihs* located in villages spread all over Darfur.

As *Muhagerin* the boys are completely dependent on food they receive as alms from villagers. After their period as *Muhagerin* most boys return to their home village, but some may continue studies to acquire reputation in Islamic learning sufficient to set up their own Qur'anic schools or even to pursue higher Islamic studies at Al Azhar University in Cairo.

Recently a Sudanese anthropologist, Bakheit Nur Mohammed (himself a Fur and a Muslim), has argued

> that Islam had historically been proselytized among the Fur by individual religious men who came from different Islamic traditions and cultures. They infiltrated into the Fur society and intermarried within the local populations. This was a process in which immigrant religious men were culturally assimilated into the local cultural context and the Fur selectively acquired values of the new faith.

Figure 6.2. Qur'an schoolboys on the way to a new *faqih* in a different village (author photograph)

The Fur took Islam into their social system by transforming it according to their own experience. The formation of Fur Islam, therefore, was a process that combined both Islamisation of the Fur and Furisation of Islam, because the Fur did not only adhere to Islam but also appropriated it according to their social situation. Such indigenisation resulted in the appearance of the distinct characteristics of the *fuqarâ*, and their unique approach to the Qur'an and its usage in various aspects of social life. This combination also led to the emergence of a unique methodology of learning in Fur Qur'anic schools. Therefore, Qur'anic learning is deeply rooted in the Fur society and it forms an important aspect of people's social and cultural life. (Nur Mohammed 2017)

It is interesting to note that although the traditional Qur'anic teacher generally practiced rules of Islamic recommended behavior, they did not make much effort to prevent consumption of local beer or to advise people to discontinue the nightly dance parties where boys/men and girls/women lined up in two lines and, in rather suggestive movements, were jumping up and down facing each other—dances ending, as they said, with sweethearts going to the forest to "search for the needle."

Introduction of Islamic traditions brought about some new practices that dealt with the same problems of vulnerability and dependence as the *bora fatta* traditions did, but based on belief in a very different source of "taken-for-granted" trust, namely the sacred writings of the Qur'an. One such practice relates to vulnerabilities to diseases. In 1966 I observed that instead of arranging *bora fatta*–related metaphors as part of curing rituals, a local *faqih* was invited to write Qur'anic verses on the wooden tablets. The ink of the verses was washed off, and the sick person drank the water—literally consuming the curing power of the sacred words. I have been informed that this practice is also used for protection against other kinds of vulnerabilities.

Another widely used practice is use of *hijab* (small leather amulets worn on the right arm containing a few Qur'anic verses written by a *faqih*) as protection against weapons like knives, spears, and even bullets, as well as against harmful consequences caused by people's evil eye or witchcraft. This is also manifested in the belief that not all *faqihs* may be trustworthy and that they may even write verses containing words that might harm you and people close to you. The fact that practices related to Islamic elements are addressing the same concerns as the *bora fatta* indicate how strong the concern about trust and betrayal is among Fur people.

On this background, it may not be so surprising that at the same time as the Fur have a reputation for having more *faqihs* than any other group in Darfur, it is also the group that until recently has resisted Arabization most strongly. Neither is it so surprising that the two traditions until recently have coexisted as alternative ways of coping with vulnerabilities. As Darfur has increasingly been affected by exposure to large-scale changes in politico-economy, education and global communication systems have confronted people with experiences stimulating a search for new ways of understanding and coping with the hazards of nature and society.

After inclusion in the Anglo-Egyptian Sudan in 1898 and particularly after World War II, the Fur people have increasingly participated in interaction systems of national and international scale—participation that exposed them to new kinds of vulnerabilities where dependencies on fellow humans are more difficult to ascertain.

The Anglo-Egyptian Sudan colonial power pursued a quite active economic policy by stimulating the growth of irrigated cotton production for export. This was mainly concentrated in the Nile valley, but the populations of the savanna also benefited because of the income they gained as migratory laborers during cotton-picking season. As Meillasoux has argued, this tended to have important macro-level consequences. It stimulated dualistic trends where the savanna cultivators have one foot in the traditional subsistence economy and one foot in the modern commercial economy, while the modern enterprises have one foot in the subsistence economy, which supplies them with cheap labor, and one foot in the world economy, which demands the products of the modern enterprises. The dynamics of such systems seem to produce similar outcomes: lack of development of forces of production on the family farms and rapid development of productive forces in the "modern" enterprises (Meillasoux 1972). In 1973, 542,000 migratory laborers (with a large number recruited from Fur lowlands) were seasonally employed in cotton harvesting in the great Gezirah project. In its extreme form the migrants' wages may be below the reproduction costs of labor, because labor is largely reproduced in the subsistence sector—this is the sector where laborers are born and grow up, and it is to this sector they return to cultivate subsistence crops when their engagement in the modern sector is discontinued. Labor migration was the dominant way that Fur lowlanders used to earn cash required to satisfy increasing cash needs. An important aspect of labor migration was that the employment situation correlated with a systematic cultural difference between the central Arab elite and the non-Arab migrants.

Coping with experiences harvested in this confusing world of macro-scale changes stimulated a search for cultural constructions that could serve as "models of" the situation people found themselves in and as "models for" actions to improve that situation. The Fur search for such cultural reconceptualization has to be seen against the background of politico-economic processes of Sudan-wide scale.

Ethnic contrasts had somehow been held at bay under colonial rule, but after independence in 1956 these problems became precarious issues. Now the government had to mobilize authority from within the country. Such mobilization is notoriously problematic when the country's population is fragmented along a multitude of economic, religious, and ethnic fault lines and where the population neither share feelings of joint national identity nor agree on the "rules of the political game." Clifford Geertz has pointed to the critical problem of creating a convincing ideological platform that explains and justifies a state-wide social order:

> Now that there is a local state rather than merely a dream of one, the task of nationalist ideologizing radically changes. It no longer consists in stimulating popular alienation from a foreign-dominated political order, nor with orchestrating a mass celebration of that order's demise. It consists in defining, or trying to define, a collective subject to whom the actions of the state can be internally connected, in increasing, or trying to create, an experiential "we" from whose will the activities of government seem spontaneously to flow. And as such, it tends to revolve around the question of content, relative weight, and proper relationship of two rather towering abstractions: "The Indigenous Way of Life" and "The Spirit of the Age." (Geertz 1973: 240)

The problem of creating an experiential "we" out of a population as fragmented as in Sudan is difficult indeed. The populations of savanna regions of the north and of the south are separated by ethnic and religious identities—Islam is dominant in the north, and Christianity is dominant among the educated elite in the south.

Articulation of "the spirit of the age" kind of ideology had a certain appeal among educated people and trade unionists. In the 1970s that spirit was closely associated with Marxist ideas. It had to some extent served to legitimize the military rule of Nimeiry. Many Sudanese, particularly those in urban employment, found the abstract principles of Marxist theory of historical development appealing because they provided a plausible conceptual model explaining the causes behind critical socioeconomic problems the independent country was facing and also served as a "model for" political action in order to eliminate these causes.

However, articulation of abstract principles like "mode of production" and "class struggle" had to confront strong interests connected to a perspective of who the "we" are, namely a perspective that is not rooted in impersonal factors but on personal identification with "an indigenous way of life." On the important arena of student politics, the Communist Party and the Muslim Brothers were the dominant groups in the Student Union at University of Khartoum. The Muslim Brothers can also be seen as a "spirit of the age" kind of ideological platform. While the Communists identified the "spirit of the age" with the assumption of eventual victory of societies based on communist principles of economic organization, the Muslim Brothers identified the "spirit of the age" with the assumption of eventual victory based on the spiritual superiority of the puritan and scripturalist Islam as Allah had revealed it to the Prophet Mohammad. An important aspect of Muslim Brotherhood ideology is that it can also be seen as the authentic "indigenous way of life" as practiced by the Prophet and his companions, but which later generations have corrupted.

The main challenge to reproduction of basic Fur cultural elements came from the expansion of the national educational system in Darfur, and these challenges continue up through the present. Members of the Muslim Brotherhood became increasingly influential in the education system, and interviews indicate that the teaching of the Brotherhood increasingly influenced Fur students from the 1960s and onward. Many of the young students saw it as a religious obligation to weed out *bora fatta*–associated *adat*. Although the Fur educated elite for a while resisted central Arab dominance by appealing to elements of Fur culture (e.g., collection of folk stories and folk songs) that could serve as markers contrasting with cultural elements of central Sudanese Arab culture (Haaland 1978), Fur resistance later became inspired also by other sources similar to the ideological platform of the central government, namely the teachings of the Muslim Brotherhood as expressed by Hassan al Turabi. One of the Darfur resistance groups, JEM (Justice and Equality Movement), probably considers much of the inventory of traditional Fur culture pretty close to idolatry and worship of natural objects. Another resistance group among the Fur was originally SLM/A (Sudan Liberation Movement/Army). The founder of the movement, Abdel Wahid al Nur, has explicitly endorsed establishment of a secular state.

These two main contemporary resistance movements seem to articulate different cultural policies in Darfur, with JEM aiming to replace traditional beliefs and practices with an Islamic cultural platform very similar to the ideology articulated by the central government. If JEM succeeds, it may lead to reduced cultural differences between the Fur and the Arabs. Although cultural differences may be reduced, the ethnic dichotomy (Fur versus Arab) may still be relevant, although of diminishing social relevance. If SLM/A succeeds, active articulation of Fur specific cultural inventory may serve as a factor in maintaining Fur-Arab ethnic dichotomization.

An important change has taken place in the symbolism of trust. Instead of being anchored in the experience-near concept of mother-child solidarity, one now increasingly finds that it is anchored in the experience-distant concept of an all-powerful but incomprehensible Allah. Instead of using the Fur words *bora fatta* as an expression of blessing, the Islamic Arabic word *baraka* is increasingly used instead. Although not a local Darfur formulation, verses of the Arab female poet Aasiyah Abdul Musawwir provide an example of imagery expressing solidarity of the global community of Muslim believers (the Ummah) with the solidarity inherent in the Fur construction of mother-child solidarity—light (*nur*) from Allah is symbolically associated with the umbilical cord:

> Arabic, you are the tongue
> of my spirit
> And Wallahi,
> it is no coincidence that
> umm, "mother,"
> and Ummah, "community,"
> come from the same root. . . .
>
> This hijab
> declares proud lineage
> not of blood—
> but of light.

Conclusion

Barth's contribution in my opinion was not to establish a grand "substantive theory" about society and culture, but rather to develop an "analytical theory" of conceptual tools that might stimulate well-corroborated leaps from fragments of observations to statements that revealed something about the complexity of the human condition wherever we encountered it.

Feedback loops between micro and macro levels are central in Barth's analytical orientation: "I urge that we . . . recognize the penetration of society deep into the privacy and psyche of the individual, and that we recognize how much of every individual is out there, dispersed in his or her previous and current relationship with others" (Barth 1987: 86).

In making such leaps Barth argued that we as anthropologists needed to focus on sociocultural reality in its "widest compass: a natural world, a human population with all its collective and statistical features, and a set of cultural ideas in terms of which these people try to understand and cope with themselves and their habitat" (Barth 1987: 87). Some of us (e.g., Levi-Strauss, Barthes) have focused on clarification of systemic features of verbal and nonverbal sign systems of cultural ideas found in particular communities; some (e.g., the structural-functional school) focused on the way corporate group organizations regulate interaction; others (e.g., Marvin Harris) searched for explanation of social forms with reference to their ecosystem implications. In contrast, Barth argued that "ideas and concepts cannot be modelled as if they were abstract, logical constructs linked together in an orderly universal science. On the contrary, they are images which are used when we engage the world—i.e., they are linked to contexts and purposes as well as to each other. Their definition inheres significantly in the rules of relevance that attach to them, the operations that are invoked. To grasp them, we should not sever them from these connections of practice and only consider them in the abstract, as thought. We must also observe them in their range of use, as knowledge" (Barth 1994b: 356).

In my sketch of lifeworlds among the Fur as they have unfolded in time and space, I have tried to place signs relating to the basic human concern about trust and betrayal in the context of dramatic changes that have taken place in politico-economic and communicative interactions system the people of Darfur participate in. The micro-macro levels have undergone far-reaching changes since Barth did his study in the Umo mountain village. In 1963 the most important interaction systems impinging on people's choices were of intermediate scale. Where I did my studies in the lowlands a few years later people were placed in interaction systems of much larger scale, connecting them to national and international markets, and to a much stronger impact of central policy making. Changes in the scale of macro-level interaction systems imply that the range of micro-level choices confronting people have been dramatically altered. In the village of Umo in the early 1960s, choices were overwhelmingly based on institutionalized taken-for-granted knowledge not requiring much rational calculation of alternatives. Today the Fur (like most others) are living in a world of global flows of material goods, political power, and communicative messages: "We now realize that global empirical variation in culture is continuous, it does not partition neatly into separable, integrated wholes. In any population we may choose to observe, we may also find that it is in flux, it is contradictory and incoherent, and it is differently distributed on variously positioned persons" (Barth 1994a: 14). This has expanded the range and the importance of choice in ways that have opened the field for entrepreneurial activities widely. On the micro level, people are faced with the agony of choice in various sectors of life. Economic careers, politico/administrative connections, as well as ethnic identifications and religious/ideological commitments are now up for choice.

On the ideological level, the fundamental choice is today largely articulated as one between secularism and fundamentalist Islam. As Peter Berger has pointed out, modernity and secularization have confronted the individual "with a multitude of choices that previously were unimaginable—choices of career, intimate relationships, political and religious values, even the very definition of one's own identity" (Berger and Zijderveld 2010: 45). The other side of freedom of choice is the agony of choice that may generate a longing for premodern certainties as manifested in the modern growth of fundamental-ist movements. Shmuel N. Eisenstadt has argued that there is a close relation between fundamentalist movements and modernity in organizational charac-teristics (tight party-like discipline, modern communication technologies, and modern propaganda techniques):

> But it is above all with respect to their ideological features, to the mode of con-struction of their ideologies, that the relations between the fundamentalist move-ments and the modern world, modernity, is most conspicuous. . . . The basic ideology of fundamentalism is antimodern: the negation of some of the basic ten-ets of modernity—of the autonomy of the individual, of the hegemony of reason, of the ideology of progress, and the like. (Eisenstadt 1995: 264)

For the anthropologist who straddles the gap between painstaking learning of cultural idioms by participating in local life and the need to understand how this life is shaped by macro-level system dynamics, this seems like an impossi-ble task. Barth addressed this problem most importantly in the book he edited, *Scale and Social Organization*:

> Large-scale society also takes place between people. By insisting on this fact, we avoid a trap into which anthropologists easily fall, that the study of local commu-nities is the study of small-scale systems, while large-scale society somehow exists only outside these loci and is to be discovered in the *interconnections between* communities in a region, between regions and states and supra-national alliances. No such hierarchy in fact obtains, and small-scale communities do not aggregate into large-scale systems. (Barth 1978: 256)

Following Wallerstein (1988), he argued for the need to unthink nineteenth-century social science that had divided different aspects of intertwining pro-cesses into fields of study allocated to separate disciplines (Barth 1992: 18).

Gunnar Haaland is Professor Emeritus in the Department of Social Anthro-pology at the University of Bergen. He began his career as an applied anthropol-ogist. His scholarly focus was on human ecology and economic anthropology, but in his applied work he soon became interested in ethnic processes, where he has made his most important contributions. In his later career he has pub-lished works on culture history in cooperation with Randi Haaland. Most of his work is based on fieldwork in Sudan and in South Asia. He is currently working on the long-term impacts of the so-called axial breakthroughs.

References

Barth, Fredrik. 1967. "Economic Spheres in Darfur." In *Themes in Economic Anthropology*, edited by R. Firth. London: Tavistock.

———. 1969. *Ethnic Groups and Boundaries: The Social Organization of Culture Difference*. Boston: Little, Brown.

———, ed. 1978. *Scale and Social Organization*. Oslo: Universitetsforlaget.

———. 1981. *Process and Form in Social Life: Selected Essays of Fredrik Barth*. London: Routledge & Kegan Paul.

———. 1987. *Cosmologies in the Making: A Generative Approach to Cultural Variation in Inner New Guinea*. Cambridge: Cambridge University Press.

———. 1992. "Towards Greater Naturalism in Conceptualizing Societies." In *Conceptualizing Society*, edited by A. Kuper. New York: Routledge.

———. 1993. *Balinese Worlds*. Chicago: University of Chicago Press.

———. 1994a. "Enduring and Emerging Issues in the Analysis of Ethnicity." In *Beyond Ethnic Groups and Boundaries*, edited by Hans Vermeulen and Cara Govers. Amsterdam: Het Spinhuis.

———. 1994b. "A Personal View of Present Tasks and Priorities in Cultural and Social Anthropology." In *Assessing Cultural Anthropology*, edited by R. Borofsky. New York: McGraw-Hill.

Bateson, Gregory. 1975. *Steps to an Ecology of Mind*. New York: Ballantine.

Berger, Peter, and Anton Zijderveld. 2010. *In Praise of Doubt*. New York: Harper Collins.

Dunbar, Robin. 2010. *How Many Friends Does One Person Need?* London: Faber and Faber.

Eisenstadt, Shmuel. N. 1995. "Fundamentalism, Phenomenology, and Comparative Dimensions." In *Fundamentalism Comprehended*, edited by M. E. Marty and R. S. Appleby. Chicago: University of Chicago Press.

Evans-Pritchard, Edmund E. 1937. *Witchcraft, Oracles and Magic among the Azande*. Oxford: Clarendon Press.

Geertz, Clifford. 1973. *The Interpretation of Cultures*. New York: Basic Books.

Greenberg, Joseph. 1966. *The Languages of Africa*. 2nd ed. Bloomington: Indiana University Press.

Haaland, Gunnar. 1978. "Ethnic Groups and Language Use in Darfur." In *Aspects of Language in the Sudan*, by R. Thelwell. Occasional Papers in Linguistics and Language Learning 5. Ulster: New University of Ulster.

———. 1990. "Øl og morsmelk (Beer and Mother's Milk)." *Norsk Antropologisk Tidsskrift* 1: 3–16.

———. 1998. "Beer, Blood and Mother's Milk." *Sudan Notes and Records* 2: 53–76.

Johnson, Mark. 1987. *The Body in the Mind*. Chicago: University of Chicago Press.

Macintyre, Alasdair. 1999. *Dependent Rational Animals*. Chicago and La Salle, IL: Open Court.

Meillasoux, Claude. 1972. "From Reproduction to Production." *Economy and Society* 1: 93–105.

Merton, Robin K. 1964. *Social Theory and Social Structure*. London: Free Press.

Musawwir, Aasiyah Abdul. 2010. "Umm and Umma." Virtual Mosque. http://www.virtualmosque.com/miscellaneous/poetry-fiction/umm-and-ummah/.

Nur Mohammed, Bakheit. 2017. *The Religious Men in Jebel Marra: The Process of Learning and the Performance of Islamic Rituals and Practices*. Berlin: LIT Verlag.

O'Fahey, Rex S. 2008. *The Darfur Sultanate*. London: Hurst.

Rappaport, Roy. 1979. *Ecology, Meaning and Religion*. Richmond, CA: North Atlantic Books.

Trimingham, J. Spencer. 1965: *Islam in the Sudan*. Oxford: Oxford University Press.

Wallerstein, Immanuel. 1988. "Should We Unthink Nineteenth-Century Social Science?" *International Social Science Journal* 118: 525–31.

Walters, Bradley. B., and Andrew Vayda. 2009. "Event Ecology, Causal Historical Analysis and Human Environment Research." *Annals of the Association of American Geographers* 99(3): 534–53.

7

Khan and Sufi
Two Types of Authority
in Swat, Northern Pakistan

Charles Lindholm

In this chapter, I will revisit some aspects of Fredrik Barth's work among the Yusufzai Pukhtun of Swat, Northwestern Pakistan. In the spirit of Barth's great essay "The Guru and the Conjurer," I will sketch two contrasting Swati modes of teaching, valorizing, and contesting authority as "ideal types . . . culturally constructed on syndromes of premises and concepts" (Barth 1990: 642). Unlike the Baktaman conjurer and Balinese guru that Barth discussed, in Swat the ideal types of khan and Sufi exist within the same social formation. The first is epitomized in the warrior ethos of the Yusufzai; the second is a spiritual ideal exemplified by Sufis. In my analysis, following Barth, I shall "focus on efficient causes: the cultural and interactional enablements and constraints that affect actors, with consequences that can be seen in the patterning of resulting acts and their aggregate entailments" (Barth 1990: 651).

But first, some personal background: I've always been proud of the fact that Barth and I did our doctoral fieldwork in the same place, albeit twenty years apart. My local informants had never met him but had heard of him. They teased me about the "Englishman" who had preceded me and spoke their language far better than I. As every anthropologist knows, his research led to a classic ethnography, *Political Leadership among Swat Pathans* (1959a), as well as a number of equally influential papers. I was privileged to be able to build on his foundation.

As for me, I went to Swat completely by accident in the late 1960s, on an unplanned side trip from my overland voyage to Japan, where I had a scholarship to study brush technique. While visiting Swat, I met and became friends with Zaman Khan, who invited me to stay in his village (in my ethnography I called it Shin Bagh—Green Garden) and introduced me to his friends and relatives who were khans of the Malik *khel*[1] subdivision of the Painda khel, the leading clan in one of the two factions (*dullah*)[2] that divided the Shamizai area of Upper Swat. As their designation as Malik (ruler) suggests, my friend's clan was once the most powerful and respected in the Painda khel, but their dominance had faded by the time I visited them. As they told me, "We are weak because we have produced no great men" (Charles Lindholm 1982: 91). However, they still proudly upheld the Pukhtun values of hospitality and generosity. I was a guest for some months in Shin Bagh and forgot about going to Japan. Instead, I returned to the United States and studied anthropology.

Eventually, I spent a total of about fifteen months living in the village, settling into my friend's compound with my wife and daughter during my fieldwork. For various reasons, I never returned but maintained my relationship with Swat secondhand, through Zaman's half brother, my friend Dr. Sher M. Khan, who was born and raised in Shin Bagh and whose autobiography (S. M. Khan 2015) I draw on for my discussion below. I have also referred to my field notes as well as other writings on Swat and on similar systems elsewhere in the Middle East. I caution the reader that this chapter pertains to the traditional society of Swat. It is a very different place today. But that is another story.[3]

The Playing Field

Like Barth, my research and writing were largely determined by what most interested the elite khans[4] who were my major informants. These were tales of former battles, political maneuvering, and the rise and fall of leaders. Almost everything I learned confirmed Barth's analyses of the manner in which political authority was conceptualized, sought, maintained, and lost in the Swati social formation, which, in theory, was an acephalous segmentary lineage system based on patterned relationships of complimentary opposition between coequal patrilineal kin groups. According to legend, these encompassing lineage relationships dated back to the apocryphal apical ancestor Qais and divided the millions of Pukhtun/Pashtun[5] into equivalent segments. On the ground, the salient reality was, as my friends explained to me, a version of the old Arabic formula of "I against my brothers; my brothers and I against our [patrilateral] cousins; my cousins, my brothers, and I against the world."

In the Swati case, the most significant and violent opposition in the narrow and overpopulated valley was between father's brother's sons who farmed adjacent plots of land and whose families often intermarried. The informal (and insulting) term for these close relatives was *tarbur*, which loosely translates as "enemy." These "close enemies" typically aligned themselves with one or the other of the two opposing neighborhood factions[6] that were named after the dominant lineages in the region. In Shamizai, as I mentioned, one of these was the Painda khel. Their traditional rival was the Mamat khel.

Although the Yusufzai speak of these dyadic dullahs as if they were concrete entities, in practice they are a statement, couched in universal and abstract terms, of the fluid oppositions and alliances among individuals. At the basic household level, a man opposes his neighboring tarbur, but he usually has several tarbur. So he can war with or remain neutral toward or even ally with one of his tarbur against the others, according to his perception of his own advantage. The dyadic dullah alliance therefore is crosscut by a shifting triadic relationship consisting of ego, his momentary allies, and his momentary rivals. This pattern is replicated at the ward, neighborhood, village, and regional level, as men pledge allegiance to the dullah of their local leaders, while their enemies support the opposing dullah. But they can also opportunistically oscillate between the two factions according to circumstances. In other words, uncertainty and betrayal are built into the system at every level (Lindholm 1986).[7]

To make matters even more complex, dullah alliances are trumped by obligations of revenge (*badal*) and honor (*ghairat*). No man would support the murderer of his tarbur or the seducer of a tarbur's sister or wife under any circumstances, even if the miscreant were a longtime dullah partner and the tarbur a detested rival. To do so would besmirch the honor of the lineage and all its members. In such cases, "close enemies" temporarily unite to retaliate against the perpetrator and his family (Lindholm 1981). Similarly, when the integrity of a larger unit was threatened, longtime opponents could temporarily set aside their differences in order to uphold their shared *ghairat*. This could extend to the whole valley, as when the armies of the British threatened Swat a century ago. As I shall discuss later, organizing such large-scale unity generally required the leadership of an outsider whose authority was validated by his sacred status as a Sufi *pir* (spiritual master—*shaikh* in Arabic).

Keeping this rudimentary sketch of the shifting polity in mind, we can investigate the "syndromes of premises and concepts" (Barth 1990: 642) that validate the power of a secular khan in Swat. As Barth states, for the khan, "it is the fact of effective control and ascendancy—not its formal confirmation or justification—that is consistently pursued" (1985: 175). In other words, the great khan who holds power has the right to power—until he doesn't. When he fails to dominate, he loses legitimacy. This is because the Pukhtun consider any secular leader simply first among equals, to be followed and obeyed when strong, overthrown and replaced when his grip loosens. Actual authority rarely lasts more than one generation, if that, since the great khan's resources of land, wealth, and prestige are likely to be exhausted during his lifetime in struggles with his tarbur and more distant rivals and even by battles with his own adult sons, who want to control their share of his patrimony.

In this competitive situation, where lasting control over others is difficult to obtain and impossible to maintain, allegiance to a great man has nothing to do with his access to esoteric secrets, as occurs among the Baktaman Barth studied. Neither is it associated with the Balinese guru's transmission of expert knowledge. Nor is authority based on his industrious pursuit and accumulation of wealth. On the contrary, the proud khan despises merchants, refuses to work for anyone else, and is admired if he spends his resources heedlessly.[8] And while membership in a noble lineage gives contestants for command a head start, it does not ensure success, since the Pukhtun knows that dishonorable behavior in the present offsets the credit established in the past, while honorable behavior today raises the status of the lowly.

For the Yusufzai, the ultimate criterion for designation as a great man is his persona as a *sakh* (real/exemplary) Pukhtun. At minimum, such a man must be a landowner and a member of a Pukhtun lineage. But far more importantly, he must exemplify in action the universally known virtues of the Pukhtun (*Pukhtunwali*). These are usually defined as *badal* (revenge), *melmastia* (hospitality), and *nanawatia* (refuge). He must protect the chastity of his women and uphold the honor of his khel. He must be brave, handsome, athletic, generous, diplomatic, intelligent, and stoic. He is also an implacable enemy who, as the pithy Pukhtun proverbs (*mataluna*) have it, "takes revenge after fifty years and says, 'I took it quickly,'" and "returns a blow for a pinch." Proper self-presentation is essential for the sakh Pukhtun, for whom, as for the Kayble of Algeria, "the innermost personality, with its uniqueness and individuality, is concealed beneath a veil of modesty and discretion ... the expression of the feelings is always carefully controlled, restrained and reserved. Generally it is seemly to dissimulate and keep silent about the natural side of life, the inner world, the affections, emotions and feelings" (Bourdieu 1974: 210, 225). As the great Pashtun warrior poet Khushal Khan Khattack cautions:

> If it's your hope never to be / Shamed before anyone
> It's best to keep within your heart / Even your least affair.
> Let your heart bleed within itself, /Khushal, if bleed it must,
> But keep your secrets well concealed / From both stranger and friend. (1965: 36)

A real Pukhtun therefore displays an impassive demeanor outside the house. He never speaks loudly in public. He holds himself erect, and like a member of the English royal family, he keeps his hands clasped behind his back when he walks. His gait is steady. He neither hurries nor dawdles. He always looks at others directly and shakes hands firmly; he is alert and lets nothing escape him, unlike those who foolishly gaze at the clouds or stare at the ground. He treats guests with respect and generosity. He shows decisiveness and has mastered the delicate art of commanding without disrespecting those commanded. Among his age-mate allies he is humorous and informal, but he demands the deference of his juniors, who cannot address him by name. Likewise, he defers to his elders by standing when they enter, not speaking unless spoken to, not gossiping or using racy language, not smoking or chewing tobacco or laughing and joking in front of them.

As Bourdieu and many others have argued, the accumulation and demonstration of the "symbolic capital" of manly honor is the predominant mode of self-assertion throughout the Middle East and, in somewhat different form, around the Mediterranean. In Swat, as elsewhere, a man becomes *beghairata* (without honor) by being cowardly, greedy, or foolish, or by losing self-control, or by being cuckolded, or by otherwise failing to uphold the recognized honor code. A casual observer will notice no evident difference in the way a beghairata is treated and the treatment offered to those who are respected. But in fact he has become a nonperson, still living in the community, but only as a shadow. He will not be asked to participate in any collective activities, his word will be disregarded, his lineage will be disgraced, his children will be shamed. Not respected by others, he can have no respect for himself. No wonder, then, that men will sacrifice a great deal, even their lives, to avoid this fate.

Learning How to Play the Game

At this early stage in his career, Barth was mainly interested in establishing the parameters and contradictions of the Pukhtun's political organization. He therefore said little about how the foundations for a man's participation in the pervasive public game of honor are first instilled in the privacy of the home. There a male child is pampered and praised; he gets the best food, wears clean clothes, is petted by his mother, is given presents, does no work, and can beat and insult his sisters, who, rather than hitting back, will cater to his wishes. A prince in the compound, a young boy can do no wrong and is given a very high opinion of himself early in life. He is trained to believe that his desires will be met if he whines and demands attention long enough and with sufficient intensity. In so doing, he must compete with his brothers and half brothers, who, like him, want to be the center of attention. It is not surprising that the first words of a Pukhtun child are likely to be *ma la*—"give me." In sum, the young boy is raised to expect indulgence from his mother and rivalry from his siblings. He gains attention mainly by nagging and crying.

At about the age of seven, when he is thought to have attained the capacity to reason, things change. Although his mother still pampers him, his father now begins to take a more active role in teaching him how to act like a true Pukhtun. The boy learns the genealogy and history of his khel. He is told that he comes from a lineage of heroes and chevaliers, staunch and fearless upholders of Pukhtunwali. It is his duty to defend this heritage. He is also trained in the rituals of greeting and politeness and harshly punished for lapses such as carelessness, clumsiness, or any kind of awkwardness. Putting one's hands near one's face, failure to stand still, or even a vacant expression is liable to lead to a hard slap and to being cursed as *bedagh* (passive homosexual). The Pashtun writer Ghani Khan succinctly expresses the philosophy underlying raising a male child: "The eye of the dove is lovely, my son, but the sky is made for the hawk. So cover your dovelike eyes and grow claws" (1958: 12). The manifest self-confidence of the "real" Pukhtun is built on the conquest of the pervasive fear that is its opposite and its dynamic.

A boy puts in practice what his father has taught him when he joins one of the gangs that freely roam in the neighborhood, spending their time fighting among themselves, playing pranks on the villagers, "abusing and complaining,"[9] stealing fruit, undergoing tests of courage, shooting birds, learning to masturbate, and battling other gangs "with sticks, punches, kicks and stones from our slingshots" (S. M. Khan 2015: 24). As I wrote in my ethnography, "In these years, they learn the skills they will need in later life. Weaker boys learn to attach themselves to those who are stronger. Leaders learn how to establish a loyal following. Boys learn stealth and bravado while their fears of humiliation are reinforced" (Charles Lindholm 1982: 176). In the gang, the strongest and most daring rule, and if a khan's son comes crying home with a bloody nose, he is likely to get a slap across the face from his father for showing fear and not fighting back.[10]

When he is a little older, a boy leaves the protection of his home permanently and moves into one of the two village *hujras* (men's houses)—the one that is associated with his father's faction. Always built next door to the neighborhood mosque, the hujra is the center for male social life. There the boy learns the etiquette of receiving and serving guests, elders, and dependents. At night he hears the rousing *char beta* verses sung and poems recited to commemorate heroes of the past and listens to his elders tell stories of the clan's great men and victorious battles. The hujra is also a place to celebrate marriages and alliances between groups, witness the proceedings of *jirgas* (counsels), and engage in clandestine sexual activity. In this all-male environment, the young man sees how the presiding elders reconcile disputes, how political decisions are negotiated, and how strategies are planned and carried out. Eventually, when he shows himself capable, he is given the chance to participate, albeit as a junior partner, in the corporation. In other words, the hujra is a kind of finishing school for young men. There they learn the actual nuts and bolts of being a "real" Pukhtun.

To recapitulate: A young khan boy is given a very high opinion of himself within the household, but he must learn to compete with his brothers and half brothers at home and with equally self-confident boys in the gang. When he is a little older, his father begins teaching him the rigid rules of decorum and restraint expected of a sakh Pukhtun and punishes him for any awkwardness or evidence of cowardice or weakness. The boy learns to hide his fears behind a hawk-like self-presentation. Later, when he moves to the hujra, he lives among men and absorbs their manners, attitudes, and practices. His socialization makes him an adult who has (or presents himself as having) the attributes of a leader. He knows how to hold himself with dignity and what is expected of his public performances; he is primed to emulate the heroic examples of his ancestors and has learned the proud self-confidence and feelings of entitlement that press him to pursue the power and position he feels he deserves as his birthright. He has also incorporated a dread of shaming that keeps him from showing fear or behaving dishonorably. He believes in the axiom that "the Pukhtun is never at peace unless he is at war."

Equality, Authority, and Jealousy

The merger of the capacities of the leader and the inculcated "natural" capacities of all khans solves the predicament of justifying superiority in a social world of ideological peers. From this perspective, the leader is simply someone who asserts his character as a sakh Pukhtun in the manly pursuit of authority over his coequals, who also wish to be recognized as sakh Pukhtun. Therefore, any secular leader's ambitions and his superiority are in no way otherworldly or awesome; he is simply a man who has most forcefully displayed the traits central to every Pukhtun's idealized vision of himself.[11] The only difference is that the leader has temporarily won the political game that all men play, just as all boys vie to lead their gangs and outdo their brothers. His authority is not institutionalized in any way. It is a momentary prize to be contested, not an eternal essence to be accepted. In this "syndrome," leaders may leave great names and glorious stories but are never more than first amidst their peers, destined eventually to be supplanted. None can claim intrinsic superiority for themselves or their descendants. As Ghani Khan explains, "A true democrat, the Pukhtun thinks he is as good as anyone and his father rolled into one" (1958: 47).[12]

Under these circumstances, poor and weak khans can lay claim to great ancestors and regard their present lowered state as the work of an unfortunate fate, to be reversed in the future. Men from these subordinate clans carry themselves exactly like their betters, and if one of them is accused of dishonorable dealing, he will defend himself, not by evidence, but by a recitation of his lineage and the cry of "Am I not a Pukhtun!" Even a landless peasant does not automatically regard himself as permanently doomed to inferiority, nor does he greatly resent the power of the khans who dominate him. Instead, he wishes to somehow manage to join them, despite his present state of servility. As a poor farmer once told me, "The landlords sit upon the necks of the poor. God grant that I may become a landlord!" Achieving this dream, while highly unlikely, is not completely impossible. There are stories of poor men who, through their extraordinary bravery, loyal service, and astute maneuvering, have been granted land by their patrons and gained respect; some eventually won the right to be addressed as khans.

Thus all Yusufzai, including even landless retainers, hope someday to gain supremacy for themselves—if not over the village or the ward, at least over their tarbur—and feel no great moral horror at the success of any of their coequals. As Barth writes:

> Independence and personal sovereignty were highly, perhaps inordinately, valued; but they were conceptualized as goods for each to seek for himself, not as rights for all, to be collectively safeguarded by all. A person who commanded effective and sufficient sanctions to dominate and exploit others was not particularly condemned and his acts were not collectively resisted—indeed he would rather be admired and sought as ally and leader, unless he was so feared for the threat he might pose to one's own autonomy that one sought to build a defensive faction against him. (Barth 1985: 169)

Because leaders lack any institutionalized legitimization of their authority over their coequals, the admiration and fear they arouse is accompanied not by moral outrage, but by intense resentment from other Pukhtun, friend and foe alike, who have been raised to believe that they too have the right and the capacity to lead. As Mountstuart Elphinstone, the first English observer of the Pukhtun, noted, "Their independence and pretensions to equality make them view the elevation of their neighbors with jealousy, and communicate a deep touch of envy to their disposition. The idea that they are neglected or passed over, while their equals are attended to, will lead them to renounce a friendship of long standing, or a party to which they have been zealously attached" (1815: 1:329).[13]

The pervasive tendency to betrayal that I mentioned earlier is therefore not only structurally implicit, it is also a deep psychological impulse, as envious subordinates desert their patrons and join rival leaders if they see an opportunity for personal advancement and (equally important) for humbling their former chief. As Ghani Khan puts it, among the Pukthun "there is an autocrat in each home who would rather burn his own house than see his brother rule it" (1958: 46). As a result of this pattern, Pukhtun dynasties have proved very short-lived and generally collapse in a welter of internal warfare, proving Elphinstone's point that "it would require less exertion to conquer all the surrounding kingdoms than [for a Pukhtun king] to subdue his own countrymen" (1815: 1:233).

The Power of Sufis

Since becoming a leader is believed to be the universal ambition for *all* Pukhtun, it is difficult to generate a moral argument against the pursuit of power by *any* Pukhtun. Paradoxically, open competition for control fosters a relative inability to resist domination when a sacralized leader takes command, as witnessed in the Swat Pukhtun's willingness to accept four generations of central authority by an immigrant lineage claiming holy status as Sufis.

As Barth noted, these rulers, as well as their historical precursors[14] and lesser religious lineages resident in Swat, are members of a second set of players who exist in a dialectical relationship with the khans and who must be taken into account in any analysis of the modes of seeking and validating authority in this internally antagonistic social structure. Barth showed that such men usually originated from non-Pukhtun or very junior Pukhtun lineages. Their sacred status came from their membership in Sufi orders and/or their inherited standing as sayyids, *miangan*, or *Sahibzadan* (purported descendants from the Prophet Muhammad or from local holy men). While many sayyids, miangan, and Sahibzada held quotidian occupations—including laborer and shopkeeper—those most important for Barth's political analysis were symbolically distinguished from the khans by their refusal to bear arms or fight or join factions, by their special turbans and robes, by their non-participation in the *wesh* (periodic land redistribution traditionally practiced by the Pukhtun and their retainers), and most especially, by their pious self-presentation. "Because it was unheard of to attack such people, whenever there were skirmishes or fighting, combatants sent their womenfolk and their other precious items to be protected by them" (S. M. Khan 2015: 45). As trusted and sanctified noncombatants outside the rivalries of tarburs and dullahs, these men also served as arbitrators in potentially destructive feuds between villages or regions, where their intervention allowed Pukhtun rivals to back off from a dangerous confrontations without undue loss of face.[15]

In return, the khans rewarded these holy mediators with strips of land (*tseri*) that lay between potentially warring villages and that served as symbolic barriers between traditional combatants. They were also given donations of money and land by khans who wished to improve their chances of getting into heaven. Holy men and their families could therefore become quite wealthy and acquire a retinue of servants and hangers-on (*kurimar*—those who are fed). Although they were ordinarily relegated to the sidelines as mediators in inter-village struggles for prestige, the most prestigious of these figures could also serve as symbolic rallying points in warfare against invaders from outside the valley. This was because they were reckoned to be above the animosities of the Yusufzai and so could unite the rival khans and their dullahs, which otherwise would split, with some members joining the invader in order to defeat their personal "near enemies."

The most famous and successful of these mediating figures in recent Swati history was Abdul Gaffur (later acclaimed as the Akhund—messenger of God—and as Saidu Baba).[16] According to his legend, he left his home as a young man, journeyed to India, and became a disciple (*murid*) of a Sufi order (the Naqsh-bandiyya). In a Sufi lodge (*tariqa*) the "band of brothers" replaces the disciple's family. Instead of sibling rivalry, they share their worldly goods among themselves and deny all distinctions. They are all united by their absolute trusting submission (*tawakkul*) to their spiritual master (pir). The ascetic disciplines of "little food, little sleep, little talk" are meant to polish away the impurities of personality, leaving the seekers nearer to the ideal state of mirror-like emptiness that was a precursor to the ultimate goal of self-loss (*fana*) in God's love.

Eventually, Abdul Gaffur was judged to have reached this goal. He was duly awarded the patched blue cloak of the Sufi and the blessing of his spiritual master and sent off to gain devotees in Swat. Following the standard path toward recognition as a saint, he subsisted on a diet of dried bread and practiced other austerities. As a result of his piety and self-abnegation, he won wide renown as a holy man possessing great *baraka* (charisma—especially the ability to give blessings) and was besieged with pilgrims seeking his favor. Naturally, a person of such great repute was in demand as a mediator. He was not the only contender for this position. Rival holy men have always risen and fallen in Swat, ranging in type from sayyids demanding leadership roles because of their religiosity and elevated lineage, to ecstatic magicians claiming to be the Mahdi (redeemer) sent to save the faithful from disaster. However, the Akhund's Sufi training, combined with his knowledge of local custom, his fairness as a mediator, his ability to interpret holy teachings, and his evident sanctity and remarkable asceticism made him the most beloved and prestigious of the holy men drawn to the valley.

His position was vastly improved by the encroachments of the British, who were threatening to invade the border region. Faced with this external danger, Saidu Baba called together the Swati factional leaders and warned them that they must unite against this dangerous opponent. His appeal was successful, and his candidate was named the leader of the confederation. It is said that Saidu Baba was asked to lead himself, but he refused on the grounds that official elevation to secular power would compromise the spiritual authority that allowed him to overcome lineage rivalries and provide the locus for the Swati resistance. Inspired and united by him, the Yusufzai decisively defeated a British invasion at the Ambela Pass in 1863.

After Saidu Baba's death, his role and his baraka were inherited by the younger of his sons, entitled Miangul (a descendant of a holy man—i.e., his father), who also served as a preferred mediator of disputes. Although his authority over the valley was never official, his influence was greatly enhanced by the Pukhtun's continued need to fight pressure from the British and their local ally, the Dir Nawab. After the Miangul's death, the Yusufzai acclaimed Sayyid Abdul Jabbar, another outsider from a religious family, as ruler, but he soon proved himself incompetent and was dethroned. Swat again disintegrated into factionalism.

The next ruler, Miangul Abdul Wadud (later acclaimed as the Badshah—great king—and also as the Wali—friend of God) was the grandson of Saidu Baba. As his two titles indicate, his tumultuous career fused elements of his grandfather's saintliness with the warrior ethic of the Yusufzai. Following the traditional Pukhtun pattern of enmity, he killed his two parallel cousins (his tarbur) who were warring against him. As he dictated to his biographer, "The only possible course open to us then was to take the initiative and put (our cousin) to death before he did the same to us" (Wadud 1962: 8). He also fought many battles against his younger brother before finally joining him in the war against the British-backed invasion of Swat by the Nawab of Dir.

In this conflict, Abdul Wadud's brother was killed, leaving him as the sole inheritor of both his grandfather's vast property and his reputation as a sanctified mediator. At the same time, he had already demonstrated all the valued characteristics of a sakh Pukhtun, as is clear in this eyewitness description of his election to rulership at a jirga meeting in 1915:

> Miangul Abdul Wadud impressed everyone when he arrived riding a horse and leapt from the saddle to the ground. When he left, he also jumped into the saddle from a distance. His athletic ability, religious background, his reputation for trust-

worthiness and credibility, combined with his status as an outsider uninvolved in dullah feuds and therefore capable of fair arbitration (and also the fact that he was in the good books of the British) led the jirga to acclaim him as their ruler. (S. M. Khan 2015: 38)

Unlike his predecessors, Badshah Sahib explicitly denied that he had any saintly powers to bless or produce miracles, which allowed him to avoid the dilemma of Saidu Baba, who could not directly assume secular power because of his religious role.[17] By renouncing his ancestral claim to *baraka*, Badshah Sahib cleared the way ideologically for transforming Swat into a centralized state under his own personal authority. Aside from his close relatives, the Badshah's major opponents to his rise to power were not landlords, but other Sufis who had personal followings among landlord factions. It is no surprise that one of his first acts on assuming power was to exile all saints not holding property, thus eliminating the class that had given rise to his own grandfather. He was also ruthless in his treatment of other spiritual figures who claimed to have baraka.[18] The Badshah's close ties with the emerging Pakistani government and his judicious use of modern technology also were vital factors in consolidating his gains.

Clearly, the Badshah was an organizational genius and visionary whose leadership résumé combined hereditary spiritual legitimacy, a heroic personal history, and a Pukhtun sense of honor. From his position of power, he was able to establish a relatively honest and efficient centralized bureaucracy and army and a modern school system, as well as build new roads, install quality hospitals, and make other improvements. In the process, he also disarmed the khans and undermined their authority by playing off dullah loyalties, using his traditional role as the final arbiter of disputes to support weaker parties against the stronger.

The Badshah's son and successor Jehan Zeb (also styled the Wali) was more up-to-date than his father. He wore Western clothes, lived a luxurious life, traveled to Europe, and married into the Pakistani elite. As is usual in Pukhtun families, he tried to enhance his own authority by shifting his faction alliances, favoring groups and people that his father had previously suppressed. However, his family could not escape the Pukhtun curse of jealousy and was torn apart by internal rivalries and the hostilities of old enemies. These internal power struggles became moot when the Swat state was incorporated into Pakistan in 1969, officially ending four generations of rule—indirect and direct—by the lineage of the Sufi saint Saidu Baba.

There is much to say about this great, but short-lived, dynasty (for a good summary, see Edwards 2013). Here, I simply want to stress its rapid secularization and assimilation into the warrior culture of the Pukhtun. Even by the time Badshah Abdul Wadud took power, his grandfather Saidu Baba's saintly baraka had all but dissipated.[19] The Badshah was not elected ruler because he had a saintly lineage, though the support of the wealthy and powerful Miangul certainly helped him, as did his reputation for integrity and abstemiousness. But more important was his warrior self-presentation, demonstrated in his victory over his lineage rivals, and his bravery and leadership in the fight against invading enemies. He kept power because of his skillful alliances, his ability to manipulate disputed settlements so as to weaken the strong and strengthen the weak, and his willingness to subdue and imprison his most implacable foes. Although he was illiterate, his pragmatic strategy was combined with a forward-thinking policy of modernization, bureaucratic centralization, education, and the general improvement of people's lives. In many senses, he stayed within the stereotypical parameters of the proud sakh Pukhtun, but in other ways he and his family, unlike the Pukhtun khans, worked hard to make the lives of ordinary people better. Perhaps the Badshah's willingness to transcend pure power politics and consider the welfare of his subjects was a remnant of the baraka his ancestor Saidu Baba had once bestowed on his devotees.

Recently other religious claimants to power have replaced saintly lineages as contenders for power in the political arena of Swat. These are mostly mullahs, who in times past were village servants occupying one of the lowest rungs on the status ladder. Their job was limited to teaching the rudiments of Islam to children and presiding over prayers in the mosque. As S. M. Khan recalls, "In Pukhtun society mullahs were not well respected, and for some unknown reason were often the butt of jokes" (2015: 43). Today the situation has changed drastically. Zealous mullahs now lead their devotees against the state, claiming sacred authority due to their supposed knowledge of the Qur'an and their call for implementation of Shari'a law.

Saints, Selflessness, and Authority

Unfortunately, I do not have the space here to explore the complex reasons for the recent political ascendance of mullahs in Swat.[20] Instead I want to spend the rest of this chapter outlining the precepts and styles of the Sufis who previously were the most important religious authorities in the valley, comparing their training and subsequent worldviews to those of the khans in a way that is parallel to Barth's later comparison between conjurer and guru. I am handicapped because the great exemplar of this type, Saidu Baba, has been dead for many years, his history is cloudy, and his successors explicitly repudiated his claims to sainthood. But there is plenty of parallel material from other Middle Eastern social worlds to show how the Sufi saint's elevation to authority is in many ways the counter-image to the warrior's and relies on a very different form of education and self-presentation to win followers.

As I have mentioned, in Swat some lineages were granted hereditary spiritual status. These are the sayyids, miangan, and Sahibzada. But, like the Pukhtun tribesman, descent is not sufficient for becoming a religious leader, and members of "sacred" lineages can easily become as secular as anyone else. Religious claims to authority need to be proved to be accepted. But the proof demanded is in many ways the mirror image of demonstration of character demanded of one wishing to be known as a sakh Pukhtun khan. Traditionally, saintly authority was achieved by following the pathway taken by Abdul Gaffur, that is, leaving one's family and friends behind, joining a tariqa, and becoming a murid of a pir. As I briefly outlined earlier, inside the lodge the murid's individual character was suppressed by cultivating unquestioning devotion and "cadaver obedience" to his spiritual master. As one typical Sufi manual puts it, "He should always obey the shaikh and he should serve him with his life and property. Nothing is achieved without love for the shaikh, and obedience is the mark of love. . . . He should not object to anything that the *murshid* [shaikh] says or does. . . . He should believe that the shaikh's mistake is better than his own virtue" (Ajmal 1984: 241).

By learning loving submission to his master within the confines of the Sufi lodge, the student gave himself up completely to selflessness, "because love, as all agree, is the negation of the lover's choice by affirmation of the Beloved's choice" (Lapidus 1984: 197). The murid's spiritual elevation was recognized only after he demonstrated to his pir that he had lost all personal will and desires. As the Pukhtun Sufi poet Rahman Baba wrote, "Intoxicated by love / My consciousness has vanished" (1977: 103). Self-immolation was confirmed by severe acts of self-denial: eating only dry bread, drinking only sips of water, sleeping only a few hours, and even self-laceration.[21] As a direct result of the murid's experience of absolute subordination to his spiritual master and his conquest of all passions save the passionate love of Allah as expressed in his selfless adoration of his pir, he could become a pir in his own right, believed by the populace, and by himself, to be the conduit for sacred blessings and part of a spiritual pyramid of holiness.

Obviously, the submission and de-individuation demanded of the Sufi initiate is in important ways the absolute antithesis of the warrior model of secular leadership, where, as Ernest Gellner observed, "if you wish to command you must learn not to obey" (1981: 28). As we have seen, in Pukhtun society the successful socialization of an adult man transforms childish weakness into the "natural" manly qualities of bravery, pride, generosity, and self-assertion. In contrast to the Sufi, the secular leader's personal identity is not lost in the pursuit of his goal; instead he revels in what he and others take to be his essential manly character, honed and strengthened through hard experience. So, while the religious acolyte gains baraka through *passive acquiescence* to a divine force that fills him with love, the Pukhtun khan gains personal power and public respect through the *active expression* of his innate impulse to struggle against and dominate his coequals.

Because of this antithesis, the Pukhtun regarded sanctified authority with deep suspicion, as well as with awe and veneration. They believed not only that holy men can bless, but that they can also curse. If train conductors demanded a fare from a Sufi, they were likely to find their trains suddenly immobilized, their watches stopped—but all came right again when abject apologies were made. Those who disturb the holy man, even unintentionally, may suddenly die miserably—in one case I was told of, a man was eaten by his own dogs. Even wandering Sufi beggars (*malang*) can kill with a curse. The Pukhtun often accuse mystics, and their more orthodox counterparts, of being frauds who hide their vices behind their long beards, seducing the foolish women who go to them for blessings. In Swat, men with birthmarks on their faces are pointed out as the products of their mothers' illicit unions with these erotic charlatans.

Because they passively empty themselves and ostentatiously deny their "natural" emotions—especially their desires for domination—the saint's values are the reverse of the Pukhtun code. Thus, the holy man, though respected and even worshipped, can also be feared and despised as hypocritical, as effeminate, and as a coward who does not fight like a man with sword or rifle, but resorts instead to his magical powers. These suspicions gain force because the authority of the saint does not spring from his "natural" self, as does the authority of the sakh Pukhtun, but from his subordination to his pir in the tariqa. He has destroyed what he was "by nature," and so has the potential to be false, whereas the ability of the secular leader to inspire loyalty and fear is thought to spring from his inborn character and to be transparently real and immediate. No one can feign bravery and manliness. He will soon be found out in the confrontations of daily life. But a pretender to piety is not so easily unmasked. As the Pukhtun say, "any fool can grow a beard."

Conclusion

In this chapter, following Barth, I have outlined two ideal types of authority in Swat: khan and Sufi.[22] I have tried to show that these ideal types are based on opposing premises, modes of inculcation, and styles of performance and result in "contrasting acts and aggregate entailments." To recapitulate: In his person the sakh Pukhtun warrior conveys a "natural masculine" character shaped by his socialization in the household, the gang, and the hujra. His heroic self is realized in *action*, specifically in the pursuit of influence over coequals, who are also seeking the same goal. They recognize the manly authority of the sakh Pukhtun and submit to him, but they never believe he is essentially different from them. His leadership has nothing to do with learning and teaching special knowledge, as in Bali, or with impressing others with his secret powers like the Baktaman conjurer. Instead, the sakh Pukhtun's power is thought to emanate from his character; it is public, personal, and immediate. Autonomy, generosity, and honor are the great virtues of the warrior. His great failings are jealousy, betrayal, and overweening pride. This ideal was sought by every Pukhtun (save those who take the religious path), including the poor and weak. Its realization is, in principle, possible for all. And its expression is immediately recognizable. However, the sakh Pukhtun is an ephemeral figure, destined to fade when he weakens and stronger rivals fired in the same mold compete for his spot.

The saint, in contrast, is someone who has repudiated his home, family, and tribe and voluntarily subdued his ambitions and desires by complete surrender to a pir, who is worshipped as a conduit to Allah. Moving through stages of renunciation and self-abnegation, the disciple strives to achieve emptiness. Becoming nothing, he can be filled with God's love as transmitted through the vehicle of the pir. Then he too can serve as a beacon for the lost. The pupil's spiritual authority is based first on the pir's official recognition of his vocation, second on the pupil's own ascetic practices, which repudiate the normal secular world. He does not gain authority through "being himself" like the Pukhtun, or by learning, interpreting, and teaching sacred texts like the Balinese guru (though that can play a part), or by referring to ever more esoteric doctrines and practices like the Baktaman conjurer (though this also can play a part), but through his own self-immolation and the baraka he earns thereby. The saint's virtues are pacifism, trustworthiness, and the power to bless. His failings are duplicity, concupiscence, and cowardice. The saintly ideal is sought only by a chosen few, its means of realization are hidden, and the results are hard to judge. Saints are both worshipped and reviled by the khans they serve and sometimes rule. But rule, of course, always means the eventual sublimation of saintly ideals[23] and the gradual progression (or regression) toward the opposing mode of authority—the mundane secular violence of the sakh Pukhtun. At the same time, as the rule of Saidu Baba and his descendants shows, the ethical precepts of service and austerity, originally inculcated by Sufi discipline, may have had a taming effect, making them more attuned to relieving the suffering of their subjects than was the case for sakh Pukhtun khans, who sought only recognition of their power.

Charles Lindholm is Emeritus Professor of Anthropology at Boston University. His books *Generosity and Jealousy* and *The Islamic Middle East* explore the implications and contradictions of asserting authority in egalitarian societies. Other books and articles examine cross-cultural experiences of charismatic relationships, romantic love, and the pursuit of authenticity in contemporary society. His two coauthored books, *Is America Breaking Apart?* and *The Struggle for the World*, investigate contemporary social movements. He also wrote *Culture and Identity: The History, Theory, and Practice of Psychological Anthropology*.

Notes

1. A *khel* is a named local segment of the larger Yusufzai clan structure.
2. Barth called them "blocs," but I will use the Pukhtun term.
3. For my perception of these changes, see Charles Lindholm 2013.

4. Because of female seclusion, I was unable to talk with women or enter into homes. My wife did have access however, and much of what I write about childhood is taken from her observations (Cherry Lindholm 1982).
5. Pukhtu and Pashtu are regional dialects of the same language.
6. There are strong similarities to the oppositional *liff* system that prevails among Berbers (Montagne 1973) and to other, even larger, dyadic divisions in the classical Middle East, such as the opposition between the Yemen and Qais/Mudar.
7. See Barth (1959b) for a somewhat different analysis.
8. This heedless value orientation may lead the great khan or his descendants to exhaust the family's resources on status items (falcons, horses, dogs, expensive weapons), on *nusha* (intoxication—usually by smoking hashish or opium), and on entertaining his retinue with extravagant musical parties featuring prostitutes and dancing boys.
9. When I asked my host Zaman Khan what the boys did, this was his answer.
10. Although too much violence against or humiliation of a khan's son might erupt into real fighting and begin a dangerous feud between fathers.
11. Similarly, in Morocco the legitimacy of the ruler depends on his "being like every other man only more exemplary, the best-of-category-representative" (Combs-Schilling 1989: 385).
12. In this, the Pukhtun resemble the Bedouin for whom "there is scarcely one among them who would cede his power to another, even to his father, his brother, or the eldest member of his family" (Ibn Khaldun 1967: 119).
13. The villagers in Shin Bagh bore out Elphinstone's insight when I included the question "Are most people jealous?" in an attitude test I administered in Swat. Out of 140 responses, 116 replied in the affirmative.
14. The most famous of these precursors is Shaikh Mali, a Sufi who accompanied the original Yusufzai invaders into the Swat Valley. He initiated periodic land redistribution that was meant to maintain equality among the various Yusufzai lineages. For a Moroccan analogy to the Swati case, see Gellner 1969, whose work inspired a voluminous literature on the relation between saints and warriors, which I cannot recapitulate here.
15. Ordinarily, disputes within the village did not require intervention by religiously sanctioned mediators. Instead, they were arbitrated by a *jirga*. Such arbitration was not binding; if no agreement could be reached, the ensuing feuds often ended with the extermination or exile of one party.
16. His tomb is presently a site of pilgrimage in the Swati capital of Saidu Sharif, which is also named after him.
17. The adoption of khan-like attributes is not unusual among saintly lineages in Swat and environs. Some have even gone to war with their Pukhtun neighbors and, aside from their names, have become wholly indistinguishable from them.
18. As S. M. Khan recounts, "A religious person in Shangla, a part of Swat, inspired many people to come to him for his blessing. The Badshah saw him as a threat to his authority, and had him dropped into a dry well and killed" (2015: 47).
19. The numbers of pilgrims to the tomb of Saidu Baba decreased considerably during the reign of the Badshah and his descendants.
20. For a contextualized account of a recent mullah-led movement in Swat, see Charles Lindholm 1999.
21. For a standard portrayal of Sufi training, see Trimingham 1971.
22. Possibly Barth's comparison between conjurer and guru was inspired by his experience of the alternative assertions of power that he had observed and described so well in Swat, but had not analyzed in terms of enculturation. I expect that most, perhaps all, societies contain contrasting ideal types of authority that would benefit from a Barthian investigation into actors' "enablements and constraints."
23. A similar pattern has prevailed in other Muslim dynasties founded by Sufis, e.g., the Safavids of Iran, as well as the Almohads and the Almoravids of North Africa and Spain.

References

Ajmal, Mohammad. 1984. "A Note on Adab in the Murshid-Murid Relationship." In *Moral Conduct and Authority: The Place of Adab in South Asian Islam*, edited by Barbara Daly Metcalf. Berkeley: University of California Press.

Baba, Rahman. 1977. *Selections from Rahman Baba*. Translated by J. Enevoldsen. Herning, Denmark: Poul Kristensen.

Barth, Fredrik. 1959a. *Political Leadership among Swat Pathans*. Monographs on Social Anthropology 19. London: Athalone Press.

———. 1959b. "Segmentary Opposition and the Theory of Games: A Study of Pathan Organization." *Journal of the Royal Anthropological Institute of Great Britain and Ireland* 89(1): 5–21.

———. 1985. With Miangul Jahanzeb. *The Last Wali of Swat: An Autobiography as Told to Fredrik Barth*. New York: Columbia University Press.

———. 1990. "The Guru and the Conjurer: Transactions in Knowledge and the Shaping of Culture in Southeast Asia and Melanesia." *Man* 25(4): 640–53.

Bourdieu, Pierre. 1974. *Outline of a Theory of Practice*. Cambridge: Cambridge University Press.

Combs-Schilling, M. E. 1989. *Sacred Performances: Islam, Sexuality and Sacrifice*. New York: Columbia University Press.

Edwards, David 2013. "More Lessons from the Swat Pathans." In *Beyond Swat: History, Society, and Economy along the Afghanistan-Pakistan Border*, edited by Magnus Marsden and Benjamin Hopkins. London: Hurst.

Elphinstone, Mountstuart. 1815. *An Account of the Kingdom of Caubul*. 2 vols. London: Longman. Reprinted 1972. Karachi: Oxford University Press.

Gellner, Ernest. 1969. *Saints of the Atlas*. London: Weidenfeld & Nicolson.

———. 1981. *Muslim Society*. Cambridge: Cambridge University Press.

Ibn Khaldun. 1967. *The Muqaddimah*. Princeton: Princeton University Press.

Khan, Ghani. 1958. *The Pathans: A Sketch*. Peshawar: University Books.

Khan, Sher M. 2015. *In Pursuit of Knowledge: A Pukhtun's Life, from East to West*. Cirencester, UK: Mereo Books.

Khattack, Khushal Khan. 1965. *Poems from the Diwan of Khushal Khan Khattack*. Translated by D. Mackenzie. London: Allen and Unwin.

Lapidus, Ira. 1984. "Knowledge, Virtue and Action: The Classical Muslim Conception of Adab and the Nature of Religious Fulfillment in Islam." In *Moral Conduct and Authority: The Place of Adab in South Asian Islam*, edited by Barbara Daly Metcalf. Berkeley: University of California Press.

Lindholm, Charles. 1981. "The Structure of Violence Among the Swat Pukhtun." *Ethnology* 20(2): 147–56.

———. 1982. *Generosity and Jealousy: The Swat Pukhtun of Northern Pakistan*. New York: Columbia University Press.

———. 1986. "Leadership Categories and Social Processes in Islam: The Cases of Dir and Swat." *Journal of Anthropological Research* 42(1): 1–13.

———. 1999. "Justice and Tyranny: Law and the State in the Middle East." *Journal of the Royal Asiatic Society* 9(3): 375–88.

———. 2013. "Swat in Retrospect: Continuities, Transformations and Possibilities." In *Beyond Swat: History, Society, and Economy along the Afghanistan-Pakistan Border*, edited by Magnus Marsden and Benjamin Hopkins. London: Hurst.

Lindholm, Cherry. 1982. "The Swat Pukhtun Family as a Political Training Ground." In

Anthropology in Pakistan: Recent Sociocultural and Archeological Perspectives, edited by Steven Pastner and Louis Flom. Ithaca, NY: Cornell University Press.

Montagne, Robert. 1973. *The Berbers, Their Social and Political Organization*. London: Frank Cass.

Trimingham, J. Spencer. 1971. *The Sufi Orders in Islam*. Oxford: Clarendon Press.

Wadud, Abdul. 1962. *The Story of Swat as Told by the Founder*. Transcribed and translated by Ashruf Husain. Peshawar: Ferozsons.

8

Values and the Value of Secrecy
Barthian Reflections on Values and
the Nature of Mountain Ok Social Process

Joel Robbins

The work of Fredrik Barth has been part of my understanding of anthropology from very early on. I arrived at graduate school knowing that I wanted to do fieldwork in Papua New Guinea, but with no idea where in that vast country I wanted to go. Over the first Christmas break, my advisor Roy Wagner assigned me three well-known ethnographies of the region to read, but he gave me no guidance as to what I should hope to take from them. When I returned from the vacation, he asked me which of the three books I liked best. I answered with little hesitation that I had found Barth's (1975) *Ritual and Knowledge among the Baktaman of New Guinea* the most stimulating. "That settles it," Roy quickly responded, "you will do your fieldwork in the Mountain Ok region where Barth worked." Having been thoroughly taken with Barth's discussion of the complex relations between secrecy, skepticism, and the sociology of knowledge among the Baktaman, I agreed to this plan immediately, and I have never regretted the decision to follow Barth to this part of Papua New Guinea.

The Mountain Ok or Min area, which spans two provinces in the far western highlands of the country, up against its border with West Papua, was the last part of Papua New Guinea to be thoroughly colonized, and in 1968 Barth was the first anthropologist to carry out sustained research among any of what the local people call the "Min" groups. By the time my own fieldwork with a Min group known as the Urapmin began more than twenty years later, much had changed in the Min region—most notably the advent of a huge gold and copper mine on Min land (mentioned also in chapter 1), and the very striking and so far enduring conversion of many Min people to a charismatic form of Christianity in a revival the swept through Papua New Guinea in the late 1970s (Robbins 2004). When I arrived among the Urapmin at the end of 1990, the men's cult Barth had placed at the very center of indigenous social life was completely gone, as was the case in most, if not all, Min groups by that time. But even before I began my fieldwork, it had become clear from the literature that later changes not withstanding, Barth had with remarkable sensitivity discovered almost all the features that rendered the Min region distinctive in relation to other parts of Papua New Guinea. It is a testimony to his gifts as an ethnographer that the themes he highlighted—in particular those having to do with the importance of secrecy as a social practice, the immense value placed on secret knowledge, and the way these two factors shape local cultures and patterns of social interaction—have never been absent from regional ethnography since he introduced them.

I will dwell on issues of secrecy, knowledge, and interaction in this chapter. But Barth never cared much for ethnography for ethnography's sake, and so I also want to bring these ethnographic themes into dialogue with a theoretical issue that occupied Barth on and off throughout his career concerning the nature of values and their role in social theory. As Barth (1993a: 31) notes in an important piece about values that he published in 1993, values were a major anthropological topic in the 1950s and 1960s when he was starting out, but soon after they became almost invisible, at best "discretely introduced into the discipline's descriptive prose without receiving due recognition in the theoretical framework." This has largely remained true until now, though there are some signs that interest in values has recently begun to grow (e.g., Graeber 2001; Rio and Smedal 2009; Otto and Willerslev 2013). In this chapter I want to start with some of Barth's (1981) earliest influential thinking about this topic, one that was in fact quite central to his famous 1966 essays collected as *Models of Social Organization* (Barth 1966). I am going to argue that the perspective on values Barth develops in those essays raises a serious problem for Min ethnography. Having set out this problem, I turn to some of his later thinking about values, and some of my own, to suggest a way of reformulating some aspects of the anthropological theory of values in order to solve it.

Barth on Models and the Study of Values

In the *Models* essays, Barth lays out his most fundamental vision of what social anthropology should aim to accomplish. It should, he tells us, explain, and not just document, patterns of action in the societies it studies by determining the ways people's strategic actions, carried out in situations in which they encounter both opportunities and constraints, generate these patterns. The key kind of social action in his model is transactions, interactions in which people reciprocally give and receive all manner of tangible and intangible goods. These goods, in turn, must have value for those who receive them, otherwise there would be no reason for them to transact. We can see the tight link between the concept of values and that of transactions in the following quotation from the first essay:

> It is meaningless to say that something has value unless people in real life seek it, prefer it to something of less value, in other words maximize value. This can only be true if they usually act strategically with respect to it, that is, make it the object of transactions between themselves and others. (Barth 1981: 39)

Values are, according to Barth's early account, what people seek to maximize in interaction, and their efforts to do so make values "the determinants from which social forms . . . may be generated" (1981: 48).

Even more than the first of the three *Models* essays, the second one is devoted to the topic of values. More particularly, the second essay focuses on explaining how the values of a cultural formation can come to be "integrated" with one another, such that their relationships to each other exist in a relatively stable pattern and knowledge of this pattern is shared by those people who transact them. Such integration comes about, Barth tells us, because individuals' values are constantly being displayed and calibrated in exchange, such that various things one might transact with others come to have agreed upon levels of worth in themselves and in relation to one another within transacting communities. What Barth has given us in his *Models* essays, then, is a consistent approach to values that finds them both motivating transactions and developing their coherence in relation to one another through them.

Knowledge, Secrecy, and Value among the Min

With Barth's early transactional model of values in place, let me turn to some Min ethnography. One of Barth's most famous discoveries in his work among the Baktaman was what he influentially labeled "the epistemology of secrecy" (Barth 1975: 217). This is the Baktaman idea that the value of any piece of knowledge, even its likely truthfulness, is inversely related to how many people know it. The fewer the number of people that possess any given piece of knowledge, the more valuable it is and thus the more that those who are interested in knowledge are motivated to obtain it. In all Min groups during the period of Barth's fieldwork, the institutional scaffolding for this epistemology was a set of elaborate men's initiation rituals. These initiations were composed of many stages, which began when boys were as young as four years old and lasted until they were in their late teens or older. The number of stages varied across the Min groups (Baktaman had seven, for example, while the Urapmin had four major ones with a number of minor ones taking place between them), but everywhere a similar pattern of handling sacred knowledge in the initiation process was in force. At each stage, boys would be given a great deal of cosmological knowledge that had many practical correlates about such things as who can eat what and what kinds of people (such as men or women) can have what kind of contact with what other kinds of people. The initiators stressed to the novices that they should not share this knowledge with women or younger men, lest they themselves stop growing and the rituals cease to be effective in prospering the staple crops of their communities. More than this, at each stage after the first, the boys were also told that key pieces of secret knowledge had been kept from them at earlier initiations. As initiators revealed this new knowledge, they also told the novices that much of the secret knowledge they had been taught during previous stages was wrong. Boys and young men who experienced such confounding revelations (or what the Telefolmin refer to as "turnings") as they moved through the initiation sequence came to recognize that they could never be sure that the initiators were telling them anything of value (Jorgensen 1990). This led to a situation that Barth found among the Baktaman, and that I and others found in subsequent fieldwork in the region, in which even the oldest men, those who were the most knowledgeable initiators, doubted that their fathers had shared their own most important knowledge with them before they died (Barth 1975: 220; Jorgensen 1981; Robbins 2004). No one, then, was fully confident that they possessed truly valuable sacred knowledge, and as Barth put it, perhaps what the whole initiation complex taught novices the most about was "the pervasiveness of secrecy and direct deception on which the structure is built" (1975: 219).

Further ethnography has revealed that among at least some Min groups the idea that little knowledge is ever securely or accurately passed between people applied not just to the practice of the men's cult. People assumed that this was also true of what happened in social interactions in everyday life. Setting side by side the religious injunction to secrecy with people's fear of offending others through sorcery, Barth had already hinted at this in his first book on New Guinea, writing that "a Baktaman will experience no social relation which can embody for him a conception of truthfulness and trust: fathers must systematically deceive sons, men deceive women and vice-versa, all public life is permeated with the protective tactfulness of sorcery fear" (1975: 219–20). And perhaps this conviction about the failure of routine social interaction to convey knowledge is rooted in more than just worries about sorcery. Among the Urapmin, at least during my fieldwork during the early 1990s, fear of sorcery was markedly less pronounced than among the Baktaman, but I nonetheless found that the Urapmin held that language can never reliably inform a person about what others know or are feeling in their hearts (*aget*), the seat of all thought. There is too much distance between the heart and the mouth, the Urapmin say, for speech to reliably tell you what people know, think, or feel. With this idea about mental opacity in place, all verbal interactions become, like the encounters between initiators and novices, events in which no fully reliable knowledge is exchanged. For this reason, Urapmin epistemology also contains the assertion that trustworthy knowledge comes only from "seeing" (*tamamin*) things and never just from "hearing" (*weng senkamin*) them. As they often put it, the things people say are "just talk" (*weng katagup*).

Having discovered the epistemology of secrecy among the Baktaman, Barth famously went on to study how such ideas about the control of knowledge set up interactional opportunities and constraints that shape knowledge systems themselves in Papua New Guinea, Bali, and elsewhere (Barth 1987, 1990, 1993b). But in the spirit of Barth's early work, I want to keep the focus on what this set of ideas about knowledge means for transactional life itself, rather than for the bodies of knowledge such transactional life might shape, and in particular for Barth's theory of the role of values in interaction.

Secrecy, Values, and Transaction

Recall that, for Barth, it is the reciprocal exchange of values that drives people to transact. In his model, one enters into exchange with another person in the hope that one will get something at least as valuable, if not more so, as what one gives. But in the face of the skeptical epistemologies of the Min, a problem arises here. If valuable knowledge of a sacred or even mundane sort never, or almost never, passes between people, why do they transact verbally at all? Do we not have a paradox here—one in which people spend a good deal of time interacting verbally with each other with no expectation that they will exchange anything valuable by doing so?

I think this is a genuine paradox that raises issues for Barth's transactional theory of value. Before considering what these issues are, however, I want to spend a moment examining some more Min ethnography, drawn mostly from fieldwork in Urapmin but in line with what others have written, that bears on how people in the region interact and that might be taken to render the paradox as I have laid it out more apparent than real.

A first point to make is that, in my experience, while Min people do perforce speak to one another quite a bit, they are not compulsive talkers. They are comfortable spending time together without the accompaniment of constant conversation, and it is notable that they mostly do not gossip (see Barth 1993a: 45). To this we might add that when the Urapmin people with whom I worked do listen to others talk, especially when they listen to people give public speeches, they tend to stress the pleasurable poetic qualities of the speaker's utterances, rather than their information-bearing ones. The rather limited role the Urapmin accord to verbal interaction is also linked to a second point, which is that the transactions the Urapmin and other Min peoples think of as most important are those in which material goods, rather than words, are the primary things that are given or received. Material gifts are precisely things one can see, unlike talk, which one can only hear. And Urapmin give and receive gifts with great frequency. I think it is fair to say that most adult Urapmin hardly get through a day without someone giving them at least a small piece of food, and often the food gifts or gifts of bows, string bags, and other material goods are much more substantial than this. When Urapmin describe what has happened to them in the recent or distant past, it is lists of material gifts of this kind received and given, rather than reports of conversations held, that dominate their accounts.[1] From this sketch, we might conclude that Urapmin do not look to transactions to transfer knowledge and that they therefore engage in them not to maximize what they know, but rather to attain other goods such as the enjoyment produced by hearing beautiful language and the relational goods that follow from giving and receiving material gifts. If this is the case, then the paradox disappears because it turns out that transactions are not about giving and receiving knowledge in any case, and thus it does not count as a problem when they fail to accomplish this.

An account like the one I have just given of Min transactions as about the exchange of items of value other than knowledge is fine as far as it goes, and I will return to a similar kind of discussion later on in my argument to suggest that we need to develop a value theory that recognizes its force. But it remains true that this account rather begs the questions raised by Barth's key findings about the importance of secrecy and knowledge for the Baktaman and other Min people. How can knowledge, an item that is never reliably transacted, and the practice of secrecy itself, which is a refusal to transact knowledge, come to be so important if values are developed and integrated only in exchange and people do not think of knowledge as something that is ever securely exchanged? And even if we subtract all the time Urapmin spend with each other without interacting verbally, the interactions in which they simply enjoy the artful qualities of one another's speech, and the many interactions in which material gifts are transferred, every Min person still engages in plenty of transactions in which they mostly exchange "just talk"—talk that is worthless in terms of conveying knowledge and that is not beautiful in itself. What is going on in these transactions, and how are people motivated to participate in them? To answer these questions, we are going to need to expand our theory of values, complementing Barth's transactional model of values with one of a different kind.

To explain what I have in mind by way of expanding our theory of values, I can begin by noting that it is possible to divide modern thinking about values, which began to take shape in the second half of the nineteenth century (Robbins 2015b), into two rough groups. In one of these groups, the emphasis is on the creation and exchange of tangible and intangible things that have value. Those who subscribe to this view, most famously Marxists, but not them alone, talk about the *production* of value, a term they tend to use in the singular. In this view, it is important that more and more value is routinely being created in the world. In the other group are those who talk not about the production of value or values, but about the *realization* of them. The image of value here is less one of making quantities of something new and more one of successfully reproducing a pattern, and those who take this view tend to identify a number of different values in any social formation and thus to use the plural form "values" rather than the singular "value." For theorists in the second group, who come mostly out of the neo-Kantian tradition, values lead people not to, or not only to, maximize the accumulation of certain goods, but to participate in bringing about states of affairs that are valuable in themselves.[2] Think, for example, of those who, though living alone, tidy up their home every night before going to bed. It is clear that they value tidiness. But they value tidiness not as something to be accumulated in maximal quantities, since they are not making or gathering more of it each night than the night before, nor do they value it as something to transact with others, since every evening they bring about this state just for themselves. For those who stress values as something to be realized, this behavior is not problematic because bringing into existence a valued state of affairs is rewarding in itself, and thus such tidying up counts as valuable. It is because of this kind of realization model that Weber (1978: 24–26) can differentiate value rational from instrumental action even though value rational action, just as much as instrumental action, aims to bring about a good by calculated means, and it is why Durkheim (1974) ends up going beyond Kant to talk about the realization of values as something people accomplish not only out of a sense of duty, but also because they desire to do so and experience pleasure when their desires are fulfilled.

In which of these two camps—the productivist or the realizational—does Barth belong in his guise as value theorist? Placing him on one side or the other is not completely straightforward. He does not stress production in his account of values, but rather the transaction of valued items between people—be these material goods, knowledge, or displays of attitudes like deference, respect, and esteem. But production theorists always care about circulation as well, and I think in his emphasis on accumulation of values in transaction and his language of maximization, Barth fits more comfortably with them. Moreover, in his 1993 piece on values, he makes a move that decisively puts the realization model out of play for him. In that essay, Barth is much less confident that values are a key to an actor's motivations than he was in the *Models* essays. "The behavioral effects of values," he argues there, "are secondary" (1993a: 44). What they are secondary to are institutions, which guide behavior without having to promise, as transactions do, that people will acquire more value than they expend in the course of acting. But it is precisely at this juncture that the realization model leads in a different direction than the transactional one. For on a realization account, acting in accordance with institutional strictures counts precisely as a way of bringing about a valued state of affairs—it is a way of realizing whatever value or values the institution represents. This kind of realization, however, is not figured primarily as "producing" a new quantity of value in the world, but as realizing in an appropriate way a value that is already established as present.

Recognizing that values can be realized, and not only produced and accumulated in varying quantities, is the key to understanding how it is that Min people, who highly value knowledge, can also highly value secrecy and can continue to interact, perhaps even transact, verbally, even though they expect no knowledge to change hands between those who engage one another in conversation. It is precisely in interaction that one realizes the value of keeping secrets.[3] Without interaction, one could never keep anything from anyone else. Hermits and loners do not keep secrets; only those who might give knowledge away but in the end do not do so can claim to have realized this value. This is one reason that verbal transactions in which knowledge is not shared are of value to Min people, and it is why young boys are taught the discipline not of withdrawing forever from the social world beyond ritual, but of living in that world without giving away the secrets of the ritual domain. But there also is another reason that Urapmin undertake verbal transactions that convey no reliable knowledge, and this follows from the fact, already hinted at above, that Min people, like many other Papua New Guineans, value relations in themselves. I have argued elsewhere that in fact relations are the things Papua New Guineans value most highly (Robbins 1994, 2004). Transacting material goods is the most important, institutionalized way to realize relations among Min people. But the simple swapping of turns of talk, even those that transfer no knowledge, also counts in this regard. Barth might see such conversations as a case in which people simply adhere to the rules of the institution that defines what counts as relationships—they are just doing what they have to do to participate in social life in their society. But at least in Papua New Guinea, I think it makes sense to see them as doing more than this—as also realizing a value not by transacting to gain more of it, but by bringing it about as a state of affairs— and the evident pleasure they take in interacting socially demonstrates that for them doing so generates the kind of emotional response theorists expect the realization of values to cause (Robbins 2015a). My point here is not to argue against Barth's transactional model of values, but to suggest that to fully understand the themes of knowledge and secrecy he first put at the center of the anthropological study of the Min peoples, we will need a realizational model of values as well.

Conclusion

I have engaged the full range of Barth's thinking about values across his career both to illuminate his work on the epistemology of secrecy in the Min region of Papua New Guinea and to lay a foundation for intervening in contemporary discussions about values by suggesting the usefulness of making a distinction between productivist and realizational approaches to the study of this phenomenon. My discussion to this point does, however, leave a number of issues related to value theory unaddressed. By way of conclusion, I want to mention two of these issues quite briefly and then finally dwell a bit longer on a third one that was of direct concern to Barth.

First, I should stress that my argument has not been that we need to choose between production and realization models of values. I think that we probably need both models to fully register the force of values in social life. Although my own thinking on this is not fully settled as yet, I borrow from Julian Sommer-schuh (pers. com.) the idea that perhaps the production model is a subset of the realization one. That is to say, it is possible to argue that producing value is one way of realizing at least some kinds of values, but that other values are realized in other ways, such as by adhering to institutional patterns. If this is the case, then all values are realized, but a value that is produced is realized in a way that allows for its realization to be meaningfully understood from a production point of view as increasing the quantity of that value that exists in the world and therefore as also allowing for the possibility that quantities of such a value can be accumulated, while other ways of realizing values do not lead to increase and accumulation in this sense.

The possibility that the production of values is but one way of realizing them raises the second issue I want to discuss, which has to do with whether the values that one produces are the same kinds of things as the values one realizes. Are we simply confusing matters by calling both of these things values? Are tidiness, on the one hand, and widgets that one might apply one's labor to producing, on the other, the same kinds of things when both are conceived of as values? Again, I do not feel fully confident in my ability to answer this question at this point, but I am for the moment proceeding on the assumption that we will end up with a much more powerful theory of values if we assume that values that are produced and those that are realized in other ways are not two or more radically distinct kinds of things. All of the things that we might call values would, in this view, share the quality of being ranked vis-à-vis one another, as well as all being ranked above things that are disvalued, and would also be capable of motivating behavior. As the Barth (1981: 39) of the *Models* era would have it, every value has the quality of leading people in "real life [to] seek it, prefer it to something of less value, in other words [to] maximize" it. At this level of generality, values that are produced and those that are realized in other ways would share crucial characteristics in common, and the theory of values would have to account both for the commonalities that link all values and those characteristics of various kinds of values that lead to them being realized in different ways.

The third issue I want to discuss has to do with Barth's reason for wanting to separate values from institutions in his 1993 piece. What worries him about the idea that institutions are directly related to values is the possibility that if this is the case, then the notion of values will cease to have explanatory power. If, Barth asks, we say that the Urapmin carry out exchanges because they value exchange relationships, what more does this tell us than we are told by a simple statement of fact that the Urapmin carry out such exchanges? Only if we reserve values for "concepts that apply to the judgment of individuals' acts and prestations, not to collective institutions" can we use values to explain the forms social life takes (1993a: 40). I understand the force of this criticism, but I do not think the explanatory failure it portends is a necessary outcome of the realization view of values as I have laid it out here. What one needs to do to protect against this danger is to recognize that values are always relative terms;

they make no sense unless in any social world there is more than one value that a person might realize (see Robbins 2013). This is elementary, of course, but it is also the case that as soon as we recognize this point, every realization of one value—including every instance of participation in a given institution that realizes a value—becomes a sacrifice of a chance to realize another value, at least for the moment. I may choose to leave time to tidy my flat, or I may choose to stay late at work and make one more widget. The choice I make depends on how I rank the value of a clean flat relative to that of accumulating one more widget or one more of whatever I would exchange for my labor or for the widget itself. Institutionalized patterns themselves do not tell a person what values to realize. All they do is define the steps one needs to take to bring about the realization of some of the kinds of values one might find oneself having chosen to pursue. There is, then, still some explanatory force that follows from answering the question why it is that people realize the values they do and not others that it is possible to pursue in their social world. I think Barth is right that to develop a fully formed theory of values, we need to know more about how values motivate individuals to do things. But I am also convinced that we are likely to make progress in this quest not only by studying their transactions, but also by considering the way institutions often concretize values in the cultural worlds of which they are a part, providing clear pathways for realizing those values, and attempting to solicit such realization through institutional participation.

One of the reasons Frederic Barth was such a towering figure in anthropology was that he, more than all but a handful of scholars, realized the disciplinary ideal of being equally a first-rate, adventurous, and indefatigable fieldworker and a searching, first-rate theoretical thinker. I have hoped to pay tribute here to these combined aspects of Barth's legacy by working with both his foundational insights into Min ethnography and his important theoretical contributions to the anthropological theorization of values. In doing so, I have discussed what is often considered the most globally unique aspect of the traditional lives of the Min peoples—the strong emphasis they place on the importance of secrecy as a social practice and knowledge as a valuable and powerful force in the world—and used their uniqueness in this regard to sharpen a theoretical approach to values that is intended to apply universally. More successfully than almost anyone else, Barth kept alive the impulse to celebrate the particular in ways that enhanced our ability as anthropologists to make universal theoretical claims. Along with all of his concrete accomplishments, this spirit that he embodied so fully is one that anthropology needs always to hold on to.

Joel Robbins is Professor of Anthropology at the University of Cambridge. His work has focused on value theory, cultural change, ethics, and the anthropology of religion. He is the author of *Becoming Sinners: Christianity and Moral Torment in a Papua New Guinea Society* and is currently completing a book on the relationship between anthropology and Christian theology.

Notes

1. I have discussed Urapmin ideas about speech and gifts in much more detail elsewhere, and I have located this discussion in relation to other literature about language ideology (e.g., Robbins 2001a, 2001b).
2. I discuss this neo-Kantian view in more detail in Robbins (2015b).
3. Note how similar this is to the understanding of secrecy in Crete outlined by Michael Herzfeld in chapter 2, although his theoretical goals are quite different.

References

Barth, Fredrik. 1966. *Models of Social Organization*. Occasional Paper No. 23. London: Royal Anthropological Institute.

———. 1975. *Ritual and Knowledge among the Baktaman of New Guinea*. New Haven: Yale University Press.

———. 1981. *Process and Form in Social Life: Selected Essays of Fredrik Barth*. London: Routledge and Kegan Paul.

———. 1987. *Cosmologies in the Making: A Generative Approach to Cultural Variation in Inner New Guinea*. Cambridge: Cambridge University Press.

———. 1990. "The Guru and the Conjurer: Transactions in Knowledge and the Shaping of Culture in Southeast Asia and Melanesia." *Man* 25(4): 640–53.

———. 1993a. "Are Values Real? The Enigma of Naturalism in the Anthropological Imputation of Values." In *The Origins of Values*, edited by Michael Hechter, Lynn Nadel, and Richard E. Michod, 31–46. New York: Aldine De Gruyter.

———. 1993b. *Balinese Worlds*. Chicago: University of Chicago Press.

Durkheim, Emile. 1974. *Sociology and Philosophy*. Translated by David F. Pocock. New York: Free Press.

Graeber, David. 2001. *Toward an Anthropological Theory of Value: The False Coin of Our Own Dreams*. New York: Palgrave.

Jorgensen, Dan. 1981. "Taro and Arrows: Order, Entropy, and Religion among the Telefolmin." PhD dissertation, University of British Columbia.

———. 1990. "Secrecy's Turns." *Canberra Anthropology* 13(1): 40–47.

Otto, Ton, and Rane Willerslev. 2013. "Value as Theory," parts 1–2. Special issues, *Hau: Journal of Ethnographic Theory* 3(1–2).

Rio, Knut M., and Olaf H. Smedal. 2009. "Hierarchy and Its Alternatives: An Introduction to Movements of Totalization and Detotalization." In *Hierarchy: Persistence and Transformation in Social Formations*, edited by Knut M. Rio and Olaf H. Smedal, 1–63. New York: Berghahn Books.

Robbins, Joel. 1994. "Equality as a Value: Ideology in Dumont, Melanesia, and the West." *Social Analysis* 36: 21–70.

———. 2001a. "God Is Nothing But Talk: Modernity, Language and Prayer in a Papua New Guinea Society." *American Anthropologist* 103(4): 901–12.

———. 2001b. "Ritual Communication and Linguistic Ideology: A Reading and Partial Reformulation of Rappaport's Theory of Ritual." *Current Anthropology* 42(5): 591–614.

———. 2004. *Becoming Sinners: Christianity and Moral Torment in a Papua New Guinea Society*. Berkeley: University of California Press.

———. 2007. "You Can't Talk Behind the Holy Spirit's Back: Christianity and Changing Language Ideologies in a Papua New Guinea Society." In *Consequences of Contact:*

Language Ideologies and Sociocultural Transformations in Pacific Societies, edited by Miki Makihara and Bambi B. Schieffelin, 125–39. New York: Oxford University Press.

———. 2013. "Monism, Pluralism and the Structure of Value Relations: A Dumontian Contribution to the Contemporary Study of Value." *Hau: Journal of Ethnographic Theory* 3(1): 99–115.

———. 2015a. "On Happiness, Values, and Time: The Long and the Short of It." *Hau: Journal of Ethnographic Theory* 5(13): 215–33.

———. 2015b. "Ritual, Value, and Example: On the Perfection of Cultural Representations." *Journal of the Royal Anthropological Institute* 21: 18–29.

Weber, Max. 1978. *Economy and Society: An Outline of Interpretive Sociology*. Translated by Guenther Roth and Claus Wittich. Berkeley: University of California Press.

9

Paradigm Change in Chinese Ethnology and Fredrik Barth's Influence

Ke Fan

In the past two or three decades, ethnology in China has experienced changes that are strong enough that I would consider them to be research paradigm shifts.[1] This chapter first examines paradigms centered in the field of ethnic minority studies from the establishment of the People's Republic of China (PRC) in 1949 to the 1990s and beyond. For this half-century-long period, Chinese ethnologists focused especially on three paradigmatic problems concerning interethnic relations: (1) what was the *essential aspect* in the history of interethnic relations in China; (2) which *stage of social evolution* each minority nationality occupied; and (3) how to describe the role of the *frontier* in each group's formation. The paradigms built around these three questions attracted almost all the academic enterprise in ethnology during that period, and the question of the frontier is now still ongoing, though with some minor changes. The need to determine social policy underlay this long period of paradigm sovereignty.

The second part of this chapter addresses how and why these paradigms changed or are changing. A new paradigm, which I call the *zuqun* (族群, ethnic group) paradigm, was established soon after Fredrik Barth's famous 1969 article (Barth 1969) was introduced to China in the 1990s (Barth 1999). This chapter examines how the paradigm shifted from the previous ones to the one centered on zuqun, why this new paradigm is relevant especially to Chinese academia, and in what ways Barth's theory influenced this shift. I suggest that Barth's theory on ethnic boundaries has significantly changed the perspectives of a number of Chinese scholars on how one sees the frontier. More importantly, this new research paradigm, under Barth's influence, has led scholars to focus less on issues of sovereignty than on those of people's livelihood.

How Did These Paradigms Come About?

In this chapter, I am using "paradigm" largely in Thomas Kuhn's sense, but with a little difference. According to Kuhn (1996), a paradigm forms when some new academic achievement breaks through earlier problems and shapes other scholars' academic enterprises. In the long run, however, such a paradigm can limit the development of a discipline, because paradigms discourage thinking along lines outside themselves. In this sense, paradigms mean making boundaries. As Kuhn suggested, every breakthrough academic achievement succeeds by overcoming the limitations or boundaries of the old paradigms. In China, however, rather than seeing a breakthrough that gets rid of the old and establishes a new paradigm, however, paradigms established in social sciences and humanities have been strongly shaped by what the state wants academia to do. In other words, the state determines the formation of a paradigm more than any academic innovation.

After 1949, the state-making and nation-building needs of the new country shaped two ethnographic projects: ethnic identification (*minzu shibie* 民族识别, 1953–87) and the social-historical investigation of ethnic minorities (*shaoshu minzu shehui lishi diaocha* 少数民族社会历史调查, 1958–64). Many ethnologists, anthropologists, historians, and scholars of other disciplines were organized to take part in these projects, along with many state cadres. The two most significant consequences of these two projects were the reconfiguration of ethnicity (Fan 2012) and the production of a systematic representation of ethnic minorities (Fan 2016).

Soon after the ethnic identification project was carried out, however, a few researchers raised a serious question: how could every "people" be considered as a nationality (hereafter *minzu* 民族) if they had to take account of Joseph Stalin's definition of what counts as a nation (Stalin 1935)? As Fei Xiaotong pointed out later on, these scholars realized that Stalin's definition had been used only as a vague frame of reference in the campaign of ethnic identification (Fei 1985). In fact, to a great degree, an official identification as a separate minzu had almost nothing to do with Stalin's definition. In order to understand what followed after the project of ethnic identification was carried out, we need to recall what Stalin's definition was.

According to Stalin, a human community regarded as a nationality should match four criteria: a common territory, common language, common economic life, and some common psychological characteristics or cultural makeup. Stalin suggested that such nations formed during the rise of capitalism. This leads to many questions, however. How can one define a group of people in China as a minzu in accordance with that definition? And, if they were to follow what Stalin said, then classifying the majority Han as a minzu is immediately open to challenge. The issue was a problem because the Chinese Communist Party (CCP) had defined the social nature (*shehui xingzhi* 社会性质) of pre-revolutionary China to be semi-colonial and semi-feudalist—that is, not yet capitalist. By asking whether the Han could actually be considered a minzu by Stalinist standards, these scholars in the 1950s thus questioned a notion that had been taken for granted in Chinese society since the turn of the century, and they challenged what minzu meant to the leadership of the PRC.

A few scholars, therefore, tried to apply other terminologies, such as *buzu* (部族, ethnos, a term used by Soviet ethnologists to refer to many ethnic groups who had not yet reached a stage of capitalism according to its social evolution theory), tribe (*buluo* 部落), and so on. These scholars, however, intentionally wanted to define the Han as a minzu and so considered going beyond the Stalinist definition. They thus went on to divide human collectivities into several kinds in accordance with the presumptive five stages of Marxist social evolution.² For example, in primitive society people were organized as tribes, those who were considered to be in slave and feudalist societies were organized into ethnos, and so on.

It is interesting to ask why, when China was preparing a set of preferential policies toward ethnic minorities, no one initially asked whether Stalin's definition was feasible in the Chinese context. I infer at least two contributing reasons. First, minzu had already been established to refer to all groups of peoples soon after the term was introduced from Japanese at the turn of the twentieth century. As Fei Xiaotong (1985) suggested, this establishment was achieved through common practice (*yueding sucheng* 约定俗成) and was therefore widespread. Second, as a consequence, the party leadership tended to regard every separate group of people as a minzu, without consideration of its size and complexity. This usage by the party was also partly due to a kind of political correctness based on communist equalitarianism. Not everyone in the party leadership, however, agreed. As a politician, Mao, among a few others, was exceptional in realizing the importance of achieving political goals through this project.

When the Central Committee of the CCP was summarizing its experience from the preceding work with ethnic minorities in 1953, Mao had keenly worried that such a division according to five stages would lead to potential risk. Mao suggested that "it could be a scientific analysis, but politically, [we] should not differentiate which one is minzu [nation or nationality], which one is buzu [ethnos] or buluo [tribe]" (cited in Liu Xianzhao 1999). In this case political utility definitely concerned Mao. It is relevant to point out that according to this story, Mao had the last word, so that only *minzu* was therefore applied in the state's social policy.

Interestingly enough, in 1954 Fan Wenlan, a well-known historian, published an article titled "On the reasons that China became a unified country in the Qin-Han Period" ("Shilun Zhongguo zi Qin Han shi chengwei tongyi guojia de yuanyin" 试论中国自秦汉时成为统一国家的原因) (Fan Wenlan 1954). This article suggests that after the Zhongyuan (Central Plain) was unified under Qin Shi Huang (秦始皇), the first emperor of the Qin dynasty, China experienced a great transformation through centralization, including a standardized traffic infrastructure, the use of the same written language, and standard measurement units. These steps, according to Fan Wenlan, contributed to the formation of the Han minzu/nationality (*Han minzu* 汉民族). He found an opportunity in the term "modern nationality" (*jindai minzu* 近代民族, in the Chinese version) as used in the Stalinist definition of a minzu/nationality. Since Stalin had specified a "modern" nationality, Fan Wenlan argued that the definition also implied the existence of a traditional nationality. He thus suggested that the Han nation formed during the Qin-Han may not have been modern, but it still qualified as a nation. His article signaled an end to the ongoing debate on how to label ethnic minorities. Fan Wenlan was a high-ranking official in academia, who had been associated with the party leadership since the Yan'an era. Without doubt, he is one of the few to have known about Mao's position on this issue at that time. His article thus delivered Mao's own idea in this way and at the same time placed the Han at the top among all the nationalities of China.

Paradigm One

It is not hard to understand why so many scholars were involved in these projects of ethnic identification and the related debates over the meaning of *minzu*. The state urgently needed to narrate histories for the new ethnic configuration that was forming through the ethnic identification campaign. Scholars were now given the task of legitimizing these newly established ethnicities by showing how they connected to forebears in ethnic groups of the historical past. In order to generate historical facts to fit the logic of this narrative, of course, scholars had to be very selective. They were required to provide material to prove the hypothesis that China had been a "unified country of multiple nations since ancient times" (*Zhongguo zi gu yilai jiu shi yige tongyi de duo minzu guojia* 中国自古以来就是一个统一的多民族国家). This hypothesis therefore became an assumption, leading to topics such as *what the essential aspect* was in interethnic relations of the historical past, how to understand the question of "China" in history, how to correctly treat "assimilation" (*tonghua* 同化) and "integration" (*ronghe* 融合), among several others. Among these topics, the concern about the nature of interethnic relations in the historical past was considered the most central. These topics, especially the central one, were extremely popular, and most of them did not fade out from academic discourse until the early 1980s. As I will discuss below, some historians have revisited some of these issues in recent years. The dynamic for these revisits stems from different sources and has been inspired especially by the study of the Qing dynasty by younger generations of American scholars. These revisits, however, have inherited almost nothing from the earlier paradigm in spite of some common interests and ideas.

Scholars supported this project first by arguing that no matter how often wars between the dynasties of the Central Plain and the polities of ethnic minorities took place, all powers involved wanted to unify China. Second, they asked whether interactions between the Han and ethnic minorities were more likely to involve cultural and economic exchanges or antagonism. Third, as a consequence of the previous questions, they studied how assimilation or integration among different peoples took place, either forcibly or spontaneously, in the historical past.

Understandably, all of these discussions and research projects had to consider what the state wanted. There is far too much research to list here. It is enough to note that at that time, with only a few exceptions, most scholars thought that whatever the party wanted must be right. I do want to cite one scholar, however, who provided one of the few exceptional voices during that period. The main points made by Sun Zuomin (孙祚民), a historian, could be summed up as follows: first, today's China is not the same as China in the past; second, wars embarked on between powers of the Central Plain and other ethnicities were always negative and only brought suffering to peoples; and third, different regimes, no matter whether they had been established by Han or non-Han, represented only the interests of the ruling class and should thus be treated differently from ordinary peoples of every minzu.

Sun's points of view, especially about how today's China differs from ancient China, encountered a lot of attacks from colleagues. Though Sun did not distinguish between the traditional state and the modern state from a perspective of social sciences, he did indeed challenge the assumptions that others were accepting. And, because wars happened so frequently between the regimes of the Central Plain and those of the ethnic minorities, his argument also implied that the so-called "essential" aspect of interethnic relations was actually negative (Sun, 1961, 1980). Nonetheless, his differentiation between the ruling classes and ordinary people left some space to appreciate that there were indeed cultural and economic exchanges between the Central Plain and ethnic frontiers.

China's opening and reform after 1978 also fostered an academic boom. Interestingly enough, the older minzu paradigm seems to be not entirely congruent with the changing situation. Nonetheless it did not completely fade out until the mid-1980s. There are at least three reasons for its termination. First, unlike in the Mao era when the orthodox interpretation of the dynamics of history was class struggle, scholars in the post-Mao era have energetically searched for and explored other topics and fields. Scholars also realize that a mono-causal explanation of history is too weak to stand up to scholarly scrutiny. Second, many research results from scholars working before 1949 and from foreign scholars finally became accessible. Communication between Chinese and foreign scholars became increasingly frequent, and many Chinese scholars were inspired by the new influx of ideas. Third, many scholars found that what they did in the Mao era actually did little more than serve the political agenda of the state. Indeed, many issues raised in the Mao era were actually tasks assigned by the central government.

Paradigm Two

The intellectual projects that took shape in the 1950s were directly followed by another paradigm. From 1958 to 1964, the Chinese government announced that there would be an investigation into the social history of ethnic minorities. The main purpose of this investigation was to legitimate the categorization of population from the ethnic identification campaign (1953–79).[3] The state also asked every provincial and ethnic autonomous district government to collect materials on ethnic minorities. This was to show off the state's accomplishments in ethnic minority affairs as part of the celebration of the tenth anniversary of the People's Republic (Fan 2016). The results would be showcased in Beijing's Minzu Cultural Palace (Minzu Wenhua Gong 民族文化宫).

The display celebrated its opening on time, although the investigation obviously had not been completed and work continued to be carried out. There were a lot of difficulties with this investigation (Fan 2016), but it did result in systematic production of knowledge, which was represented by five series of concise books and many documentary films, in addition to numerous materials collected during the investigation and countless reports.

This investigation was influential in the creation of paradigm two. The key questions had now become the following: How should we narrate the history of every separate nationality? How can we understand every nationality as a historical entity or category? And, how can we construct their histories as parts of the history of the Chinese nation (*Zhonghua minzu* 中华民族)? These had now become the central issues for scholars, although many concerns from the first paradigm remained relevant.

One will find, when reading works produced during that period, that all share the same basic shape and framework. For example, they have to start with the statement that China has been a unified country of multiple nations since ancient times. This formula establishes a framework in which every separate minzu is tied together. Nevertheless, they had to be treated differently according to the ideology of the party-state. The framework accomplishes this by differentiating each minzu in accordance with the five stages of social evolution, so as to construct an ethnic hierarchy that existed within a kind of family metaphor, such that those who were socially and economically advanced should help those who were backward. The Han was of course the most advanced group and therefore the oldest brother, and so burdened with the mission to help all ethnic minorities. The others were scrutinized in order to locate each of them on a stage represented by their degree of social development. This was the main task for the social historical investigation of ethnic minorities and was emphasized in the outlines of the investigation. Since the investigation was partially for the celebration of the tenth anniversary of the establishment of the People's Republic, all notices sent out from the central government stressed the importance of defining every minzu's stage of social evolution. In that juncture, the party-state wanted to show how hard the government had worked on helping minority peoples to successfully leap over developmental stages (*kuayueshi fazhan* 跨越式发展); some minorities were defined as on the stage of so-called late primitive society but could develop by jumping over intermediate stages to enter socialism directly. This included groups such as the Jingpo, Dulong, Wa, and several others. The Yi of Liangshan was defined as a slave society, Tibetan society was labeled as a feudal serfdom, and so on.

Influenced by these projects, many scholars put their energies for a long time into the examination of social evolution according to a formula outlined in a textbook of Soviet Communist Party (Bolshevik) history. Even those who were trained in the West were also engaged in this topic, such as Lin Yaohua (林耀华), Yang Kun (杨堃), and Weng Dujian (翁独健), to mention just a few. They were working on a grand theory of social evolution and basically returned to the classic evolutionism formulated by figures such as Edward B. Tylor, Louis Henry Morgan, and James Frazer. For understandable reasons, their approach tended to be closest to that of Morgan. For them, rather than culture, society was the research object, and Marxist formulas, such as "men's social existence determines their consciousness," or "the economic base determines the superstructure," were taken for granted. In a word, their works taught us little about culture, but a lot about the division of labor, production relations, and the analysis of classes.

Since the boundary of each minzu was firmly fixed after the ethnic identification project, most scholars for a long time primarily provided materials to prove the reality of those boundaries by examining the historical longevity, evolution, and genesis of some particular customs of each separate minzu. Examination of the stage of social evolution indeed worked as a paradigm that shaped many research results. One noteworthy effect of all this research (far too much to cite here), whether disseminated by the governmental propaganda machine or by scholars, was to produce and strengthen stereotypes of ethnic minorities.

As a consequence, people often still use terms from these publications or other representations whenever they mention minority people. In Yunnan, an ethnically diverse province, different peoples criticize each other using terms fraught with meanings produced by these official publications, such as "backward," "childlike," and so on.[4] I would like to provide some experiences of mine to illustrate this point.

I once interviewed a Tibetan woman who was a cadre in the Cultural Bureau in Diqing City, Yunnan Province.[5] I wanted to understand what kind of impact such ethnic research had on ordinary people, especially since Diqing was considered a model of the good handling of interethnic relations. I started with questions about which minzu people most wanted a spouse from. She answered that if the local Tibetans had to marry a non-Tibetan, then the priority should go to the Han; non-Han minzu would be acceptable too, but not any of the mountain people. I asked what she meant by mountain people. She said, "I just use the term to refer to the Lisu and Yi. They live in the mountains, and they are very backward in all respects, lazy and ignorant."

In 2007, with an anthropologist from Taiwan, I visited a park called "Ethnic Minorities Garden" (Shaoshu Minzu Yuan 少数民族园) in Kunming, the provincial capital of Yunnan. The Jingpo of Yunnan have long been regarded as a very backward group in their social organization and daily life, so we went directly to see the "Jingpo house" after we entered the park. A young woman in Jingpo ethnic costume came to interpret the display. She took us to an object seemingly used in ritual situations, and said, "We Jingpo people have practiced primitive religion." Before she could go on, we asked, "Do you understand what primitive means?" She answered, "Doesn't it mean being very backward culturally and economically?" "Who was telling you all this?" "Everyone says it, and it's what they taught us in our job training."

Another case took place in Yangshuo, a famous tourist city in Guangxi. I was visiting a tourist spot named Shiwai Taoyuan (世外桃源, which they translated as Xanadu). It was a scene of karst landforms, with the beauty of natural mountains and water. It was a pleasant place to visit, and the main activity was to float on a boat that passed through many caves. When coming out of caves, tourists could see different views of the mountains. Oddly, however, there were quite a few half-naked Wa people running around, dancing and singing along the water to entertain the tourists. The tour guide on our boat explained, "The Wa people are the most primitive in China, and they are the happiest." I asked her if she knew that Wa people are not native to Guangxi. "Yes," she said, "they are originally from Yunnan." "Why did you put them here if they have nothing to do with Guangxi?" Her answer was just a surprising repetition: "Because they are the most primitive and so are the happiest people in our country. We need them to show their primitiveness and the backwardness of their life. They are simple, so they are happy."

Elsewhere, anthropologists have found the same situation. For example, Jingpo live in the mountains, and the neighboring Han and Dai, who live in the flatlands beneath the hills, have traditionally looked down on them, calling them *shantou* (山头, mountaintops) in the past. But, after the ethnographic investigations I have discussed, they instead started calling Jingpo *zhiguo* (直过, those who pass directly). This means that the Jingpo, as a minzu, has to be helped in order to move on to the socialist stage directly from the late primitive stage without passing through the slave, feudal, and capitalist stages.

Paradigm Three

The third paradigm is the frontier model (*bianjiang fanshi* 边疆范式). Though it appeared much earlier than the other two, this paradigm is still influential and even dominating to a certain extent. The appearance of this paradigm traces back to the republican era (1911–49). Since the establishment of the republic, the state was urgently concerned with nation-building within the framework of a nation-state. One imperative in the construction of a nation-state is the emphasis on sovereignty (*zhuquan* 主权). This notion, however, did not exist in almost any Chinese dynasty until the late Qing in the nineteenth century. In imperial China, state power was understood to decline toward the edges of the territory. State power could not reach regions that were far away from the core areas. Sometimes the state had no presence at all in such areas. The relative absence of the state on the edges of the empire helped to preserve demographic and cultural diversities. For imperial rulers, territory thus had no hard borders, but was more like a picture that faded into vagueness at the edges. The frontier of an empire actually overlapped with land shared with other political units; it was a space where people could easily move back and forth.

According to Anthony Giddens (1989), a significant difference between modern and the traditional states is that the former have borders rather than frontiers, and the latter are the other way around. All nationalist movements as well as nation-states claim to have a national boundary that overlaps with a cultural one. Accordingly, in the particular Chinese context, as Prasenjit Duara (1995) argues, the first question for a nationalist movement is how to make a hard social boundary out of a soft one. Due to the concerns with sovereignty, "frontier" turned out to be an important concept in the republican era and was written into much of the representation of nation-building and state-making. The republican government even established a semi-political body to handle issues relating to the frontier and set up a research field named *bianzheng jianshe* (边政建设, construction of frontier politics) in the 1930s. The field attracted many anthropologists, sociologists, and ethnologists at that time, and almost all of the well-known scholars did research and published on the topic, writing papers for a journal entitled *Bianzheng Gonglun* (边政公论, Public forum on frontier politics) and organizing conferences. This academic interest continues even today for at least three reasons. First, sovereignty is still a vital concern in state politics. Second, as a consequence of the first, ethnic minorities are always involved. Third, the field has been reinvigorated to a great degree by an academic approach toward the Qing (1644–1911) in the United States.

Let me expand briefly on the third reason. Since the 1990s, Chinese historians and anthropologists started to learn about new contributions from a few American historians in Qing studies. These scholars of so-called New Qing History (*xinqingshi* 新清史) have taken a new approach to Qing history. They reject the concept of Sinicization and see the Qing and its Manchu rulers in a much larger context. They regard the Qing not only as a Chinese empire, but argue that it should be considered an inner Asian empire as well.[6] This view challenges what "China" means and also redirects attention to the issue of the frontier. Partly because of the debate with the New Qing historians, some ethnographers and historians in China have reconsidered the frontier, but no longer as a place of rule without sovereignty, but instead as a symbol of the sovereignty of the Beijing-centered Chinese state. That is, the concept of frontier has sometimes become a tool to argue against the New Qing History view of the Qing as an inner Asian empire and emphasize instead that the center of gravity for the Qing was central China. Today, not everyone who is engaged in the study of frontiers necessarily intends to debate with New Qing historians. Nonetheless, the debate has helped make the frontier paradigm into a hot topic again.

Currently, although scholars who are concerned with the issue of the frontier have maintained many interests that go back to the republican era, they also show a very new concern with how to maintain stability in the frontier areas inside of the country. The state has been busy in showing off its benevolence and its authority in minority areas. In practice, this means that state penetration in Xinjiang and Tibet has grown far deeper and stronger in recent years. The state worries that those regions have been influenced by movements associated with overseas Uyghur and Tibetan secessionists. With the situation getting worse, a field called frontier security studies (*bianjiang anquan yanjiu* 边疆安全研究) has emerged, with a primary emphasis on preventing nation-state unity from being broken by secessionists. In practice, however, the focus often shifts to the trustworthiness of ethnic minorities. I think this situation resulted in part from the long history of mutual construction between the concepts of frontier and ethnic minority. In other words, in the view of the state and those scholars who are in line with it, the frontier is not a site for cultural contact, but instead a dangerous and highly unstable place. It faces potential transborder challenges at national and subnational levels from issues like ethnicity and religion.

That is, the problem that the issue of the *bianjiang*/frontier has brought to Chinese academics and policy makers is that it inevitably intertwines with the concept of minzu. The bianjiang/frontier has long been defined as an area of ethnic minority habitation, so of course it is reasonable to think of minzu when talking about bianjiang and vice versa. Ethnic minorities spread over 60 percent of China's territory, which is much larger than the area of so-called China proper. Nevertheless, ethnic minorities constitute less than 10 percent of the national population. Under the influence of social Darwinism in the early twentieth century and working with the state-making and nation-building agenda of the republican government, such a situation naturally led officials and scholars to worry about whether ethnic minorities are trustworthy. Xu Yitang (徐益棠), a student of Marcel Mauss and a well-known ethnologist in the republican era, expressed this concern. In an article, after a brief introduction and discussion, he pointed out:

> In the past, we all thought that the frontier problems came about because of imperialists stirring up trouble behind the scenes. . . . Now, we know that the factor of minzu [nationality] is really serious in China's frontier problems, and among other things, cultural backwardness is the essential cause. (Xu 1941)

Other scholars of *bianzheng*/frontier politics showed the same attitude. Ke Xiangfeng (柯象峰; Ke, 1941) argued that because frontier peoples are much more backward in all respects than those of China proper, they should be seriously studied in order to solve the problem of *bianhuan* (边患, troubles on the frontier). Obviously, as long as sovereignty concerns drive the importance of the frontier in the eyes of the state, the fate of the ethnic minorities there will be carried along. Therefore, ethnic minorities were called *bianmin* (边民, frontier people), which thoroughly conflates frontiers and minorities. This term even came to be applied to ethnic minorities living in China proper, such as the She (畲), the Dan (疍, a boat people of Guangdong and Fujian), and the Hakka (*kejia* 客家), even though some of them are classified as part of the majority Han minzu. From files dating back to the early 1950s, found in the Fujian Provincial Archives, we know that the term "frontier people" in the official documents refers to all groups of peoples who were considered to have been excluded from mainstream Han society. The term "frontier people" lumps peoples together no matter how different they are in religion, ethnicity, and other cultural aspects; it also includes those Han living in frontiers regions. Accordingly, the "frontier"/*bianjiang* in "frontier politics" studies responded to the agenda of nation-state construction that the republican government had launched as early as their 1911 revolution to overthrow the Qing court. The crucial continuity is the implied link to sovereignty. All peoples living in the frontier areas were called *bianmin* (frontier people) without consideration of their ethnic variations; this seems to have intentionally ignored the ethnic diversities of these areas.

Bianjiang/"frontier" thus became a term juxtaposed with *minzu*/"nationality," and to a great degree one can replace the other cognitively; they are inseparable in current representations. For a long time after the social-historical investigation of ethnic minorities, all descriptions and narratives about ethnic minorities in media, textbooks, and other sources portray them as economically and culturally backward. These representations of ethnic minorities always occur in association with the conditions of frontiers. This inseparability continues even in professional Chinese ethnology today. Frontier and minzu have mutually constructed each other; at the same time they serve as metaphors for each other.

Since the state is so concerned with sovereignty, the frontier has become a special category in academia. Just like the category of minzu after the ethnic identification project, the frontier has also become a fixed concept. People imagine it as something that existed forever. This is quite different from some other places, like in the United States, where the frontier is understood as a process that no longer existed after the initial westbound expansion. The frontier in this process was a contact zone (Redfield, Herskovits, and Linton, 1936), in which cultural exchange took place between European migrants and native peoples. The fate of the frontier, however, has been completely different in the Chinese context. Soon after China began to construct itself as a modern state, the frontier was no longer a free zone of interaction, but became a crucial site for the display of national sovereignty. This symbolization has been so deeply planted in people's minds that it has affected their behavior. For example, as long as sovereignty concerns continue to be dominant, policy makers are supposed to prioritize national security over anything else. People's livelihoods are thus secondary, which in the long run may lead to trouble in those areas.

The discussion so far provides a rough picture of Chinese ethnology before Fredrik Barth's understandings of ethnic boundaries were introduced to China. Let me turn now to an account of how Barth's theory of ethnicity has influenced Chinese academia and what changes have been ongoing in ethnology and anthropology since that introduction.

Barth and the *Zuqun* Paradigm

Roughly speaking, popularization of the term "ethnic group" (*zuqun* 族群) in Chinese academia started in the 1990s. There are two sources for this. The first is racial and ethnic studies in US sociology. The Beijing University sociologist Ma Rong, who holds a PhD from Brown University, was possibly the first one to systematically introduce and apply a US-style sociology of ethnicity in his research (Ma 2007). In a controversial article he called for the depoliticization of the idea of minzu. He argued that the term had taken on a purely political status rather than an analytic one. His argument was clear and powerful: the official ethnic classifications had shown so many problems after decades of practice that they could potentially harm the integration of the nation. It was therefore urgent to depoliticize minzu through a replacement of the concept with zuqun/ethnic group. Ma Rong showed clear Durkheimian motives in his primary concern with national social integration, rather than with the daily interactions among ethnicities. Barth's approach, on the other hand, is not at all Durkheimian. Ma did mention Barth's ethnic boundary work a little in his book (2004), but to him, Barth was not crucial to the argument. Ma cites him mostly because Barth's work could not be ignored in any study of ethnicity since the 1970s.

The second source, however, does draw directly from Barth's work, specifically from his 1969 edited book (Barth 1969). Barth had long been established in Western anthropology before his 1969 work, but most Chinese anthropologists were not yet aware of him. In 1998, Chiao Chien (乔健), then professor of anthropology at the Chinese University of Hong Kong, may have been the first person to introduce Barth into Chinese scholarly circles. In 1998, during the fourteenth IUAES congress in Williamsburg, Virginia, Chiao and Chee-Beng Tan (another anthropologist, also included in this volume) strongly recommended Barth's introduction to Chinese attendees, suggesting to Xu Jieshun (徐杰舜), an ethnologist, that Barth's theory deserved to be translated into Chinese. Later on, Gao Chong (高崇), then a graduate student of anthropology at the Chinese University, translated Barth's famous introduction of the 1969 book (Barth 1999). After this, people became far more aware of Barth's work, but Chinese scholars continue to regard *Ethnic Groups and Boundaries* as his masterpiece.[7]

For Barth, ethnicity is an intersubjective phenomenon, and ethnic boundaries do not assume the absence of mobility, contact, and encounters with others. In contrast to the minzu concept, an ethnic group is not formed because of the isolation of the group and defined by its cultural distinctions; instead it always involved encounters with the other. Ethnicity thus is a practice of categorization by interacting people rather than a set of shared cultural traits (Brubaker 2009).

So far, we are still not sure who was the first to put the Chinese characters *zu* (族 clan, group) and *qun* (群 group, crowd, school, etc.) together to translate "ethnic group." It seems most likely to have been either in Taiwan or Hong Kong. In ethnohistorical research in China, some scholars had already been using the term *zuqun* to refer to many peoples whose cultures are similar and who live side by side in a geographic area, such as the Baiyue (百越), for example. *Zuqun* in this sense referred to many groups of peoples living next to one another and whose cultures are similar. It is something more like a cultural cluster, rather than an ethnic group, and so is completely different from what ethnic group means in English. Nonetheless, the emergence and popularization of this term in its current sense should certainly be attributed to Barth's work directly or indirectly. There are two reasons. First, since the opening and reform after 1978, more and more foreign anthropologists came to China, and many of them had been doing field research among ethnic minorities. They introduced the concept of zuqun/ethnic group in their research and especially in their talks. Second, Western academic literature has become far more directly accessible than it used to be.

Introducing the concept of ethnic group to China has led to a lot of discussion, both criticism and appreciation, because it has certainly opened a new space for studying ethnic minorities. The concept of ethnic boundary, though welcomed by students, has been met with some difficulties. First, in my opinion, are some problems caused by misunderstanding of the concept. For Chinese, boundary is usually imaged to be physical rather than nonphysical. Thus after "ethnic boundary" (*zuqun bianjie* 族群边界) was introduced, many students of ethnicity have tended to look for "physical boundaries," so to speak. That is, they used visible cultural characteristics to define boundaries, and that is exactly opposite to what Barth suggested.

Second, some Chinese scholars may not fully understand the whole context of Barth's theory. They criticize the theory as focusing on an individual level and forgetting the group issue. It seems that for those who holding this view, shared culture is the first factor in formation of an ethnic group. This view has been popularly held among Chinese ethnologists for a long time and stems from the legacy of the minzu concept.

Nonetheless, "ethnic group" and "ethnic boundary" have brought an entirely new paradigm, and many things people used to take for granted have now begun to receive serious scrutiny. The introduction of Barth's insights about ethnicity has stimulated students to look into cultural or ethnic diversities that go beyond the limitations of fifty-five official ethnic minorities, even though, for some of them, their understanding could be only partial. As a result of Barth's work, many scholars have had second thoughts on how people were categorized in the ethnic identification campaign and how this categorization has changed ethnic configurations in China. More importantly, many scholars are questioning how national, ethnic, or any other kinds of collective identities have been constructed and reconstructed. For years now, zuqun has been a hot topic in Chinese ethnology, though the term *minzu* is still in use. One result of the change is that the fifty-six minzu are no longer each considered homogeneous and bounded by a unique cultural character.

Barth's work has opened up a new space beyond the category of minzu as it is defined through China's state and party power structures. All kinds of new topics have become popular to scholars, especially PhD students. These include finding diversity and variation within ethnic categories, seeing how livelihoods vary within ethnic groups, asking how different groups of peoples even within a single official minzu define or see themselves, examining how different parts of a separate minzu see each other, and so on. Numerous articles and books on these topics have come out every year since the mid-1990s. "Barth" is appearing in writings all the time, especially if we include those done by graduate students.

Frontiers after Barth

In the remainder of this chapter, I would like to revisit the issue of frontiers and the bianjiang/frontier paradigm again, because Barth's theory gives us the potential to deconstruct the concept of bianjiang. This could take us beyond the previous understandings of bianjiang as a symbol of sovereignty that juxtaposes or overlaps with minzu. The idea of zuqun/ethnic group has the potential to elaborate as well as downplay minzu, which implies a reworking of how we think about the bianjiang issue. This is especially true when we examine the complex diversities of Southwest China. Many of these areas have been considered to be frontiers since the republican era.

Barth's perspective could also help students understand the frontier in a different way—to examine how different subjects practice boundary-making or categorization when encountering one another in a zone of cultural contact. In a word, Barth's perspective on ethnic boundaries helps scholars to go beyond the boundaries demarcated by the nation-state, seeing and thinking how various subjects—religious, ethnic, national, and so on—interact, communicate, exchange, and negotiate with each other. Many religious and ethnic groups were crossing borders well before modern times. The historical connections and heritages of these crossings, however, still remain, even among those groups who were split apart or lumped together by modern nation-states, sometimes becoming different nationals (Harrell 2000). All the nation-states concerned have tried their best to limit or even erase these historical heritages, narratives, and connections among those now split apart and lumped together in different countries. Through a Barthian perspective, studies of bianjiang can go beyond the existing academic paradigms to explore the "new frontier" (Kennedy 1991: 101) of "every day ethnicity," which is ethnicity "without groupism" (Brubaker 2009; Brubaker, Loveman, and Stamatov 2004).

Even though Chinese scholars have been concerned with bianjiang since the republican era, the livelihood of peoples inhabiting those areas did not receive equal attention. Concern with peoples actually living in these areas has always been secondary and barely a by-product of the issue of sovereignty under state-endorsed academic paradigms. Nonetheless, since sovereignty has been such a central concern, people who are living in the borderlands still receive attention and oversight for security reasons. It is feared that they might otherwise cause problems if they are not treated well. Underneath this logic is the question of whether these non-Han people are trustworthy. In other words, there has long been an attitude toward non-Han peoples expressed in the adage that "those who are not part of the we-group must have a very different mind" (*feiwo zulei, qixin biyi* 非我族类，其心必异). In modern times, however, the idea has shifted. Now the reason that they are considered not trustworthy is because of their rugged environmental ("frontier") conditions, which have led them to be "backward" in all aspects of their lives. These poor conditions make them vulnerable to being cheated or stirred up. Situated in such "frontier conditions" (*bianjiang tiaojian* 边疆条件), they are thus considered to be an unstable factor for sovereignty, social integration, and national integrity. This is also an important reason why both party-states of the twentieth century had to carry out policies of control: the "frontier politics" (*bianzheng*) project in the republican era and the ethnic identification project in the PRC era. It also explains the rapid creation of preferential social policies toward ethnic minorities soon after the communists attained the power (Fan 2012).[8]

As mentioned in the previous pages, scholars on *bianzheng*/frontier politics of the republic had contributed a lot to, as well as consulted with, policy making at the regional or national level, offering advice on how to balance domination and livelihood in the governance of the frontiers. It seemed as if a deal had been made between the power-holders and the ordinary people, benefiting the people first in order to buy popularity and loyalty. These scholars hoped that through these policies, the non-Han would ultimately become emotionally attached to or even self-identified with the regime and the nation under construction. Apparently, this approach of coping with ethnic minorities has persisted through today, though with ups and downs over the years.

Deal-making between the CCP and ethnic minorities took place as early as the Long March (1934–35), in which the Red Army passed through several minority areas. Not only did this experience allow the CCP to realize what the real situation of China's ethnicities was, but it also provided opportunities to buy popularity from ethnic minorities. The result of this experience in "ethnic areas" (*minzu diqu* 民族地区), such as Qinghai, parts of Sichuan, Yunnan, Guizhou, and Guangxi, was that many of the first generation of cadres after the establishment of the PRC were people who had assisted the CCP in the revolutionary era (Zang 1998). These newly assigned officials were not necessarily party members. This situation was just like a contract signed between the state and those who were claiming to represent ethnic minorities; one's position was given by the state and so one must be faithful to the state. That is similar to an older imperial way of handling minority issues through indirect rule, but it shifted toward direct rule soon after that earlier revolutionary generation passed away, especially in recent years.

For a long time, the state has shown its double faces of benevolence and authority through its preferential policies toward ethnic minorities, although they are of course not always in balance. Just how much someplace counts as a "frontier," however, appears to be measurable in accordance with perceptions of national security, as long as sovereignty concerns loom so large for the state. For example, Xinjiang has often been treated differently from other places, such as Yunnan, Inner Mongolia, or elsewhere, because the region is perceived to have a greater potential for chaos or even secession; the same is true for Tibet. This means that Xinjiang and Tibet are considered to be even more frontier than other frontier areas. And therefore, more often than not, in these two regions in particular, the central state tends to dominate local governance of these regions, even though administratively these are ethnic autonomous regions.

After unrest took place in Lhasa on 14 March 1998 and in Urumqi on 5 July 2009, the state has increasingly strengthened its domination in both Tibet and Xinjiang. The government has of course been most worried about the integrity of the national territory, and sovereignty has therefore become the key issue again. In recent years, partly due to globalization, some conservative Islamic forces from outside of China have entered and developed in Xinjiang. As a result, some Uyghur people, especially those who are living in rural conditions, have begun to practice Islam in a way that has little in common with what they have inherited from their own tradition.

This situation has further stimulated the state. However, some policy makers have realized that there is an urgent need to improve people's lives as the only way for the government to regain its popularity. This approach has also been promoted by a number of scholars, especially anthropologists. In brief, does the state treat both Xinjiang and Tibet as if they were fundamentally different from elsewhere? And, if that is the case, to what extent have both regions been treated differently? Some scholars have even called for de-frontierization (*qu bianjianghua* 去边疆化) in order to have a new look at the concept of bianjiang.

As a category, bianjiang, in the sense of an environment that binds a minzu together, already has a long history in China. These two categories have greatly affected how people think, with an impact that certainly includes both policy makers and numerous scholars. As a consequence, policies shaped by these ideas place a heavy weight on the role of state power. In the short run, this could bring some results. In the long run, however, the situation could only get even worse. We can see this in other parts of the world, like Puerto Rico in the past, or the nations of the former Yugoslavia and USSR in recent decades, just to mention a few.

At this juncture, Barth's ethnic boundary theory could help to open a "new frontier" for students by encouraging them to examine how and in what way modern power has changed things for the people concerned, including their social life, their relation to the state, how they see themselves and others, and how state policies have changed their livelihood. Anthropologists and ethnologists have a new way to look at ethnicity by focusing on things usually ignored, on what Roger Brubaker (2009) calls "everyday ethnicity."

A Brief Conclusion

The foregoing discussion has examined how paradigms have changed over time in Chinese ethnology and the degree to which the work of Fredrik Barth has played an influential role. I have argued that paradigms formed in Chinese academia arise not so much because of breakthroughs, new discoveries, or leading scholars' contributions, but more by determinations by state power. Therefore, these paradigm changes more often than not are congruent with changing sociopolitical circumstances. By scrutinizing how these three paradigms changed in Chinese ethnology, this chapter has provided an unfolding picture of how Chinese academia has connected to the state and has roughly delineated how a scholarly ecology changed through time. By calling for a de-frontierization of the "frontier," this chapter suggests that we need to be more concerned with the livelihood of the people in question. We need to know what they are really thinking about rather than what potential risks a few among them may produce, even though we also need to be alert for risks.

Michael Moerman's research career exemplifies some of the issues related to what I have discussed above and elsewhere (Fan 2017). Through three articles he published in 1965, 1967, and 1989 (the last coauthored with P. L. Miller), Moerman examines how an ethnic group in the "frontier" of Thailand changed their attitude toward the state. During his visit in 1989, he found that the attitude of the Lue people he studied had almost totally reversed over the three decades he had been working there. The Lue no longer spoke with nostalgia of their "old country" (said to be Sipsongpanna of Yunnan province, China). The Thai state had instead become a source of merit—not just a tax collector, but a provider of education, welfare, food, medication, and so on. The state has thus become increasingly popular, and the Lue people have begun to downplay their ethnicity. They identify instead as Thai citizens, though Moerman regrets that to a degree the Lue's culture has merged into mainstream Thai culture. This turn of events was not inevitable and would not have occurred without state encouragement. Michel Foucault (2000) argued that modern states are above all concerned with "men and things," that is, with governmentality. In this context we need to understand governmentality as the art of governing in a way that could allow people who are subjected to the state to feel comfortable with their lives and thus to believe that under state leadership their lives could get better every day. The problem is how to encourage the Chinese government to realize that good governance requires knowing how their actions might bring real benefits to the people they claim to be concerned with.

Ke Fan is Professor of Anthropology, Nanjing University, and a faculty member of the Johns Hopkins-Nanjing Center. He received his PhD in anthropology from the University of Washington. He has published several books (in Chinese) and numerous articles (in both Chinese and English) on issues such as historical and cultural changes among south Fujian Muslim communities, identity politics, globalization, and political anthropology. His most recent publication is *Understanding Ethnic Identification in a Comparative Perspective* (Zhishi Chanquan, 2019).

Notes

1. Anthropology and ethnology are institutionalized as two separate fields in China. In recent years the Ministry of Education has classified all academic disciplines into two rankings according to their size and position in the state curricula. The social sciences, sociology, political science, and ethnology, among several others, are counted as first class (*yiji xueke* 一级学科), while anthropology is placed into the second class (*erji xueke* 二级学科). Anthropology is thus subordinated to both sociology and ethnology. There have been a lot of debates challenging the rationality of such a classification, and in anthropology many scholars argue that the term "ethnology" is completely out of fashion and should therefore be replaced by "anthropology." They also argue that ethnology in China is not fully ethnological since much research under that rubric has little to do with what "ethnology" conventionally means. I am using "ethnology" here in a much broader sense for the following reasons: First, the term has been used in China since the 1920s. Second, many of the scholars engaged in projects this chapter discusses consider themselves as ethnologists rather than anthropologists. This does not mean they necessarily refuse an identity as anthropologists, but it is just that they have been regarded as ethnologists for a long time. Third, the projects and research I discuss here are exclusively ethnological rather than anthropological. Fourth, scholars engaged in the projects were not exclusively ethnologists or anthropologists. They often came from other disciplines with overlapping interests in ethnic minorities, such as arts, economics, and others.
2. Marx never outlined social evolution as such. The five-stage doctrine was first outlined in chapter 4 of *History of the Communist Party of Soviet Union (Bolsheviks): Short Course*, edited by a Commission of the C.C. of the C.P.S.U.(B), authorized by the C.C. of the C.P.S.U.(B.)1938 (Moscow: Foreign Languages Publishing House, 1951).
3. It was officially announced in 1987 that the government decided no longer to carry on further ethnic identification (Huang and Shi 2005).
4. In these representations, terms used in Chinese usually are "simple" (*chunpu* 纯朴), "pure" (*danchun* 单纯), "naïve" (*tianzhen* 天真), or "kindhearted" (*shanliang* 善良).

5. The interview was conducted during the Forum on the Protection of Intangible Cultural Heritage in China, Hangzhou, 28 June 2013.
6. Recently, however, Mark Elliott (one of the founders of New Qing History) has questioned whether the Qing should really be considered an empire in a Chinese source (Ou 2017).
7. I have discussed in another paper Barth's contributions to anthropology and how his thinking about ethnic boundaries could help us to rethink the issue of the frontier in a Chinese context (Fan 2017).
8. Today, because of globalization, a number of scholars and officials consider certain groups of people to be stigmatized almost to the point of being thought as separate from the nation.

References

Barth, Fredrik. 1969. Introduction to *Ethnic Groups and Boundaries: The Social Organization of Cultural Difference*, edited by Fredrik Barth, 9–38. Boston: Little Brown.
———. 1999. "Zuqun yu bianjie." Chinese translation of Barth's 1969 introduction, translated by Gao Chong, Zhou Daming, and Li Yuanlong. *Guangxi Minzu Xueyuan Xuebao [Journal of Guangxi University for Nationalities]* 1: 21–32.
Brubaker, Rogers. 2009. "Ethnicity, Race, and Nationalism." *Annual Review of Sociology* 35: 21–42.
Brubaker, Rogers, Mara Loveman, and Peter Stamatov. 2004. "Ethnicity as Cognition." *Theory and Society* 33: 31–64.
Duara, Prasenjit. 1995. *Rescuing History from the Nation*. Chicago: University of Chicago Press.
Fan, Ke. 2012. "Ethnic Configuration and State-Making: A Fujian Case." *Modern Asian Studies* 42(4): 919–45.
———. 2016. "Representation of Ethnic Minorities in Socialist China." *Ethnic and Racial Studies* 39(12): 2091–107.
———. 2017. "Heyi bianwei—Barth bianjie lilun de qidi" [How boundaries are made: Inspirations from Barth's theory]. *Xueshu Yuekan* [Academic monthly] 7: 99–110.
Fan, Wenlan. 1954. "Shilun zhongguo zi qinhan shi chengwei tongyi guojia de yuanyin" [On China becoming a united country of multiple ethnicities during the Qinhan Period], *Lishi Yanjiu* [Historical studies] 3: 15–25.
Fei, Xiaotong. 1985. *Shehui Diaocha Zibai* [My experiences and thinking on social investigation]. Shanghai: Zhishi Chubanshe.
Foucault, Michel. 2000. "Governmentality." In *Power*, edited by James D. Faubion, 239–97. New York: New Press.
Giddens, Anthony. 1989. *Nation-State and Violence*. London: Polity.
Harrell, Stevan, 2000. *Ways of Being Ethnic in Southwest China*. Seattle: University of Washington Press.
Huang, Guangguo and Lianzhu Shi. 2005. *Zhongguo Minzu Shibie* [Ethnic identification in China]. Beijing: Minzu Chubanshe.
Ke, Xiangfeng. 1941 [2016]. "Zhongguo Bianjiang Yanjiu Jihua yu Fangfa zhi Shangque" [A discussion on the plan and method of frontier studies]. In *Zhongguo Jindai Bianjiang Minzu Yanjiu Fangfa yu Lilun* [Frontier and ethnic minorities in modern China: Theory and method], edited by Duan Jinsheng, 21–35. Kunming: Yunnan Renmin Chubanshe, 2016.

Kennedy, John F. 1991. *Let the World Go Forth: The Speeches and Writings of John F. Kennedy 1947–1963.* Compiled by Ted Sorensen. New York: Dell.

Kuhn, Thomas. 1996 [1962]. *The Structure of Scientific Revolutions.* Chicago: University of Chicago Press.

Liu, Xianzhao. 1999. "Guanyu minzu de jige jiben lilun wenti" [A Few fundamental and theoretical questions about minzu]. *Minzu Yanjiu* [Ethno-ethnic studies] 2: 1–12.

Ma, Rong. 2004. *Minzu Shehuixue—Shehuixue de Zuqun Guanxi Yanjiu* [Sociology of ethnicity: Sociological study of ethnic relations]. Beijing: Beijing Daxue Chubanshe.

———. 2007. "A New Perspective in Guiding Ethnic Relations in the Twenty-First Century: 'De-politicization' of Ethnicity in China." *Asian Ethnicity* 8(3): 199–217.

Moerman, Michael. 1965. "Ethnic Identity in a Complex Civilization: Who Are Lue?" *American Anthropologist* 67: 1215–30.

———. 1967. "A Minority and Its Government: The Thai-Lue of Northern Thailand." In *Southeast Asian Tribes, Minorities and Nations*, edited by Peter Kunstadter. Princeton: Princeton University Press.

Moerman, Michael, and Patricia L. Miller. 1989. "Changes in a Village's Relations with Its Environment in Thailand. In *Culture and Environment in Thailand: A Symposium of the Siam Society.* Bangkok: Siam Society.

Ou, Lide [Elliott, Mark]. 2017. "Chuantong Zhongguo Shi Yige Diguo Ma?" [Was traditional China an empire?] *Dushu* (Reading) 1: 29–40.

Redfield, Robert, Melville Herskovits, and Ralph Linton. 1936. "Memorandum on the Study of Acculturation." *American Anthropologist* 38: 149–52.

Stalin, Joseph. 1935. *Marxism and the National and Colonial Question.* Moscow: Co-operative Publishing Society of Foreign Workers in the USSR.

Sun, Zuomin. 1961. "Zhongguo gudaishi zhong youguan zuguo jiangyu he shaoshuminzu de wenti" [On questions of the motherland territory and ethnic minorities in China's ancient history]. *Wenhui Bao* [Wenhui daily], 4 November.

———. 1980. "Chuli Lishishang Minzu Guanxi de Jige Zhongyao Zhunze—Du Fan Wenlan 'Zhongguo Lishishang de Minzu Douzheng yu Ronghe'" [A few important principles in dealing with interethnic relation in the history: Some remarks on "Interethnic conflict and integration in Chinese history" by Fan Wenlan]. *Lishi Yanjiu* [Historical studies] 5: 37–46.

Xu, Yitang. 1941 [2016]. "Shinianlai Zhongguo Bianjiang Minzu Yanjiu zhi Huigu yu Qianzhan" [Retrospection and envision: Chinese studies of frontier and ethnic minorites in the past 10 years]. In *Zhongguo Jindai Bianjiang Minzu Yanjiu Fangfa yu Lilun* [Frontier and ethnic minorities in modern China: Theory and method], edited by Duan Jinsheng, 1–20. Kunming: Yunnan Renmin Chubanshe.

You, Zhong. 1985. *Zhongguo Xinan Minzushi* [Ethnohistory of Southwestern China]. Kunming: Yunnan Renmin Chubanshe.

Zang, Xiaowei. 1998. "Ethnic Representation in the Current Chinese Leadership." *China Quarterly* 1 (January–March): 107–27.

An Overall Generative Approach
Fredrik Barth's Contribution to Anthropological Research and Writing

Chee-Beng Tan

Fredrik Barth's research in very diverse regions—Europe, the Middle East, Central Asia, New Guinea, Bali, and Bhutan—was always both ethnographic and theoretical.[1] There is a common theoretical interest in all his work, that is, the concern with processes that give rise to cultural forms, or broadly, the concern with studying social organization rather than social structure. At first his focus was on the study of transactions in social relations, which "hinged on the importance of observing the behavior of actors at the moment of action" (Barth 2007: 8). In later years, he took up the study of meaning. This shift, according to him, was due to the anthropological interest in meaning by the late 1960s and because his proposal to study transactional relations had "limited purchase" on that topic (Barth 2007: 9). For Barth, meaning "can only be interpreted when it is located in a social organization and a praxis of communication" (Barth 1987: 85).

"Process," "social organization," "interaction," and "communication" are thus key concepts in Barth's work. Process refers to "the aggregate consequences of events of communication" (Barth 1987: 79). Culture is always an ongoing process; it is "an ongoing system of communication and contains a corpus of replicated messages" (Barth 1975: 15). The study of Baktaman (New Guinea) rituals may seem a very different undertaking, but its aim was to study the generation of a tradition of knowledge, theoretically "to develop ways of analysing ritual as a mode of communication and, behind that, a mode of thought" (Barth 1975: 11). Searching for a generative model in each ethnographic setting provided Barth with a theoretical approach to do anthropology, and this surely helped him to engage with such a wide range of ethnographic research. The generative models are first outlined in his *Models of Social Organization* (Barth 1966). Perhaps not much read by postgraduate students today, it is actually essential for understanding Barth's pathbreaking anthropological work.

This chapter pays tribute to Fredrik Barth for his contribution to anthropology with his call for a generative approach. His contribution in this respect has to be seen in the context of his lifelong work, in which he applies and refines this approach in diverse ethnographic settings. What Barth has inspired in us is an approach, not a theoretical formula or a theoretical concept that can be understood easily and be applied. His is an approach that informs us about how to do dynamic anthropology in local and regional settings. By studying Barth's works over the years, one can have a clearer understanding of his overall generative models that study processes and cultural forms as well as knowledge and cultural variation.

Background

Fredrik Barth's anthropological career began in 1946 when he enrolled as an anthropology student at the University of Chicago. His father, a geochemist, was invited to the University of Chicago to take up a visiting professor position, at a time when Barth had just completed his high school in Norway, and so he was able to follow his father to Chicago (Barth 2007: 2). At Chicago, Barth received training from such distinguished anthropologists as Robert Braidwood, Fred Eggan, Robert Redfield, Sol Tax, Sherry Washburn, and Lloyd Warner. In 1951, Barth joined Braidwood in his research in Iraq. This led him to conduct his first serious anthropological research, on the Kurds. He wrote up this research later when he spent a year at the London School of Economics, where he met Edmund Leach. The research on the Kurds and his connection with British anthropology played a significant part in Barth's anthropological career.

Barth mentions that he admired the work of British social anthropologists then, Raymond Firth in particular (Barth 2007: 3). At that time, some British social anthropologists, including Leach and Firth, had begun to rethink about the then dominant anthropological theory, as represented by the influential anthropologist Radcliffe-Brown, that put much emphasis on the rather static analysis of structure. They were exploring ways to study culture in a more dynamic way that also would take into consideration analysis of individuals and change. Edmund Leach, for instance, in his book *Political Systems of Highland Burma* (1954), proposes to analyze facts in an "*as if* system of ideas," treated as if they were part of an equilibrium system" (1954/1965: ix) even though "real societies can never be in equilibrium" (1954/1965: 4). In other words, anthropological descriptions are "largely *as if* descriptions" that "relate to ideal models rather than real societies" (1954/1965: 285). Leach's attempt to build a model that takes into consideration that real society is "a process in time" (1954/1965: 285) may have inspired Barth. But as pointed out by Raymond

Firth, Leach's dynamic theory "is still largely a special, not a general, one" (Firth 1965: vii). It was Barth who proposed a general dynamic model, the generative model, not just the one he proposed in 1966, but one that he had continued to formulate in his thought as he marched on in his anthropological profession, as this chapter tries to illustrate.

Leach's other significant influence in anthropology and on Barth is his emphasis on the need to locate the study of culture in the context of ethnic interaction. He calls for greater attention to the impact of ethnic interaction on a group's social organization (Leach 1954/1965). It is worthwhile to note that Edmund Leach was Fredrik Barth's doctoral supervisor in Cambridge, and his teacher's work, which Barth admired, must have influenced his study on ethnic groups and identities. Furthermore, Barth's research in Middle Eastern and Central Asian tribal regions had some similarities to Leach's research in Burma in that they worked among people who interacted among diverse ethnic groups that occupied hills and lowlands, even though the Central Asian regions and upland Burma were culturally and ecologically different.

Barth's own reflection eventually led him to propose the generative model, which he outlined in his 1966 publication *Models of Social Organization*. This approach was inspired by his own field experiences among the Kurds, Swat Pathan, and the nomads of South Persia, as well as the influence of Firth and Leach (see also chapters 5 and 7 in this volume). In his article "Some Principles of Social Organization" (Firth 1964; originally published 1955), Raymond Firth introduces the idea of social organization to complement the static social structure concept. "In a narrow context, organization implies a systematic ordering of positions and duties," writes Firth, and in a broader context, social organization refers to "that continuous set of operations in a field of social action which conduces to the control and combination of elements of action into a system by choice and limitation of their relations to any given ends." Toward the end of the essay, he writes, "In the widest sense the actions of any individual resulting from his choices and decisions and involving the actions of others can be regarded as social organization" (Firth 1964: 85).

The key terms in Firth's approach to studying social organization include "choices and decisions," "actions of others," "role of mediator," and "allocation of rights and duties." "Organization is to be regarded as a primary aspect of co-operation, a co-ordination of individual behavior for economic and social purposes," writes Firth (1955/1964: 61). These key words are important in Barth's generative models and in his transactional approach to studying ethnic interaction and identity. Barth introduced the concept of process in his generative model, meaning process that produces or reproduces cultural form. In *Balinese Worlds* (Barth 1993), Barth calls this process "cultural and social construction of reality" (Barth 1993:4).

In fact, after his one-year fieldwork among the Pashtuns in Swat, Pakistan, Barth spent two years in Cambridge, where he submitted his dissertation. There he had proposed an alternative approach to his analysis of Swat political system, which emphasized choices. "Instead of seeing political organization in the traditional anthropological manner as an 'institution,' based on rules and norms and defined by its function for society, I wanted to describe it as an outcome of the choices and alignments made by its participants," writes Barth (2007: 3). Although he did not write up his Swat materials at Cambridge to illustrate his generative perspective, his focus on individual alignments is obvious.

It may be noted that in 1953, two years before the publication of Firth's noted article on social organization, Barth had already published his *Principles of Social Organization in Southern Kurdistan*. While in this early work, Barth had already shown interest in studying individuals, leaders, and political organization, his ideas of choice in social interaction as well as process and cultural form were developed later, and thus Firth's article on social organization may have played an important part in his conception of generative models. His study of entrepreneurship in Northern Norway obviously played an important part in his understanding of transactions and actors "who make choices and pursue strategies" (Barth 1963: 7), although the foundation of his anthropological insight is really derived from his research among the Pathans.

Barth writes about the significance of research among the Pathans, which was his second and "proper fieldwork," as follows: "Swat Pathans have figured prominently in my writing, and perhaps at times overmuch in my thinking in anthropology" (Barth 1981b: 1). He provides more details about the impact of his research in the Middle Eastern region on his anthropological career: "Middle Eastern tribals taught me the turbulence and pragmatics of politics and the powerful constraints of ecology; the diversity of their modes of livelihood challenged me to think about comparative economics; and their situation as embattled minorities on an enormous continent forced me to face the problematics of ethnicities and boundaries" (1994b: 361). The research on Pathans provided him with field data to write about leadership, social organization, and especially ethnic interaction and identity. His generative models are based on a wider range of ethnographic research, and it is significant that the first volume of his selected essays is entitled *Process and Form in Social Life*, which is what generative models are about.

Barth is also very much influenced by the symbolic interactionism of American sociology, especially the works of G. C. Homans and Erving Goffman, and so the concepts of roles, exchange, and cooperation in social interaction are further reinforced in his generative approach. In his earlier theoretical formulation, he further added game theory to his theoretical approach, since choices are regulated by rules, as there are rules in a game that affect participants' choices (Barth 1959b).

Barth's early study of entrepreneurs in Norway provided the ethnographic experience of paying attention to entrepreneurs and leaders, and this is a convenient way of studying the roles of significant individuals. In the study of ethnicity, he later describes this focus as the "entrepreneurial role in ethnic politics: how the mobilization of ethnic groups in collective action is effected by leaders who pursue a political enterprise" (Barth 1994a: 12). Note that he extends enterprise as an economic activity to the political sphere, as a "political enterprise." The study of leaders and mediators is an early approach of Barth in analyzing local societies. This is well illustrated in his study of Swat Pathans (Barth 1959a, 1985). In this study of political leadership, he identifies two categories of leaders, Pakhtun [Pukhtun] chiefs and saints of holy descent. The saints' followers cut across descent groups and are spatially more widely distributed. Thus, they play the important role of mediator, and "they are continually active in arranging compromises and reducing tensions which the chiefs are unable themselves to resolve" (Barth 1959a: 134). In the study of ethnicity, this focus on leaders mobilizing ethnicity makes the study of ethnic groups and identities more comprehensive.

Regional Perspective

It is necessary to understand Barth's overall approach to the study of anthropology and his application of generative models through reading his various ethnographic works, and not just by reading his *Model of Social Organization*. Most significant is his location of his study in a regional ecological setting. He never studied only one village but always two or more villages within an ecological region. Of the anthropologists of their time, who mainly studied in a particular community, Leach and Barth were significant in introducing a regional framework of analysis in anthropological study. Leach was of course influential in inspiring anthropologists who studied valley and upland peoples in mainland Southeast Asia. The other anthropologist who introduced a regional approach in the 1960s was G. William Skinner. Studying rural China, Skinner called for the study of local social relations in relation to hierarchical levels of central places: standard market town at the lowest level, intermediate market town, and central market town, which is generally a large city in a region. In this way the peasants in a standard market town community are studied in the context of a regional marketing system (Skinner 1964). This was an important proposal for the study of China at a time when anthropologists still largely focused on single communities only. However, Skinner's model is inclined toward marketing, one of the two hierarchical systems—the other being administration—that he considers enmesh the middle range of traditional Chinese society's social structure (Skinner 1964: 43). In this regard, Barth's model is more useful, as it focuses on process and at the same time allows incorporating a wide range of forces of political economy that impact on a region.

To understand Barth's regional ecological approach, we need to note his work on the nomads of South Persia (Barth 1961). The research on nomads necessitates locating the study in a larger ecological setting that the nomads travel and also that involves both nomads and settlers. It is thus significant that he begins his book with the chapter "History, Ecology and Economy." His chapter on chieftainship (chapter 5) shows similarity to Leach's illustration of valley politics influencing upland Kachin political organization. It also somewhat shows his generative model approach. A quote suffices to illustrate this point:

> I have tried to analyze some of the political processes that play a part in producing the form of centralized organization found among the Basseri nomads. . . . Throughout the analysis, I have emphasized the relevance of certain aspects of the total environment in which the Basseri live, and their pastoral form of subsistence, to their form of organization. Important in this chapter has been the fact that the Basseri travel thinly dispersed over areas with large sedentary populations entirely unconnected to the tribal organization. . . . This opens a niche for the political figure we have been concerned to analyze here: the omnipotent Khan or chief. Through him, as a bridge of communication, the nomads' relations with sedentary society may be mediated. (Barth 1961: 89–90)

The study of the local in a larger setting is clearer in his more theoretical paper on nomad-sedentary relations in the Middle East (Barth 1973). Here he points out that the study need not be confined to merely nomads versus settled people in a total environment; one can analyze them in terms of differences in their system of production, and so the focus is thus shifted from differences between groups to activities. The analysis examines a common regional economy as well as class relations between nomads and sedentary people. The local situation is analyzed not only in the regional context (such as modernization of regional economy) but also in relation to state structure, especially policies that affect the local. Here lies the significance of Barth's regional ecological perspective. It locates a local study in a larger system that includes not only regional economy but also the state and, by extension, global influences. The process of generating cultural and identity formation can be analyzed in relation to an overall political economy.

Ethnic Group and Boundary

Fredrik Barth is most known for the theoretical concept of "ethnic boundary," which he introduced in the famous introduction to the book *Ethnic Groups and Boundaries*, edited by him and published in 1969. The "ethnic boundary" concept calls for investigation on "the ethnic boundary that defines the group, not the cultural stuff that it encloses" (Barth 1969a: 15). This theoretical concept helps to draw attention to how members of a group imagine and draw boundary between them and other ethnic groups, and how individuals of a group use cultural features or historical events to make distinction between themselves and others. Boundary-making involves imagination of belonging to a group, as does the use of cultural symbols to articulate ethnicity. Barth mainly studied ethnic groups in direct interaction, although in a modern state, members of an ethnic group may be distributed all over a country or in a wide region.

To Barth, ethnic groups "are best seen as a form of social organization," and he defines ethnic group thus: "To the extent that actors use ethnic identities to categorize themselves and others for purposes of interaction, they form ethnic groups in this organizational sense" (Barth 1969a: 13–14). Barth's model of ethnicity is influenced by his ethnographic study, but seeing ethnic groups as a form of organization reflects his interest in studying social organization and using his generative models, which emphasize process, choice, strategy, and "the *transactional* nature of most interpersonal relations" (Barth 1966: 3) that is largely based on reciprocity.

Students of ethnicity often forget that Barth's model of studying ethnic groups includes his generative perspective, which stresses the need to explore "the different processes that seem to be involved in generating and maintaining ethnic groups" (Barth 1969a: 10). This is an approach that researchers can follow, although Barth himself was then guided by his own transactional model, which assumes individuals make choices of best advantage under specific constraints and opportunities. In his description of Pathan identity, he shows that "critical factors are connected with the actor's own choice of identification" (Barth 1969b: 125). Thus, in Pathan-Baluch contact situations, where Baluch chiefs are willing to incorporate new members into the tribe, there is a flow of Pathan individuals to Baluch groups. This illustrates clearly Barth's use of the concept of transaction, which he defines thus: "One may call transactions those sequences of interaction which are systematically governed by reciprocity" (Barth 1966: 4). We have no reason to doubt Barth's ethnographic study, but the behavior of ethnic groups in nation-states is often not characterized by rational calculation of advantage in matters ethnic.

The debate on rationality in ethnic interaction cannot be discussed adequately in this chapter. Our concern here is Barth's application of generative models to the study of ethnic group and identity and his contribution to a comprehensive approach in doing anthropology. His later reflection on boundary maintenance helps to orientate attention on ethnicity as "produced under particular interactional, historical, and economic and political circumstances" (Barth 1994a: 12). This consideration significantly relates the study of ethnicity to political economy, history, and the role of the state, which indeed he does in his own review of his concept of boundary.

Overall Barth's model of studying the process that generates ethnic expression remains useful. However, it is possible to transcend ethnic boundaries, for as Barth has also pointed out, ethnic identification need not always involve drawing a boundary. Indeed, it is possible to feel proud of belonging to an ethnic identity without excluding or discriminating against individuals of other ethnic identities. This is where "rooted cosmopolitanism" as discussed by Kwame Anthony Appiah (1997) is relevant to our understanding of transcending ethnicity.

Transaction and Maximizing Values

Building on rethinking anthropology at that time and on his own innovative research, Barth contributed to anthropology his generative model approach. The models seek "to discover and describe the processes that generate the form," "to describe and study change in social forms," and to "facilitate comparative analysis" (Barth 1966: introduction). Inspired most probably by Firth's distinction between structure and organization, Barth's model emphasizes choice influenced by incentives and constraints in the process of transactions. In such an interaction, value and strategy are important factors. There are rules of strategy that negotiate values gained and lost, so as to "maximize value" (Barth 1966: 5). His early study of entrepreneurs in Norway had led him to incorporate the study of cultural brokers and intermediaries in his generative models, and this is evident in his various ethnographic studies, as in the study of the Swat leadership and the roles of mediators in cultural variation in Papua New Guinea. One need not follow the details of his arguments about transaction, but the suggestion of focusing on process that generates cultural form in a particular ecological setting or environment is a fruitful way of doing anthropology.

While anthropologists are all familiar with Barth's ethnic boundary concept, fewer students now read his other work, and so his theoretical influence is so far rather limited. Most associate him with a transactional theory that is also considered out of date, considering it a form of methodological individualism. In fact, labeling his approach as transactional has led scholars to neglect his generative models, and criticism against his work has largely focused on issues surrounding transaction. In particular Barth's mention of maximizing value in transaction and his reference to game theory have led to much criticism of him as seeing humans as always seeking maximum profit (e.g., Paine 1974; Akbar Ahmed 1976; Kapferer 1976a; Kapferer 1976b). Barth noted the attention on "transaction," and in his "'Models' Reconsidered," he pointed out that what he wished to focus on was "'generative,' or 'process' and not 'transaction,'" and that the concept of "transaction" was not intended "to become the central focus of a substantive social theory"; also "transaction" was introduced to conceptualize a process in social life (Barth 1981a: 76–77). "'Models' Reconsidered" (Barth 1981a) is an important work to read alongside his original proposal (Barth 1966) to see his rare response to critique and to understand his reflection and clarification about generative models.

Our concern is Barth's proposal of a generative model that allows studying individuals in their real lives, and not following every detail of his ethnographic analysis and assumptions. Other than his *Models of Social Organization* (1966), his *Political Leadership among Swat Pathans* (1959) has been critically discussed by a number of prominent scholars, including Talal Asad (1972) and Akbar Ahmed (1976). One can find shortcomings in good works, too, since all works are positioned, and an author can conclude in one of a number of ways. We learn from Asad that Barth fails to distinguish clearly authority from power, that he uses a Hobbesian model that emphasizes sovereign domination, and that Barth should have paid more attention to historical and class perspective. We learn from Ahmed that Barth's analysis of Pathan leadership largely ignores Islamic values and the roles of charismatic Islamic leaders, that he reduces Pathan society to the Yusufzai people that he studied, that he focuses too much on Yusufzai khans, and so on.

All these are very useful comments that give us insight into possible other perspectives of Pathan society. However, this criticism does not devalue Barth's work or negate his generative approach. As Michael Meeker points out, Barth's analysis of calculation of self-interest helps in understanding the disruptive processes, although he criticizes Barth for failing to analyze them sufficiently and "to place the problem of force and coercion in a proper historical perspective" (Meeker 1980: 685). More recently, David Edwards analyzes Barth and his critics' discussion, and he finds that Barth's emphasis on individual initiatives and choice is more useful for understanding Afghanistan than a class perspective. He points out that the world of the Afghan Islamic leaders in the 1980s "bears a much closer resemblance to Barth's model of rational political actors carving out blocs of supporters and savaging rivals than it does to Ahmed's more idealized image of charismatic visionaries imbuing their followers with an exalted vision of a more perfect society" (Edwards 1998: 720). Self-interest is undoubtedly an important value guiding human behavior. Perhaps the concept of value maximization can be read, as suggested by Wikan (1982: 298), "as an admonishment to identify the proximate goals which behavior aims, rather than an obviously unsupportable thesis that people are perpetually and relentlessly struggling to wring the last fraction of advantage from every encounter and incident."

Barth must have learned from his critics even if he might have disagreed. Instead of debating on transactionalism and rational calculation, his later focus on meaning and knowledge is significant. *Balinese Worlds* may be seen as a product of his lifelong reflection on doing anthropology that incorporates the study of real people and how they use knowledge to construct their social world in local settings in a global world. Both *Balinese Worlds* and Unni Wikan's *Managing Turbulent Hearts* (1990) are excellent anthropological studies of Balinese lives, of how they live and act in a living society. Unni Wikan's work, in fact, illustrates how one can study the emotional life of people in their everyday life, about people who "face choices, and choose, that they may conduct their lives with dignity" (Wikan 1990: 38).

Summarizing Barth

Barth often mentions generative models in the plural. We can take this to mean that he does not seek to propose any specific model that limits writing anthropology according to a particular formula. The generative models as outlined in his 1966 publication have influenced his own research and writings, which in turn helped to illustrate and refine the models. Barth moved on and followed the development of anthropology over time, and his ethnographic works written in different time periods show this, especially in his use of narrative expressions. He was able to refocus to take note of new developments in anthropology, and he did not waste his time on defending his theoretical position or to establish authority over a particular theory. He wrote, "I needed to refocus rather than continue to plug my particular views on the study of strategy and choice" (Barth 2007: 9). I did not have the honor of knowing him personally, but he seems to me a man who was open to criticism, with which he might agree or disagree. He noted the comments on his work, observed the trends in anthropology, and continued to engage in new anthropological research, always providing new insight from his observation of ordinary people. As such he did not reformulate his models of social organization in a way that we can follow easily without reading all his works. We need also to note that there is no particular model to follow exactly; what Barth has offered is an approach of doing anthropology, as illustrated by his various works, and anthropologists can each come up with their own models based on this general approach that focuses on process.

While Barth has provided us with a lot of insights and reflection about studying process and cultural reproduction and cultural formation, he did not outline his overall approach in a way that takes into account his later reflection. We can summarize his contribution to an overall generative approach and analytical framework in doing anthropology as follows, and I shall do this by citing his words used in *Balinese Worlds*, his last major ethnographic work that benefits from development in anthropology over the decades and his lifelong engagement with the discipline. The work may be considered his best presentation of the generative models that takes note of the advance in anthropological theorization, which has paid more attention to the roles of the state and globalization since the 1980s. The overall generative approach may be described as follows:

1. To study processes that generate cultural forms, or in Barth's terms, to look for generative models "that capture the existing world as gracefully and economically as possible" (Barth 1993: 13).
2. In empirical research, this means "on the one hand to observe and depict the events that take place around and among people, and the actions of particular persons in these various situations; and then successfully to join them as they, through their own interpretations, endow these events with the meanings that become salient realities in their lives" (Barth 1993: 286). Barth advises that in acknowledging "the fundamental subjectivity and consciousness of human beings, it is safest both to begin and to end up with people acting—if we take care to depict the ways people are embedded in the social organizations that empower them" (Barth 1993: 339).

3. In focusing on "the processes of social and cultural construction of reality," "variation should emerge as a necessity from our analysis" (Barth 1993: 4). The generative processes in cultural formation "take place in a world of considerable disorder and within a broad field of variation between people and groups where knowledge and particular concerns are differentially distributed, and most events of interaction are predicated by limited and partisan perspectives among the actors and agencies involved" (Barth 1993: 102). This emphasis on internal cultural variation might have been inspired, too, by Edmund Leach, who attempted "to represent Kachin cultural variations as different forms of compromise between two conflicting systems of ethics" (Leach 1965: 292). Of course Barth had gained this insight more comprehensively and in his own way from his experiences of research in different regions. This is most evident in his emphasis on studying bodies of knowledge/tradition and internal cultural variation of the Baktaman and the Balinese.

4. There is a need to emphasize "the importance of acknowledging flux and of conceptually merging the analysis of processes inside and outside the local context" (Barth 1993: 339). I have shown how Barth's approach allows linking up with the political economy approach and thus provides a more dynamic and wider perspective that also takes account of individual actions.

The last point on processes outside the local context is an aspect of the generative models that Barth has expanded on over the years. In reviewing his own work on ethnicity, Barth further clarified his view of the need to combine the local and the macro. He proposed three levels of analysis, namely, a micro level that focuses on "persons and interpersonal interaction," a median level that is "the field of entrepreneurship, leadership and rhetoric," and a macro level that focuses on state policies (Barth 1994a: 21). This is a useful way of doing anthropology, and it clarifies his generative models more clearly. We need, however, to note that the levels interpenetrate, as Barth himself describes. The state, for example, acts through officials and local elites, and in the case of China, for instance, the state that impinges on local ethnic relations and identity formation may be understood in terms of the roles of the local cadres, local elites, and other cultural brokers, such that the state and the medial levels are interpenetrating levels.

In his earlier research, the particular persons (point 2 above) that Barth focused on were cultural brokers and leaders. In *Balinese Worlds*, citing Unni Wikan, his wife, who accompanied him to do her own research in Bali, Oman, and elsewhere, he writes about the need to attend to "the concerns of particular and positioned persons" (Barth 1993: 297; Wikan 1990: chap. 2). He reiterates, "We need to focus precisely on the fine details of the events that engage particular, positioned persons, the interpretations they give to those events, and the experience that thereby ensues" (Barth 1993: 287). "Positioned persons" is a narrative made popular by postmodernist scholars, and the use of this term makes it more broadly useful in doing field research, in learning from ordinary individuals. While Barth has written about leaders in his earlier work, in his field research he learned from ordinary people, a point that he himself had pointed out (see chapter 1 in this volume), and this focus on ordinary people is most evident in *Balinese Worlds*.

Overall, Barth's lifelong anthropological study produced an approach that involves using field data "to produce valid models of how people act, communicate, and construct meanings together" (Barth 1994b: 359). Barth's analytical framework is general enough to allow the incorporation of relevant theoretical concepts that have been developed as anthropology advances. The concept of power has become an important theoretical concept in anthropology, thanks to Foucault (cf. Foucault 1980), although in anthropology in the early 1970s, Abner Cohen had already pointed out that power "is an aspect of all social relationship and is not limited to the politics of the state" (Cohen 1974: 122). A major criticism of Barth's early model is his neglect of power or, in the view of Robert Paine, his neglect of power "as a variable of exchange" (Paine 1974: 7). Barth agrees that he fails to introduce "an abstract concept of power" into his discussion (Barth 1981a: 88), but he points out that he has assumed the significance of power in his characterization of statuses and tasks, such as between Swat landowners and tenants. Anyway, anthropology has since paid more attention to the analysis of power in social relationships, and this needs to be incorporated into Barth's generative models, which, by the way, emphasize the study of interaction.

Significance of Barth in My Baba Research

Like many students who studied ethnicity in the 1970s, Barth's concept of ethnic boundary had a strong influence on my study of the Baba in Melaka, Malaysia. The Melaka Baba is a small community of highly localized Chinese who speak among themselves a creolized Malay dialect called Baba Malay, unlike the mainstream Malaysian Chinese, who speak their respective Chinese language such as Hokkien (Minnan or Southern Fujian dialect), Hakka, Cantonese, and so on, while those who have received some Chinese education speak Mandarin (Putonghua in China but called Huayu in Malaysia), too. Except for a few who have learned Hokkien and Mandarin, the Babas generally speak Baba Malay, while many speak English, too. Since the non-Baba Chinese in Melaka do not speak Malay among themselves, the Babas stand out as a distinct category of other Chinese. The non-Baba Chinese draw a boundary between themselves and the Babas, regarding them as not quite Chinese. In racially polarized Malaysia, the Chinese perceive themselves as discriminated against by the Malay-dominated government, and they are culturally defensive. In addition, the non-Baba Chinese are hostile to fellow Chinese speaking Malay among themselves. This is a phenomenon of the present-day ecology of ethnicity in Malaysia.

We have noted that Barth points out that ethnicity is produced under particular interactional, historical, economic, and political circumstances. We can use this point to understand Baba ethnicity. As explained above, the politics of ethnic interaction in Malaysia makes the Malay-speaking Babas an other category of Chinese. But why do the small population of Babas in Melaka continue to identify themselves as "Baba"? In the first place, as long as the Babas speak only Malay among themselves, albeit Baba Malay, they remain excluded by the mainstream Chinese as a separate category of Chinese, who are labeled as Baba. But why do Baba individuals cling to this identity despite being ridiculed and despised by the non-Baba Chinese? Here one needs to note that ethnicity cannot be explained merely by rational choice, as emotional attachment plays an important part, too. Baba Malay has remained a language of intimacy for those who grow up as Babas speaking the language and feeling attached to their identity, and they distinguish themselves from the non-Baba Chinese, referring to them derogatorily as Cina Gə, sort of "Chinamen." Nevertheless, this maintenance of Baba identity is possible because the distribution of the Baba is concentrated in the small state of Melaka, which allows them to have close interaction. This close interaction among the Babas is reinforced by their close network of kin relations, which is partly a result of marrying relatives of different family names, as discussed in Tan (1984). However, outside Melaka Baba individuals may not reveal their Baba identity by speaking English to fellow Chinese. Here there is rational choice in the interest of avoiding inconvenience in interaction that may not be sympathetic to Baba identification.

How did the Baba identity come about in the first place? Toward the end of the nineteenth century and the early twentieth century, it was the Babas who drew the boundary between themselves and the poor Chinese immigrants, who were referred to derogatorily as *sinkeh*, or "new arrivals"; even the English term "Chinamen" was used to refer to the low-status Chinese immigrants. Originally offspring of early Chinese immigrants with local women (Malay, Balinese, and other migrants from Indonesia), the small population of the early mixed Chinese were easily acculturated to speak bazaar Malay with Indonesian influence, which later became Baba Malay. While by the end of the nineteenth century with the arrival of more Chinese immigrants, the Babas were able to find among Chinese migrants spouses for their children, including arranging matrilocal marriages, the offspring of such unions continue to speak Malay. The Babas were among the earliest to send their children to English schools, making it possible for many of them to join the colonial civil service, while English became the language of literacy for the Baba. The Baba merchants engaged themselves as compradors in the colonial economy, and so the well-off Babas, as Straits Chinese, became influential business leaders among the Chinese.

This was an important factor in explaining why the Babas became a respectable ethnic status. This higher ethnic status also applied to the English-speaking Chinese in Penang who spoke a localized Hokkien that used a significant number of Malay and English loan words. This localized Hokkien may be loosely referred to as Penang Hokkien. In the nineteenth century, the term "Baba" became a label that distinguished the local-born Chinese with certain local features as seen in language, cuisine, and dress. Being local and more directly connected to the British colonial regime, the well-off Chinese merchants then were mainly Babas who were Straits-born Chinese in the British settlements of Penang, Melaka, and Singapore. The Babas in Singapore mostly originated from Melaka and so, unlike those in Penang, spoke both Baba Malay and English, while the Penang Babas spoke Penang Hokkien and English.

Thus the Malay-speaking Chinese communities formed in the context of early Chinese migration and the interactional context in the Malay world. The establishment of Baba as a respectable category of Chinese separate from the later Chinese immigrants took place in the economic and political context of British colonialism. The fortune changed after the well-off Babas lost their fortune during World War II, and with Malaya's independence in 1957, the Baba lost their privileged position in the colonial economy. Since then, the Baba were not able to define their status as respectable Straits Chinese. Only in Melaka do the Malay-speaking Babas continue to remain as a living community, while those in Singapore are merging into the mainstream Chinese community of the Singaporean society in which English has become a common language, albeit Singaporean style. Most younger people from Baba families in Singapore hardly speak Baba Malay anymore. Penang Hokkien has become the lingua franca for the Chinese in Penang, and it is difficult to identify a separate Baba community there, except when some activities are organized to showcase the glorious Baba heritage of the past.[2]

Inspired by the idea of subjective identification as well as from observation of how the Baba in Melaka use cultural features to express their Chinese identity and their Baba identity as a localized Chinese identity, my study distinguishes ethnic identification and cultural identity, that is, how the Baba perceive themselves and are perceived by others as Baba and how they use cultural features to project their identities. The posting of Chinese couplets at the main entrance of their house and the celebration of Chinese festivals as well as observing Chinese religious rites and symbolism closely all serve to highlight their Chinese ethnic status, while speaking Baba Malay and the rhetoric of Baba refinement (in contrast to non-Baba Chinese behavioral coarseness) as well as praising delicious Nyonya food (Baba food) are ways Baba individuals emphasize their Baba-ness. The Melaka Babas thus identify themselves as both "Baba" specifically and "Chinese" generally. The Baba case illustrates very well not only Barth's idea of ethnic identification but also the relevance of culture to ethnic identity. While Barth emphasizes the concept of ethnic boundary in his study of ethnicity, he does not neglect the "cultural features that signal the boundary" (Barth 1969a: 11). What he seeks to stress is that "we can assume no simple one-to-one relationship between ethnic units and cultural similarities and differences" (Barth 1969a: 10).

Conclusion

In his comprehensive biography of Fredrik Barth, Eriksen (2015: 199) points out that "Barth is a more complex and dialectical thinker than many claim. He continuously oscillates between interpretation and explanation, between the universally human and the locally particular, which can only be grasped through deep observation and participation." Overall Barth's contribution to anthropology needs to be seen in the context of his whole career and not piecemeal. He refined the conception of generative models over the years. Along with Clifford Geertz, Sidney Mintz, and Marshall Sahlins, he may be regarded as one of the great modern anthropologists whose general theoretical models have been quite influential in anthropology.

Barth's approach to studying anthropology takes into consideration all the major factors that influence cultural forms: individual action, political and social constraints, process of exchange and interaction, ecology, and ethnicity as well as the local and the regional. We can add the global to this model to make it more comprehensive. In particular, Barth's analysis of the roles of different traditions of knowledge in the study of cultural variation and the "cultural conventions of communication" (Barth 1975: 15), whether among the Balinese or among the Ok people, is truly enlightening.

Anthropology students, when not writing about ethnic groups and identities, have cited Pierre Bourdieu, for instance, more than Barth. Both provide ways of overcoming the problem of studying social structure as a static jural system without ignoring its constraints. Bourdieu does this through his innovative use of the concepts of habitus, strategy, and cultural reproduction, which beautifully also takes care of the agency of individuals. Barth focuses on the behavior of individuals acting under constraints, thus introducing agency in his own way, and his generative model provides a way to study cultural formation in the context of physical and cultural ecology, as well as interaction between individuals of different ethnic groups. In particular, Barth's analysis of the roles of different traditions of knowledge in the study of cultural variation and the "cultural conventions of communication" (Barth 1975: 15), whether among the Balinese or among the Ok people, is enlightening. In years to come, anthropology students are likely to rediscover Barth's great contribution, not the generative model that he originally proposed in 1966, but the one that he has reflected over the years, that is, the general cultural approach to the study of anthropology that I have illustrated.

Chee-Beng Tan is Professor in the Department of Anthropology, Sun Yat-sen University, and former professor in the Department of Anthropology, the Chinese University of Hong Kong. His research interests include ethnic groups, identity, religion, food, and the Chinese overseas. His publications include, as author, *Chinese Religion in Malaysia: Temples and Communities* (Brill, 2018) and, as editor, *Routledge Handbook of the Chinese Overseas* (Routledge, 2013).

Notes

1. I am grateful to Prof. Robert P. Weller and Prof. Unni Wikan for reading the draft of this essay and giving useful comments.
2. The description here is based on my study of the Baba, see Tan (1988) and Tan (2004: 69–90). Other relevant studies include Clammer (1976) and Rudolph (1998), while Cheah (2010) provides a good updated study.

References

Ahmed, Akbar S. 1976. *Millennium and Charisma among Pathans: A Critical Essay in Social Anthropology*. London: Routledge & Kegan Paul.

Appiah, Kwame Anthony. 1997 (2005). *The Ethics of Identity*. Princeton: Princeton University Press.

Asad, Talal. 1972. "Market Model, Class Structure and Consent: A Reconsideration of Swat Political Organization." *Man* 7(1): 74–94.

Barth, Fredrik. 1953. *Principles of Social Organization in Southern Kurdistan*. Universitetets Etnografiske Museum Bulletin 7. Oslo: B. Jørgensen.

———. 1959a. *Political Leadership among Swat Pathans*. Monographs on Social Anthropology 19. London: Athlone Press. First paperback edition, with corrections, 1965.

———. 1959b. "Segmentary Opposition and the Theory of Games: A Study of Pathan Organization." *Journal of the Royal Anthropological Institute of Great Britain and Ireland* 89 (1): 5–21.

———. 1961. *Nomads of South Persia: The Basseri Tribe of Khamseh Confederacy*. Boston: Little, Brown.

———. 1963. Introduction to *The Role of the Entrepreneur in Social Change in Northern Norway*, edited by Fredrik Barth, 5–18. Bergen: Norwegian Universities Press.

———. 1966. *Models of Social Organization*. Royal Anthropological Institute Occasional Paper 23. London: Royal Anthropological Institute.

———. 1969a. Introduction to *Ethnic Groups and Boundaries: The Social Organization of Culture Difference*, edited by Fredrik Barth, 9–38. Boston: Little, Brown.

———. 1969b. "Pathan Identity and Its Maintenance." In *Ethnic Groups and Boundaries: The Social Organization of Culture Difference*, edited by Fredrik Barth, 117–34. Boston: Little, Brown.

———. 1973. "A General Perspective on Nomad-Sedentary Relations in the Middle East." In *The Desert and the Sown: Nomads in the Wider Society*, edited by Cynthia Nelson, 11–21. Berkeley: Institute of International Studies, University of California, Berkeley.

———. 1975. *Ritual and Knowledge among the Baktaman of New Guinea*. New Haven: Yale University Press.

———. 1981a. "'Models' Reconsidered." In *Process and Form in Social Life: Selected Essays of Fredrik Barth*, vol. 1, 76–104. London: Routledge & Kegan Paul.

———. 1981b. *Features of Person and Society in Swat: Collected Essays on Pathans; Selected Essays of Fredrik Barth*, vol. 2. London: Routledge & Kegan Paul.

———. 1985. With Miangul Jahanzeb. *The Last Wali of Swat: An Autobiography as Told to Fredrik Barth*. New York: Columbia University Press.

———. 1987. *Cosmologies in the Making: A Generative Approach to Cultural Variation in Inner New Guinea*. Cambridge: Cambridge University Press.

———. 1993. *Balinese Worlds*. Chicago: University of Chicago Press.

———. 1994a. "Enduring and Emerging Issues in the Analysis of Ethnicity." In *The Anthropology of Ethnicity: Beyond "Ethnic Groups and Boundaries,"* edited by Hans Vermeulen and Cora Govers, 11–32. Amsterdam: Het Spinhuis.

———. 1994b. "A Personal View of Present Tasks and Priorities in Cultural and Social Anthropology." In *Assessing Cultural Anthropology*, edted by Robert Borofsky, 349–61. New York: McGraw Hill.

———. 2000. "Boundaries and Connections." In *Signifying Identities: Anthropological Perspectives on Boundaries and Contested Values*, edited by Anthony P. Cohen, 17–36. London: Routledge.

———. 2007. "Overview: Sixty Years in Anthropology." *Annual Review of Anthropology* 36: 1–16.

Cheah, Hwei-Fe'n. 2010. *Phoenix Rising: Narratives in Nyonya Beadwork from the Straits Settlements*. Singapore: NUS Press.

Clammer, John R. 1976. "Overseas Chinese Assimilation and Resinification: A Malaysian Case Study." *Southeast Asian Journal of Social Science* 3(2): 9–23.

Cohen, Abner. 1974. *Two-Dimensional Man: An Essay on the Anthropology of Power and Symbolism in Complex Society*. Berkeley: University of California Press.

Edwards, David B. 1998. "Learning from the Swat Pathans: Political Leadership in Afghanistan, 1978–97." *American Ethnologist* 25(4): 712–28.

Eriksen, Thomas Hylland. 2015. *Fredrik Barth: An Intellectual Biography*. London: Pluto Press.

Firth, Raymond. 1964. "Some Principles of Social Organization." In *Essays on Social Organization and Values*, 59–87. London: Athlone Press. [Previously published in *Journal of the Royal Anthropological Institute* 85 (1955): 1–18.]

———. 1965. Foreword to *Political Systems of Highland Burma*, by Edmund Leach. Boston: Beacon Press.

Foucault, Michel. 1980. *Power/Knowledge: Selected Interviews and Other Writings 1972–1977*. New York: Pantheon Books.

Kapferer, Bruce, ed. 1976a. *Transaction and Meaning: Directions in the Anthropology of Exchange and Symbolic Behavior*. Philadelphia: Institute for the Study of Human Issues.

———. 1976b. "Introduction: Transaction Models Reconsidered." In *Transaction and Meaning: Directions in the Anthropology of Exchange and Symbolic Behavior*, edited by Bruce Kapferer, 1–22. Philadelphia: Institute for the Study of Human Issues.

Leach, E. R. 1965 (1954). *Political Systems of Highland Burma*. Boston: Beacon Press.

Paine, R. 1974. *Second Thoughts on Barth's Models*. Royal Anthropological Institute Occasional Paper 32. London: Royal Anthropological Institute.

Rudolph, Jurgen. 1998. *Reconstructing Identities: A Social History of the Babas in Singapore*. Aldershot, UK: Ashgate.

Sahlins, Marshall. 1985. *Island of History*. Chicago: University of Chicago Press.

Skinner, G. William. 1964. "Marketing and Social Structure in Rural China." *Journal of Asian Studies* 24: 3–43, 195–228, 363–99.

Tan, Chee-Beng. 1984. "Kin Networks and Baba Identity." *Contributions to Southeast Asian Ethnography* 3: 84–97.

———. 1988. *The Baba of Melaka: Culture and Identity of a Chinese Peranakan Community in Malaysia*. Petaling Jaya, Malaysia: Pelanduk Publications.

———. 2004. *Chinese Overseas: Comparative Cultural Issues*. Hong Kong: Hong Kong University Press.

Wikan, Unni. 1982. *Behind the Veil in Arabia: Women in Oman*. Baltimore: Johns Hopkins University Press.

———. 1990. *Managing Turbulent Hearts: A Balinese Formula for Living*. Chicago: Chicago University Press.

Afterword

A Rooted Cosmopolitan Remembered

Ulf Hannerz

In times when much of the academic world seems inclined to follow fashions—star authors much cited one year, forgotten three years later—it is a pleasure to see the longevity of the influence of Fredrik Barth's work, not only in his own corner of the world, but from Beijing to Boston. It is now seen to foreshadow later developments in varied ways: postmodernism, "the ontological turn," the importance of trust, infrastructure studies, and others. And while several authors of chapters in this book—Barfield, Haaland, Lindholm, Robbins—have more or less followed in Barth's footsteps, to fields where he worked or adjacent to these, others take a trip with his ideas to apply them and adapt them elsewhere. More than ever, this is Barth going global.

I first met Fredrik Barth when he came to lecture in Stockholm in 1965, and I interviewed him on Swedish radio later that year, in connection with a Stockholm conference of Scandinavian anthropologists. (As I remember it, at the end of the official conference buffet, Fredrik loaded surplus sandwiches into his wrapped umbrella, and a group of us went off to continue the party elsewhere.) From then on, we met in different places, under different circumstances, in Bergen, in Oslo, in Stockholm, at various conference sites elsewhere in the world—once even by chance in a Mexican hotel lobby. I refer to him in the following mostly by his first name, since I think of him as a personal friend, not only as an important colleague, although he was certainly that as well.

Our research clearly took us to different sites and different topics. (If I may try to summarize my own work, it has been mostly in the United States and in West Africa, and briefly in the Caribbean, not close to Fredrik's fields; and it is urban, concerned with the transnational and the global, and "studying sideways," scrutinizing forms of knowledge in neighboring fields from an anthropological point of view.) Yet despite obvious differences in the materials we were dealing with, I think there have been underlying similarities in basic assumptions—and here, of course, I had my recurrent moments and periods reading and listening to Fredrik and contemplating his suggestions. There had been a time, too, of late 1960s upheavals in Sweden, when I found myself academically liminal, and Fredrik had invited me to join the department in Bergen; as things worked out, however, I remained in Stockholm.

I remember with special pleasure a dinner we had some years later, just the two of us, in a seafood restaurant next to the Bergen harbor. We exchanged opinions and reflections on personal experiences and choices. At earlier points in our scholarly careers, we had both chosen to remain in or return to our Scandinavian home grounds. As he explained it, if he had joined one of the larger, conventionally central departments in the world of anthropology, he might have had to function as a reliable cog in the wheel of a perhaps involuted division of labor and knowledge. (He illustrated the metaphor dramatically with his hands.) In Bergen and in Oslo, he could roam freely as he explored new lines of thought.

True, as he would later point out, he had been "aware of the danger of isolation in a small, provincial university" (2007: 7). And in chapter 1 in this volume, Unni Wikan notes that Barth's father, an Oslo professor, had been against the son's move to Bergen. Yet not only the intellectual freedom, but also the challenge of starting the first department of modern social anthropology in Scandinavia, was irresistible. (And by the time he came to Boston University, several decades later, where some of the contributors to this book met him, he was of course of a scholarly stature that allowed him to continue exploring, wherever he was.)

The years in Bergen, from the early 1960s, indeed showed his capacity for intellectual and organizational leadership. Beginning with few students and a high-caliber, flexibly recruited staff, intellectually open toward both a wider scholarly world and the surrounding national society, the department may have functioned in its early years rather as a think tank; it soon gained a reputation as "the Bergen School." As the department's reputation grew, there would be more students, including those on academic pilgrimage from other Scandinavian countries. From a distance, the homogeneity of the "school" was probably overestimated. It included scholars with a variety of backgrounds and interests, fully capable of doing their own thinking. Yet Fredrik was clearly in the middle. I remember, too, one occasion when the department colleagues gathered for their usual daily lunch, always at the same table in the same café. That day, Fredrik was off for a meeting in Oslo. So the chair that was usually his, at the center of the table, remained empty.

Unni Wikan's account, in chapter 1 of this book, of decades of life shared with Fredrik is necessarily unique in its personal insights. A step away, there is Thomas Hylland Eriksen's (2015) biography of Fredrik Barth, by a younger colleague, not quite a Barth pupil, but a Norwegian compatriot with a clear view of academic scenes in their country. My perspective is from across the border, from another Scandinavian country, but with the border between them easily and often crossed.[1]

I find Fredrik's review of sixty years as an anthropologist in *Annual Review of Anthropology* (Barth 2007) especially revealing in what it tells us about his early years of getting into the discipline, becoming a fieldworker, and developing a stance toward the relationship between field experience and theory. The start was certainly privileged, arriving at the University of Chicago as the son of a foreign visiting professor. That father, a geologist, had undoubtedly already had some influence in communicating a stance toward scientific knowledge and work, and the boy had already taken an interest in zoology. What Fredrik later identified as his "naturalist" approach to observation would come fairly readily out of this. As an undergraduate, he learned a little of everything in the American four-field conception of anthropology, went with archaeologists to a dig in Iraq, and then when the archaeologists had left, he stayed to do ethnography. After that, in one field after another in Iraq, Iran, and Pakistan in his early work, he developed his approach as a participant observer in the strictest sense. Well-informed about most branches of anthropological and other relevant social thought, he would insist on confronting them with actual human diversity. Much of his prominence within the anthropological vocation probably came from his consistently demonstrating a field grounding of analytical efforts—for one thing, it offered an attractive way out for many who did not want to become sequestered in whatever intellectual or ideological silo happened to be strong in local academic life.

There is also his emphasis on a close-up understanding of interactions and relationships and the outcomes of these. Those who have labeled him a "methodological individualist" seem to miss the point. As the title of this volume has it, "it happens among people."

Again, my perspective is from just across one Scandinavian border. While many of his scholarly followers elsewhere cannot read Barth in Norwegian, we Scandinavians can read each other's languages. In 1989, linked to Fredrik's sixtieth birthday, there appeared a *Festschrift* in Norwegian where nearly twenty of his compatriot anthropologists took stock of a quarter-century of anthropological studies on Norwegian society. It was a rich work, with remarkable breadth of topics, but I have been especially impressed by a concluding conversation between Fredrik and the two editors of the volume, both very visible on the local public scene: Ottar Brox, an early member of the Bergen group, and Marianne Gullestad, who was of a somewhat later cohort (Brox and Gullestad 1989).[2] It was an intellectual exchange between three people who clearly knew each other well, marked by respect and personal trust. At a time when Fredrik could already look back on many of his own prominent achievements, and he and his interlocutors could also review the growth of a national anthropology, it was an admirably searching discussion of strengths and possibly remaining challenges. For one thing, forever constructively impatient, Fredrik could argue that he still wanted his younger colleagues to take more of their work to the international anthropological community, thereby not only expanding their own scholarly reputations, but also contributing Norwegian ethnography and its wider implications to the global inventory of anthropological knowledge and thought.

In what follows, from my near-neighbor point of view, I will not attempt to comment on so many of the preceding chapters, but rather focus on a few topics.

The Editor as Entrepreneur

While most of the preceding chapters may have dealt primarily with Fredrik Barth as ethnographer-thinker-author, I want to dwell for a moment on Barth the editor. At the time when Fredrik started out as a professor in Bergen, anthropology was widely taken to be a study of "non-Western," even "primitive" peoples and cultures. The notion of "anthropology at home" only gained more acceptance considerably later (Jackson 1987). His department certainly had an international profile in its choice of field sites. Yet Fredrik was also already committed to showing the relevance of his discipline to an understanding of Norwegian society, and so one of his early undertakings was pulling together a slim volume that got the title *The Role of the Entrepreneur in Social Change in Northern Norway* (1963). Apart from his own introduction, there were four contributors: three from Bergen, one from Oslo. This volume is little known outside Scandinavia, and is mentioned only briefly in the present volume. In Norway, however, it succeeded in making social anthropology noticeable in scholarship and public discourse.

There is something entrepreneurial about editorship in itself. An editor can bring together a team, recruit allies for a point of view. He or she can also stimulate colleagues, young and old, who might otherwise not have gotten around to putting pen to paper (to use an expression that may by now be outdated). Not least, readers can become followers.

Northern Norway, at the time this volume was prepared and came out, was a region of mostly small coastal communities, making their living through fishing and household farming. One of the contributions focused on the Saami (then referred to as Lapps), a stigmatized ethnic minority. Entrepreneurship in the region was in large part a matter of brokerage between these communities and the institutions of the wider society.

Here are clear-eyed studies of local life. Yet at the same time, the editor especially could make references to Paul Bohannan on spheres of exchange among the Nigerian Tiv and to the predicament of chiefs in Uganda according to Lloyd Fallers. Exotic peoples in Africa and local Norwegian villagers were in some ways comparable, after all. And the editor's introduction ends by noting that the chapters following it "should demonstrate the great scope for research along these lines in the study of local communities, and the promise it holds for theoretical and applied results" (Barth 1963: 18).

Between Fredrik's first and second edited volumes, his prominence in the international anthropological community had grown. His plenary lecture on the study of social change at the American Anthropological Association meetings in Pittsburgh in 1966 was very well received; I was there and remember the enthusiastic comments afterward (Barth 1967). From about this time, it would seem that Fredrik's organized contacts were getting closer with American anthropology and a little more attenuated with British social anthropology.[3]

About *Ethnic Groups and Boundaries* (1969), which remains his best-known book, not so much needs to be said here. Most of the chapter contributors were among his Norwegian colleagues (one of whom had also been in the previous book), and there were two Swedes. They could offer ethnography and analyses that were well in line with Fredrik's overall reasoning, but his introduction was certainly most important. Here he problematized the relationship between ethnicity, as collective identity and a form of organization, and "culture"—the distinction has remained basic in anthropology ever since. With materials ranging from southern Mexico via Ethiopia to Laos, but still including Norway as well as the Pathan (Pashtun, Pukhtun—we have seen that spellings vary) life, it was possible to dwell on varied relationships between ethnicity and social stratification, and the anomalous fact that people could change ethnic identity.

Fredrik began his introduction by noting that ethnicity was "a theme of great, but neglected, importance to social anthropology." That may indeed have been so, although his references, for example, to Furnivall on Southeast Asian plural societies as well as Mitchell on the Central African Kalela dance showed that he knew what was already there. The success of the new book, however, clearly had something to do with its appearing "just in time." The 1960s were a period when Europe was increasingly opening up to transnational and transcontinental migration, making ethnicity a topic of public interest, while America was moving "beyond the melting pot."[4]

And then attention to the book just spread and spread. I was pleased to read Ke Fan's account of its more recent centrality in Chinese anthropology, where it seems that in a way, as a theorist of ethnicity, Fredrik Barth succeeded Josef Stalin.

The third major edited volume was *Scale and Social Organization* (1978). Some forty years after its appearance, its fate seems somewhat enigmatic. Beginning as a Wenner-Gren Foundation conference, at the foundation's Burg Wartenstein in Austria, it took on a big question—as Fredrik asked in the introduction: "How can anthropologists study and describe large-scale social systems without losing sight of real people and their life situations?" (Barth 1978: 9). His interest in the variable scales of social life could have been inspired by the encounter, at one extreme, with the Baktaman, that "nation of 183 persons." Yet the contributors to the book shifted freely across variations of scale and complexity.

The conference was held in 1972, so it took some time for the book to appear, with a Norwegian publisher (although in English, of course). There were a number of senior anthropologists at the conference—Americans, Europeans, one Indian—but not quite all of them contributed to the volume.

Perhaps it was a bit like herding cats? Their chapters tended to move in rather different directions. So the volume did not offer as unitary, coherent a message, as *Ethnic Groups and Boundaries* had done, with its all-Scandinavian cast. It is referred to in few places in the present volume and gets no extended attention. It may be, too, that by the time it appeared, Fredrik's own interests were moving on, toward more preoccupation with the anthropology of knowledge.

Nonetheless, I find it, too, very worthwhile to return to once in a while. That question in the introduction about what it might take to move from the bottom up toward a big picture remains intriguing—from a perspective of almost a half-century later, one can conclude that most writers, usually not from anthropology but from history, political science, or journalism, offering even global scenarios toward the present and the future, start more or less at the top and make at best hurried and impressionistic visits to small-scale scenes.[5]

All the chapters in *Scale and Social Organization* have something to offer, although here I will comment only on Fredrik's own chapter (apart from the brief introduction and the conclusion) and one of the others. The former has its point of departure in some auto-ethnography: an experiment in documenting his personal network, not concealing methodological difficulties.

To my knowledge Fredrik had not made much explicit use of the emerging body of network thinking before this chapter—despite the fact that it had more or less begun in Norway, with John Barnes's (1954) field study in the coastal parish of Bremnes. Perhaps, as it grew quickly, with possibly exaggerated claims, he just had his usual doubt about academic fads. Then, as a part of network analysis took the path of a highly technical and quantitative style of work, it may also have seemed remote from his interests. But it seems he soon realized that it could also be well in line with his understanding of social life. For the chapter in *Scale and Social Organization*, anyway, he had taken careful note of all his own interactions, including telephone calls and written correspondence, over a two-week period. He was surprised at his findings: if an investigating anthropologist had asked him to generalize about his network, Fredrik concluded, he would have been a poor informant.

Two of his observations, I think, deserve some comment here. One was that "English-speaking anthropologists above 40 years of age make up a small world of high density" (Barth 1978: 177).

Some decades later, this appears strikingly untrue—evidence of the global growth of the anthropological discipline in the intervening years. The other was that "Norwegian 'public' persons in arts, sciences and mass communication are largely known to each other" (Barth 1978: 177). This suggests a certain transparency or intimacy of the national scene.

I come to think here of the fact that Fredrik had several contemporaries in Norwegian academic life who were also internationally prominent social scientists and widely recognized on the national scene as public intellectuals as well: the peace researcher Johan Galtung, the political scientist Johan P. Olsen, the criminologist Nils Christie. I do not believe they worked so closely together, but together they provided a sense among the public that social science had something to say that mattered to everybody. The fact that Norway is a fairly small country may have had a part in this wider national impact, but far from all small countries have been so richly endowed with scholarly leadership at one point in time.

The other chapter in *Scale and Social Organization*, by one of the invited contributors, that I want to point out has to do with the concept of culture. One way Fredrik and I differed, I want to note parenthetically, was in our stances toward the culture concept. Fredrik was reluctant to use it, generally preferring "knowledge."[6] In this he may have been influenced by his early roots in British anthropology (particularly with Raymond Firth and Edmund Leach), where the culture concept has played a smaller part than in American anthropology.[7] He was also critical, however, toward the easy assumption of cultural uniformity and sharing that has indeed tended to be dominant in the latter. As my early exposure to professional anthropology was rather more in the United States, I tended to accept a vocabulary of culture more readily. But that also meant that I became aware of debates over the concept and its uses, as well as more reformist understandings of it.[8]

Theodore Schwartz's chapter in *Scale and Social Organization* —developing out of research in another classic anthropological field site, Manus (where Margaret Mead had once worked for *New Lives for Old*)—exemplified the latter, in a discussion of distributive models. In such models, "culture is conceived of as complexly distributed among the individuals, groups, categories, statuses, and other segments or designates of a society . . . a distributive model of culture is needed for conceptualizing culture over the entire range of societal scale and evolution" (Schwartz 1978: 215). Fredrik did not discuss Schwartz's contribution at any length in his conclusion to the volume, but the mere fact that he had been invited to the conference could suggest an awareness of the possibility of bringing an understanding of "culture" closer to his view of the actual complexity of social life.

The Pashtun, Over Time

The three editorial endeavors came relatively early in Fredrik Barth's career, basically initiated within a ten-year period. I also want to reflect briefly on one longer-term engagement—stretching from his doctoral fieldwork to his last book. *Political Leadership among Swat Pathans* (1959) documented his first period of extended field research in Swat and what that society was like at midcentury. Twenty-five years later (and with a number of visits in between), Fredrik would return to Swat to sit down with its aging chieftain for two weeks of intensive interview sessions, resulting in *The Last Wali of Swat* (1985). (Lindholm, in chapter 7, mentions this ruler rather in passing.) It offered a view of a period when Swat was slowly becoming incorporated into the new postcolonial state of Pakistan.[9] At a micro level, there would be the internal family politics, as the young man was taking over leadership from his father. As years passed, the Wali showed foresight and personal diplomatic skill. His reminiscences also offered a view of British colonialism, soon to depart, with its own opaque internal complexity, including class prejudices between higher- and lower-level staff brought along from the mother country.

Personally I enjoyed reading this for the comparisons it allowed me with accounts of British colonial rule in Nigeria, with comparable misunderstandings, internal divides, and moments of personal experiences of power. But I also wondered what the elderly Wali thought about that European sitting across from him, listening to him for hours and hours, interjecting questions that showed his interest? As a young man, the Wali-to-be had heard the rumors about Oxford and Cambridge, beginning to reach his corner of the British Empire, and had long wanted to go to one of them. Now here was this scholar who had indeed gone to Cambridge and got a doctorate there, and he wanted to hear the Wali's story. Probably, for one thing, the Wali felt flattered.

After *The Last Wali of Swat*, Fredrik would again have reason to draw on his knowledge about the Pashtun, Central Asia, and local and global Islam a number of times. In a Nobel symposium on post–Cold War nationalism and internationalism, held in Stockholm in 1997, he took on the question of how to understand Islamists. Again, he emphasized existing diversity, and the consequent different potential outcomes:

> Given the Islamists' organizational form and the range of ideas, in its present position of opposition it might move either towards compromise or an escalating confrontation and violence; a greater fragmentation into national agendas or a Messianic, expansive internationalism within Islam. . . . In the unequal battle with a regime's repressive powers, terrorism is an ever-present countermeasure. (Barth 2000: 62)

This was before so many people had heard of Osama bin Laden. And then in his last published book, in Norwegian, *Afghanistan og Taliban* (2008), in a hundred pages, he again took the Pashtun grassroots point of view, scrutinized its complicated relationship to Taliban policies, warned against Western misunderstandings, and pointed to infrastructural development needed to make Afghanistan a viable nation. As Unni Wikan notes in chapter 1, there was a reason he wrote this book in Norwegian. There were Norwegian soldiers among the NATO troops in Afghanistan, so the Norwegian public should know what they were up to and up against.

A Rooted Cosmopolitan

In fact, *Afghanistan og Taliban* had been preceded just a few years earlier by another book in Norwegian, *Vi mennesker* (2005). Here Fredrik offered a very personal account of his life as an anthropologist and his widespread field experiences. It is an accessible, inspiring book, which could appeal to many readers curious about what it is really like out there—and might start the younger among them imagining their own futures as anthropologists.

That he took on the challenge of pulling together these experiences and insights in Norwegian also tells us something about who Fredrik was. As Unni Wikan also points out, "there was no doubt in his mind of where he wanted to *live*."

Recently, in public commentary over much of Europe and North America, apropos such events as the Brexit referendum and the election of Donald Trump as U.S. president, there has been a suggestion that there is a new deep social divide, between a well-educated, globally oriented category of people who can be at home anywhere and a less-educated category with deep roots and commitments somewhere in one particular locale and in their home country (see, e.g., Goodhart 2017). With regard to the former, one may easily be reminded of the old epithet of the "rootless cosmopolitan" and its dubious political uses in history.

I like a comment on that notion in the context of an earlier debate about cosmopolitanism. It was entirely possible, argued the philosopher Kwame Anthony Appiah (1996), to find satisfaction in one's own country and its way of life, and yet appreciate the diversity assembled as others made their own choices. So he saw himself as a "rooted cosmopolitan." Appiah could speak with some personal authority here: he was an American academic, but he had been born and grown up in what is now Ghana, with a West African father and a British mother (and a grandfather who had been a prominent minister in the British cabinet after World War II). It was especially his father, politically prominent at the time of the Ghanaian struggle for independence in the 1950s, who had impressed on his children the fact that one could be both a patriot and a citizen of the world at the same time.

Fredrik Barth indeed seems to me to have been another rooted cosmopolitan, at home in Norway and the world.[10] But it was not his style to keep the two as separate spheres. He aimed at exchanges between them, and in that way he could also serve as a model for other anthropologists: serving as cultural brokers, in the best sense of that concept.

Ulf Hannerz is Professor Emeritus of Social Anthropology, Stockholm University, and former Chair of the European Association of Social Anthropologists. His research has been especially in urban anthropology, media anthropology, and transnational cultural processes, with field studies in West Africa, the Caribbean, and the United States. A study of the work of foreign correspondents drew on field studies in Jerusalem, Johannesburg, and Tokyo. Among his books are *Soulside* (1969), *Exploring the City* (1980), *Cultural Complexity* (1992), *Transnational Connections* (1996), *Foreign News* (2004), *Anthropology's World* (2010), *Writing Future Worlds* (2016), *Small Countries* (coedited with Andre Gingrich, 2017), and *World Watching* (2019).

Notes

1. I draw to a limited extent on my obituary of Fredrik Barth in *American Anthropologist* (Hannerz 2016a).
2. Gullestad, unfortunately too early deceased, would contribute importantly to studies of home and neighborhood life and of gender, immigration, and growing cultural diversity. Brox, forever a transdisciplinary anthropologist/sociologist/economist, and a public intellectual, would serve briefly in the Norwegian parliament. Here I also want to acknowledge another Festschrift, a couple of years later, in English, edited by three of Fredrik's early students, with contributions by a large number of Norwegian anthropologists, but apparently not as well-known in the international scholarly community, because it came out with a local publisher (Grönhaug, Haaland, and Henriksen 1991). Across the border, too, the Swedish Society for Anthropology and Geography celebrated Fredrik's sixtieth birthday with a Vega Day symposium, resulting in an issue of the journal *Ethnos* (Barth 1989, Hannerz 1989).
3. Early in the new millennium, at a conference when a new center of anthropological research was opened at Halle/Saale—as it happened, a neighboring city to Leipzig, where he was born—Fredrik offered his overview of the changing fortunes of British anthropology. He suggested that 1945–70, had been "the golden age" and what came after was more internally diverse, but less impressive; also, he saw more of a convergence between British and American anthropologies (Barth, Gingrich, Parkin, and Silverman 2005).
4. We should not forget either that there was a parallel anthropological interest in ethnicity growing out of Abner Cohen's (1969) study of the Hausa community in Ibadan, Nigeria, followed by a conference volume on urban ethnicity, in the book series of the British-based Association of Social Anthropologists (Cohen 1974). Cohen's own view of ethnicity was more narrowly focused on ethnic groups as interest groups.
5. I have dealt with this myself in a scrutiny of global future scenarios (Hannerz 2016b).
6. See on this, for example, his 2000 Sidney W. Mintz Lecture (Barth 2002)—also noted in Weller's and Wu's introduction to this volume—and his brief 1995 statement.
7. One could note that he could be critical of the omnibus notion of "society" as well, as in his plenary lecture at the first conference of the European Association of Social Anthropologists (EASA) in 1990 (Barth 1992).
8. It has seemed to me that anthropologists need to engage with the notion of culture because of its questionable proto-anthropological, quasi-anthropological, pseudo-anthropological uses in public life; to the extent that anthropologists have any intellectual authority here, we need to be there to blow the whistle. With regard to views of culture that might have appealed to Fredrik Barth, I come to think of that formulated by Eric Wolf: "Cultural sets, and sets of sets, are continuously in construction, deconstruction, and reconstruction, under the impact of multiple processes operative over wide fields of social and cultural connections" (Wolf 2001: 313). Wolf also endorsed a conception of culture formulated quite early by the psychological anthropologist Anthony Wallace (1961). Culture had tended to be seen as a "replication of uniformity," Wallace noted, but we are frequently better off seeing it as an "organization of diversity." To map that "organization of diversity" in all its aspects, and to understand how it works, must be a central and continuously challenging task of anthropology. In a lecture prepared for the symposium "Culture in Complex Societies," referred to in note 2, Barth (1989) clearly does align himself with such a view.
9. Apart from Charles Lindholm's work on the Pathan, as exemplified in chapter 7 in this book, I want to note one other contribution to research on this group: *The Pathan Unarmed* (2000), a view of some of the Pathan at a particular time in history, by Mukulika Banerjee, a young female Indian anthropologist, later active in Britain. In the period between the world wars, there was a Muslim movement inspired by Gandhian principles on

nonviolence and dedicated to Indian nationalism—all quite different from the dominant view of the Pathan.

10. Appiah, one could note, remained in the United States, most recently as a philosophy professor at New York University; even for him, with a privileged personal background but coming from a conflict-ridden and not-so-rich West African country, that was probably a more natural choice than staying abroad had once been for the young anthropologist from prosperous Norway.

References

Appiah, Kwame Anthony. 1996. "Cosmopolitan Patriots." In *For Love of Country*, edited by Joshua Cohen. Boston: Beacon Press.

Banerjee, Mukulika. 2000. *The Pathan Unarmed*. Oxford: James Currey.

Barnes, John A. 1954. "Class and Committees in a Norwegian Island Parish." *Human Relations* 7: 3–58.

Barth, Fredrik. 1959. *Political Leadership among Swat Pathans*. Monographs on Social Anthropology 19. London: Athlone Press.

———, ed. 1963. *The Role of the Entrepreneur in Social Change in Northern Norway*. Bergen: Norwegian Universities Press.

———. 1967. "On the Study of Social Change." *American Anthropologist* 69: 661–69.

———, ed. 1969. *Ethnic Groups and Boundaries: The Social Organization of Culture Difference*. Boston: Little, Brown.

———, ed. 1978. *Scale and Social Organization*. Oslo: Universitetsforlaget.

———. 1985. With Miangul Jahanzeb. *The Last Wali of Swat: An Autobiography as Told to Fredrik Barth*. New York: Columbia University Press.

———. 1989. "The Analysis of Culture in Complex Societies." *Ethnos* 54: 120–42.

———. 1992. "Toward Greater Naturalism in Conceptualizing Societies." In *Conceptualizing Society*, edited by Adam Kuper, 17–33. London: Routledge.

———. 1995. "Other Knowledge and Other Ways of Knowing." *Journal of Anthropological Research* 51: 65–68.

———. 2000. "Are Islamists Nationalists or Internationalists?" In *Nationalism and Internationalism in the Post-Cold War Era*, edited by Kjell Goldmann, Ulf Hannerz, and Charles Westin. London: Routledge.

———. 2002. "An Anthropology of Knowledge." *Current Anthropology* 43: 1–18.

———. 2005. *Vi mennesker: Fra en antropologs reiser*. Oslo: Gyldendal.

———. 2007. "Overview: Sixty Years in Anthropology." *Annual Review of Anthropology* 36: 1–16.

———. 2008. *Afghanistan og Taliban*. Oslo: Pax.

Barth, Fredrik, Andre Gingrich, Robert Parkin, and Sydel Silverman. 2005. *One Discipline, Four Ways*. Chicago: University of Chicago Press.

Brox, Ottar, and Marianne Gullestad, eds. 1989. *På norsk grunn*. Oslo: Ad Notam.

Cohen, Abner. 1969. *Custom and Politics in Urban Africa*. London: Routledge & Kegan Paul.

———, ed. 1974. *Urban Ethnicity*. London: Tavistock.

Eriksen, Thomas Hylland. 2015. *Fredrik Barth: An Intellectual Biography*. London: Pluto Press.

Goodhart, David. 2017. *The Road to Somewhere*. London: Hurst.

Grönhaug, Reidar, Gunnar Haaland, and Georg Henriksen, eds. 1991. *The Ecology of Choice and Symbol*. Oslo: Alma Mater.

Hannerz, Ulf. 1989. "The Vega Day Symposium 1988: Culture in Complex Societies." *Ethnos* 54: 119.

———. 2016a. "Obituary: Fredrik Barth (1928–2016)." *American Anthropologist* 118: 704–6.

———. 2016b. *Writing Future Worlds*. New York: Palgrave.

Jackson, Anthony, ed. 1987. *Anthropology at Home*. London: Tavistock.

Schwartz, Theodore. 1978. "The Size and Shape of a Culture." In *Scale and Social Organization*, edited by Fredrik Barth. Oslo: Universitetsforlaget.

Wallace, Anthony F. C. 1961. *Culture and Personality*. New York: Random House.

Wolf, Eric R. 2001. *Pathways of Power*. Berkeley: University of California Press.

Index

www.ingramcontent.com/pod-product-compliance
Lightning Source LLC
Chambersburg PA
CBHW070922030426
42336CB00014BA/2492